Thanks for the Memories...
The Serra Family Tree and Stories

ISBN: 0-9749291-0-7

Dedications

Serra Family Dedication:

*To Giovani Serra and Bartolomea (Lazzaro) Serra
and the Entire Serra Family*

Especially Domenico Serra, for being the first to come to America!

Christopher Obert Dedication:

*To my mother Giovannina,
my wife Nancy,
and our children, Shari and Jason.*

Without them, I would be nothing.

Thanks for the Memories…

The Serra Family Tree and Stories

Compiled and Edited by

Christopher Obert

Contents

Contents

Acknowledgements

The book you hold in your hands was the work of many people. I would first like to thank my wife Nancy and our two children, Shari and Jason. The three of them helped me gather, sort and review all of the material in this book. They also put up with me as I spent months working on the computer. I would also like to thank my mother Giovannina, she allowed me to have access to all of her photos and paperwork. If I had to say who helped me the most, I would have to say, Mary and Frank Goldrick. They were the source of much of the material in this book. They not only found me stories, photos, documents and family contacts, they also fed me, my mom and my family as they did it. The seven of us would sit down over dinner, tell family stories and take notes. It was those old time Italian dinners that are the reason for this book.

I would also like to thank all of the extended family for their help. I have been in contact with so many of them through e-mail and each have helped me on more than one occasion. Some of them were involved in the Serra Family Reunion (and did a great job), while others sent in photos and stories: I especially want to thank Angela and Sophie Villanti, Jerry and Margherita Eggleston and the Di Grandi Family. They have been a great source of information on their side of the family as well as other family information.

I want to specially thank my cousins Dominick Charowsky, Janice Charowsky and Kathleen Wilson. They have helped me with family photos and stories. I would also like to give exceptional thanks to Maria (Charowsky) Dombrowski. It was her "Life History Report" (included in this book) that got me first started working on the family tree.

I also want to thank my mother-in-law Agnes Blanchette, my sister Mary Fortin and my father Norman. They have helped me not only with the Serra family tree, but the Obert family tree, the Blanchette family tree and the Fitzgerald family tree. I would also like to thank Denise Grayson for help on the Obert family tree. I would also like to thank Rena Wischhusen for showing me my first example of a researched family tree.

Last but not least, I would like to thank Lorraine Charowsky and Tony Serra. They have been great friends and have always helped me with all of my projects. Every time I'd talk about giving up they would talk me out of it.

With this many people all working on this project, I was thinking about giving the entire extended Serra family credit for writing this book. I decided not to do this however. It is not because of pride or vanity but because I wanted to take sole responsibility for any errors. You will see that I have given credit to the author of the story and to the supplier of photos throughout this book. However if you find anything wrong with the names, dates, spellings or listings they are my fault only. I do not want this book to start any family feud. But at the same time if you love this book and find that it is a nice family heirloom, thank all of the people that have contributed to this work. I would also like to apologize to any person that I may have been hard on while gathering and compiling this book. It was a very stressful, and at times, difficult project and I may have taken out my frustration on others. I would also like to apologize to anyone that I may have missed. With the amount of information that I have received over the last two years, I am sure that someone was inadvertently omitted. To those unnamed heroes, I want to say thank you.

I would like to make a special dedication of this book to the families of Santa (Costa) Augustus, Rose (DeAngelis) Vandi and Charlotte (Simms) Serra. Santa, Rose and Charlotte died while this book was under construction. I did not know Santa and I wish that I had started this book earlier so that I could have gotten to know her. I had met Rose at many family events and she was always very nice to me. She was one of the extended family that I liked to see the most. Before Rose died, she had sent in information on the family and I am forever grateful to her effort. Charlotte was from my part of the family and I knew her very well. She was extremely nice to me and my family for as long as I can remember. She always went out of her way to make me feel loved and special. She submitted information for the book and family tree. She also came to visit me, even though she was weak, a few short weeks before she died. She did not want to miss a chance to visit and look over the Serra Family book. This book, I hope, is a small way to honor them and their families.

I would like to thank the following people, groups and sources for information...

Book Team:
Nancy, Shari and Jason Obert, Giovannina Obert, Mary and Frank Goldrick, Tony Serra, Angela and Sophie Villanti, Jerry and Margherita Eggleston, Lorraine Charowsky, Patty DiGrandi Hohmann and Christine DiGrandi Jones

Serra 2002 Reunion Committee:
Jerry & Margherita Eggleston, Angela Villanti, Bill Eggleston, Betty Bonaiuto, Sharon Turcotte, Frank Bonaiuto, Joe Bonaiuto and Nancy Obert

Family Stories and Photos:
Mary Fortin, Kathleen Wilson, Danielle Serra, Dominick Serra, Charlotte Serra, Grace Bonaiuto, Nathan Bonaiuto, Peter Clemenzi, Dominick Charowsky, Christine DiGrandi Jones, Joe Bonaiuto, Shari Obert, Francine DiGrandi, Cheryl Comstock, Giovannina Obert, Mary Goldrick, Jerry & Margherita Eggleston, Rose Czarnecki, Jackie Serra, Tony Serra, Angela and Sophie Villanti, Carolyn Marletta, Rose Vandi, Josie Keenan, Maria Charowsky, Donna Lorusso, Catherine Constantelo, Donald Clemenzi, Peter Clemenzi, Ann Clemenzi, Donia Blanton, Lorraine Charowsky, Jennifer Comstock, Amy Comstock, Nancy Costa Desmond, Danielle Desmond, Gavin Keean, Patty DiGrandi Hohmann, Marrieta DiGrandi, Diana DiGrandi, Deana DiGrandi Jones,

E-Mail Help and Photos:
Lorraine Charowsky, Mary Goldrick, Francine Di Grandi, Ann Clemenzi, Elizabeth Garreffi, John Costa, Elaine Bonaiuto, Betty Bonaiuto, Faye Sienkiewicz, Sharon Turcotte, Donia Blanton, Christine DiGrandi Jones, Dominick Serra, John Serra, Donna Lorusso, Jackie Serra, Sophia Villanti, Catherine Constantelo, Maria Parent, Jo Buckley, Patty Hohmann, Lisa Marletta Groleaa, Dean Darr, Josie Keenan, Barbara D'Elia, Lena Serra Scibetta, Gayle and Don Clemenzi, Michael and Elena Charowsky, Bill Eggleston, Mary Khalil, Faye Friedman, Peter Clemenzi, Dominick Serra, Joe Bonaiuto, Frank Bonaiuto, Maria (Charowsky) Dombrowski, Dominick Charowsky and Janice Charowsky, Robert Charowsky

Other Family Trees:
Frank Goldrick, Agnes Blanchette, Rena Wischhusen, Laurie Lawn, Norman Obert, Mary Fortin, Lorraine Charowsky, Janice Charowsky and Denise Grayson

Other:
Norma Ayers, John B. Serra and Mary Serra, Mike Goldrick, John and Charlotte Serra, Lorraine Charowsky, Lucia Clemenzi

Special Dedication:
The families of Santa (Costa) Augustus, Rose (DeAngelis) Vandi and Charlotte (Simms) Serra

Charlotte Serra and Rose Vandi at the 2002 Serra Reunion

Groups and Sources for Information:

Mike LaBella and the Haverhill Gazette, Haverhill, Massachusetts.

The Beverly Times.

Christopher Group and Group Travel Enterprises, Inc. and their web site Travel-Italy.com

Arcangelo Nicotra and The Treasures of Italy – Houses for Vacation, and his web site ITesoridItalia.it

Tom Elliott and the Interactive Ancient Mediterranean Web Site, for the use of one of their maps.

Northern Essex Community College, Haverhill, MA

Haverhill Public Library, Haverhill, MA

Family Tree Maker software by Broderbund

Ellis Island Foundation and their web site

EA Games, Medal of Honor Allied Assault

Nova Development Corporation's Art Explosion 600,000.

National Park Service: Statue of Liberty National Monument

The American Heritage New Illustrated History of the United States (Volume 12 – A World Power)

Arte Photo Graphic Oreste Ragusi Muggiò (Milano)

Miramax Films

My Great Recipes

Walt Disney Company

"The Italian-Americans" by Luciano J. Ioizzo and Salvatore Mondello

"Ellis Island Interviews in their Own Words" by Peter Morton Coan

"Ellis Island, An Illustrated History of the Immigrant Experience" by Ivan Chermayeff, Fred Wasserman and written by Mary J. Shapiro"

"Images of America – Jersey City 1940-1960 The Dan McNulty Collection" by Kenneth French

Poet, Elizabeth Bishop

"The Aeolian Isles in ancient times" brochure by the Aeolian Museum, Lipari

The Story of the Serra Family Book

Many years ago I wanted to find out more about my family tree. While I was visiting in New Jersey with my Mom, I would talk with Mary Goldrick, John Serra and Bea Charowsky. I learned much but wanted to know more. I received a few papers from Mary Goldrick, such as the report Maria Charowsky wrote on our grandparents. Years passed with not much work on the family tree. One day we received a package from Rena Wischhusen. She was a relative on my wife's side of the family. She had done tons of research on the Blanchette Family and gave us a copy of her material. I was very impressed with her work. I bought software for our computer and began to input our family trees. As time passed I would very slowly gather information on the family trees. When I bought a new computer, I bought a new family tree software package called "Family Tree Maker." With this new software I could seriously work on the family tree and accomplish more research. Up until this time it was still a project that I wanted to work on, but never really spent much time actually doing.

In the early part of 2002, I received an E-Mail from Janice Charowsky. She was passing on information about a Serra Family Reunion. The E-Mail was from the reunion committee and asked questions about when people wanted the reunion and what they wanted to eat. I sent in my selections and mentioned that I was working on the family tree. It was this E-Mail that would change my life for the next two years. People thought that because I was working on the tree that I had lots if information helpful for the reunion. At that time I only had maybe 200 people in the family tree and 60% of that was the Blanchette Family… not the Serra Family. I began to receive E-Mails asking for information and addresses. I did not have this information but I started to write to many people and started to gather information and then pass it along to others. I started to keep files containing this new information. At one point I was receiving up to ten E-Mails every day, day after day for months. Because of all of this communication people started to think I was running the reunion. I would be asked for information about the reunion and I would forward the requests to the reunion committee. One day the committee invited Nancy and me to attend the next reunion meeting. I do not remember ever having met any member of the committee before accept Angela Villanti. When I went to the meeting, I brought all the material that I had been collecting to show them. They loved the photos and short stories. I decided to try to put together some kind of display and hand out for the reunion. The committee invited Nancy and me to join them on the committee. We agreed but mostly only worked on the family tree. When the reunion finally came I had made lots of posters, hand outs and CDs that I gave out to family members. At the reunion a few people looked over all the material and asked when the "book" would be done. "What book?" I said. Many people said that hand outs and disks were nice but this material needs to be in a book.

Around Christmas of 2002, I decided to look into the possibility of putting all of this material into a family book. To tell you the truth, I was expecting it to be too expensive and too difficult to make a book. What I found out was that it was just the opposite. To make a small book the size of a Reader's Digest, about 100 pages long would be less than $2,000.00. I started to put all the material in book form. I sent out letters and E-Mails to every family member I could to ask for more information and family stories. The book quickly grew to the size it is today. Many people sent me information and the book truly turned into a work of love.

John Serra, Mary Goldrick and Giovannina Obert reviewing family information

Family Tree Get-Togethers…

I want to thank everyone that helped at the Serra Family book get-together held at Mary and Frank Goldbrick's house. We got together to review the book, gather new material, see if there were any major mistakes and look over the book layout. In attendance throughout the three days were: Mary and Frank Goldrick, Dominick Serra, Tony Serra, John Serra, Patty DiGrandi Hohmann, Christine DiGrandi Jones, Kathleen Wilson, Lorraine Charowsky my wife Nancy and me. Janice Charowsky could not make it but dropped off a large box of her mother's and father's (Bea and Mike Charowsky) old photos and keepsakes the day before. We had great fun looking at photos, telling stories and eating. What a great time we had!

Dominick Serra (standing) Mary Goldrick, Patty DiGrandi Hohmann, Christine DiGrandi Jones,
Nancy Obert and Chris Obert

Left photo: Dominick Serra (standing) Mary Goldrick, Patty DiGrandi Hohmann, Christine DiGrandi Jones, Lorraine Charowsky (standing) and Nancy Obert   Right photo: Tony Serra and Lorraine Charowsky

Mary Goldrick dressed in her mom's (Maria Concetta Costa Serra) clothes.

15

In addition to the Goldrick get-together, we had two more, at the home of Sophie Villanti. I would like to thank those people that came to the Villanti house to help me with the Serra Family Book: Sophie Villanti, John and Mary Serra, Angela Villanti, Maria and Dennis Parent, Catherine Constantelo, my wife Nancy and my mom, Giovannina Obert. We once again looked at photos, told stories and ate great food. It is meetings like this which made the Serra Book possible.

John Serra, Sophie Villanti and Giovannina Obert

Maria Parent, Sophie Villanti, Angela Villanti

16

The last meeting that we had was in July at the Goldrick's house. Although we did go over the book and material, we mostly talked, laughed and swam… and of course ate! In attendance were myself, my daughter Shari and my wife Nancy, Mary and Frank Goldrick, their daughter Kathleen, and her husband Robert, their two children, Grace and Julia, Peir-Lian Charowsky, and her daughters Lorraine and Eileen, John and Charlotte Serra and their children, Dominick and Tony, Janice Charowsky, Bobby and Patty Charowsky and their children Robert and Heather. We had a great time and wished it could have lasted longer…

Mary Goldrick and John Serra
(note Charlotte (Simms) Serra reviewing the "editing version" of the Serra Book, on the right of the photo)

The Purpose of this book.

The first goal of this book is to be fun and informative. The main reason for this book was to record some of the Serra Family stories before it was too late. As I gathered information, I sadly realized that for many stories, it is already too late. But because of the family's combined efforts, many stories have been saved. It was also the purpose of this book to serve as a starting place for a more detailed research into the history of the Serra Family. I hope that someone will pick up the banner and create a "Serra Family Book - Volume Two", with even more information, a larger and more distant family tree and information on Antonio Serra, the "Lost Serra." Another project that would be nice is a "Serra Family Photo Book." This book could contain some of the hundreds of photos of the Serra Family that did not make it into this book. Anything is possible now that a starting point has been created in this book. I hope that this book is the first of many other family projects…

With Love, Chris Obert
September 2003

Part One

There is history in all men's lives.

--William Shakespeare, *King Henry IV*

History
Paints Our Lives with Color

A Preface to Genealogy

Genealogy

Written by Shari Obert
Photos by Nova Development Corp.

Why should we explore our past? Why would we want to find out the history of our families, our ancestors? What could be either exciting or useful about knowledge of long dead relatives, especially those who died long before we were born, or when we were too young to recall anything about them? Genealogy might seem to be a dry and dull subject, only of significance or interest to older generations, in their attempt to recall times long past and striving to remember events and people that now exist only in their memories.

Yet it is precisely for this reason that studying family history is so vital. Do we want to let these past lives, stories- stories of love, births, hardships, marriage, adventures and losses- be lost to us forever? Searching through an album of faded photographs, or listening to someone speak fondly or wistfully of a long dead relative or close friend, wouldn't it be wonderful if we could share in these memories with them, if we could recall these stories and people – to learn that Domenico Serra was only 12, yet set bravely out to make a life for himself in America, that Maria Concetta Serra loved to crochet and was brilliant at it, only needing to see a new pattern once to replicate it perfectly, that your own curly hair or short stature or sense of humor were shared by an aunt, grandfather or great-grandmother of yours? Looking at the past, we find ourselves. In exploring our ancestors, we are rediscovering our own close family and becoming aware of the unconscious forces that have been working on us our whole lives, making us intimately connected with this line of family who came before us, even though we are not usually aware of it. All the dreams and ideas and actions of these people have combined and built upon one another to create the wonderful, thriving family we have today. Therefore, when looking back into our past, remembering good times and bad, hearing stories of success and of disappointment, I think we always need to remember that these were the people who made what we have possible, to respect them for their faith and perseverance and to continue building upon those dreams for our family in the future.

Discovering one's genealogy, one's family history, is not at all dull or boring, but is an exploration into a shared consciousness. It is not merely collecting names of ancestors, complete with birth, marriage, and death dates, recording specific relationships and arranging them into a neat and succinct order. It is a dynamic and ongoing adventure, encompassing all of the present and future, as well as the past. In fact, genealogy may have more to do with the present and future than with the past. For, we now in the present are the ones who care about these roots, this heritage. It is we who do not want the story of who we are to be forgotten. As the generations follow us, ever more distant from those ancestors, so similar to ourselves yet so different, who took their lives in their hands (made a place in the world for us, for which we will ever be in their debt) and made the best life they could, not for themselves, but for us and for all the generations after them.

An American Icon, The Brooklyn Bridge, greeting the new arrivals to America

Looking Back

Written by Christopher Obert

"To be ignorant of what happened before you were born is to be ever a child."

-- Cicero De Oratore

Throughout this book there are quotes from some famous people. The quotes reflect their opinion on life, relationships, history and family. These quotes say, in a way I never could, that our lives are a great gift. I have added them to remind us just how important the past is to each and every one of us. During the last few years, as I have worked on the family tree and this book, I have come to know the Serra Family better, and in doing so, I have come to know myself better. I have come to realize that life is a short and precious thing. We need to make the most of each and every day.

Here are a few more quotes that you can reflect on...

"The history of every country begins in the heart of a man or woman." – Willa Cather (1873-1947)

"People are trapped in history and history is trapped in them." – James Baldwin (1924-1987)

"All things from eternity are of like forms and come round in a circle." - Marcus Aurelius (121-180)

"It is not I that belong to the past, but the past that belongs to me." – Mary Antin (1881-1949)

"The destruction of the past is perhaps the greatest of all crime." – Simone Weil (1909-1943)

"We forget all too soon the things we thought we could never forget." – Joan Didion (1934-   )

"History is the witness that testifies to the passing of time; it illumines reality, vitalizes memory, provides guidance in daily life and brings us tidings of antiquity." – Cicero De Oratore

Remembering the Past…

Written by Christopher Obert

One of the goals of this book is to serve as a source of stories but also as a place to record new and missing stories. Just as the family Bible was used to record births and deaths; I hope that this book will not just sit on the shelf but be used to record family events, your own memories and information. It was my aspiration to create a book that can be a treasure that you can pass on to future generations.

As you gather your thoughts and collect family data here are a few hints that may help you…

First of all, there is no right way or wrong way… the only requirement is to be organized.

When you start to climb your family tree, you start in the present and work your way back in time.

Don't forget to record your own stories and facts.

Your local library and the internet are a great source of information but do not over-look anyone in your family. Contact as many people as possible, you never know who may surprise you.

Have fun!

What memories from your past will you record in this book?

One last note, if any of you out there want to take this book even further, I have gathered a small research library on Genealogy. I would love to assist you in your work!

Genealogy Notes:

If you would be loved, love.

--Hecato, *Fragments*

Our Family
and the Aeolian Islands

The Story of the Island of Salina

The Aeolian Islands - Home

Written by Christopher Obert

The Island of Salina, one of the Aeolian Islands

Up until a few years ago, I always thought that my grandparents and the Serra Family in general, were from the Island of Sicily. I had heard the names Italy, Sicily, Messina, Lipari, Salina, Leni and Malfa many times in conversations but I never fully understood how all the names came together. It was only after working on the family tree that I began to put the pieces in their proper place. I was not sure if other people in the Serra Family had the same problem as me, and were not too familiar with the land of our ancestors' birth, so I decided to include a section of the Serra Family book on their homeland. Now as you read this, please remember that I have never been to the "Isol Eolie", or as they are called in English, "The Aeolian Islands", and I may have a mistake here or there but this section should give you a better idea of where our ancestors originated from…

As we all know, our ancestors are Italian; that means they are from Italy. "Italy" is the name of the country, just as The United States is the name of this country. Sicily is a part of Italy, just as New Jersey or Massachusetts is part of the U.S. The different parts of Italy (and Sicily) are divided further, just as states are divided into counties, (for example Essex and Middlesex counties in Massachusetts), into smaller sections called provinces. One of these smaller provinces is called Messina. It is the area located around the town of Messina on the Island of Sicily and includes the Aeolian Islands. The Aeolian Islands are a small archipelago of seven islands located northeast of Sicily. It is these islands that were home for much of the Serra Family.

As I said before, up until a few years ago, I thought that my grandparents were from the Island of Sicily. I knew that Domenico Serra was from a small village called Malfa and that Maria Concetta (Costa) was from another small village called Leni. But whenever I looked on a map of Sicily, I could not find these small villages. I also had heard the name Messina mentioned many times and was told that Leni and Malfa were part of Messina. I could find Messina but not Leni and Malfa. What I did not know was that Messina was not just a town but a province; and that these villages were not located on the "big" island of Sicily but on a smaller island, called Salina, part of the aforementioned Aeolian Islands, located off Sicily's northeast coast. As I found this new information, things began to make sense. Leni and Malfa were two villages located on the Island of Salina. Salina was one of seven small islands making up the Aeolian Island chain. This group of islands was a part of the Province of Messina. Messina was one of a group of provinces on the Island of Sicily. Sicily was one of the largest sections of the country of Italy. I finally got it! Now I set out to gather information on the Aeolian Islands and Salina in particular.

The first thing I discovered was that the Aeolian Islands had more than one name associated with them, so it could be confusing. They are called "Isole Eolie" in Italian or "The Aeolian Islands" in English. They are also called "The Eolie Islands". The biggest island in the group is called Lipari; this is why they are sometimes referred to as the "Lipari Islands". Whichever name you choose to call them, just remember that they were home to the Serra Family.

Spectacular views from the Aeolian Islands

The Aeolian Islands

Written by Christopher Obert

Note: much of the information for this section was taken from many sources.
All of the ancient facts are from the brochure "The Aeolian Isles in Ancient Times" written by the Aeolian Museum, Lipari.

The first people that settled the islands lived on Lipari and Salina in the 5th millennium before the Common Era (BCE). This was the middle of the Neolithic era and the people were attracted by an important natural resource, obsidian. This is a black volcanic glass used for tools. Before man started working metal, obsidian constituted the sharpest material which could be utilized, and was therefore very sought after. Obsidian is found only in a few places in the Mediterranean. It was exported to Sicily and Southern Italy and other points in great quantities. For more than 2000 years this trade brought prosperity to the island and created a society centered around the trade.

In 1948 archaeologists started excavations to establish the succession of civilizations that flourished on the islands through the millennia. The Neolithic civilization reached its peak around 3000 BCE, at the same time the smaller islands of the archipelago began to be inhabited. After a few centuries of strong economic and demographic recession, the islands had another period of great prosperity. Another population, this time coming from mainland Greece, settled on the islands. The Greeks brought with them the knowledge of metallurgy. Trade and exchanges passed between the island group and Greece, as proved by the Aeolian Islands mentioned in Homer's Odyssey in the episode of Aeolus.

Around 1430 BCE a new population settled the archipelago, this time from Sicily. These people brought with them an entirely new culture. Relations with Greece continued but new trade now began with the Italian peninsula. Towards 1270 BCE, another group populated Lipari, the Ausonians, coming from the Campanian coast. The other islands became largely uninhabited.

Around 900BCE the settlement on Lipari was destroyed and the island mostly became uninhabited. By 580 BCE the Greeks attempted to found a colony but encountered firm opposition from the Elimians from Segesta. The Greeks withdrew to Lipari and were welcomed by its few inhabitants fearing incursions by the Etruscans. This started a sea war that lasted for more than 100 years. By the 5th Century BCE, the Etruscans seized Lipari, but the people succeeded in freeing themselves. The naval battle of Cuma in 474 BCE put and end to the threat to Lipari.

A new period of prosperity began again. The smaller islands were repopulated. This opulence lasted until 252-51 BCE when the Romans conquered Lipari and brutally slaughtered many. The Roman destruction put an end to this splendid flourishing civilization. Lipari and the islands were reduced to an insignificant and poor provincial area.

I am currently researching information on the history of the islands after the fall of the Roman Empire but have not found any records; I will add some material as I find it… Since the 1970's the islands have been one of the major tourist attractions of southern Italy, and tourism has become the main source of economic activity in the archipelago. Many members of the Serra Family have gone back to visit the islands and all have raved of its beauty. The islands are a beautiful and peaceful place to relax, as the brochure "IsoleEolie" puts it…

> "If you are looking for a real adventure holiday in a world lost to time, face to face with nature, these seven islands with their endless beaches, bays grottoes, inlets and rocks, and the incomparable variety and richness of the sea-bed are certainly made for you. The natural beauty together with the many geological and volcanic aspects of seven–thousand years of history which you will discover when you visit the prehistorical villages and the archeological museum of Lipari contribute to making the archipelago with its modern tourist organization a real dream holiday spot all year round."

Salina basic facts

Location: 38.635°N, 014.877°E

Salina is politically independent and has three individual towns: Santa Marina di Salina, Malfa and Leni.

"The Green Island" hosts the highest mountain of the Aeolian Islands and offers marvelous landscapes, panoramic views, lovely villages, and the charming crater of Pollara. Although its most recent eruption occurred about 11,000-13,000 years ago, it is not certain whether the island is to be considered volcanically extinct.

The two volcanoes are separated by the "Val di Chiesa" (Valley of the Church) with a 17th century church located there.

Extreme northwest tip of Salina, Punta di Perciato is formed by a beautiful natural arc cut into the mafic lavas of the initial Pollara activity.

Part of the island has beautifully sculptured pyroclastic flow deposits from the Pollara eruption. Such outcropsings are abundant along the extremely scenic road from Malfa to Pollara.

In 1974 Gerard and Margherita Eggleston made a trip to the Aeolian Islands. They very graciously allowed me to have access to some of their slides from that trip. I had the slides made into photos and have included some of them here. I hope you enjoy them.

Gerard and Margherita Eggleston 1974 Trip to Salina photos

Margherita Eggleston

Gerard and Margherita Eggleston 1974 Trip to Salina photos

Margherita Eggleston in front of some local architecture

Salina is known as "The Green Island"

Photo of one of the ferries that transport people and goods to the islands.

Ocean views

Salina – More Information

Salina

The following are a few excerpts from books and other sources…

"Off the north-east coast of Sicily are the Eolie or Lipari Islands: Lipari, Vulcano, Salina, Panarea, Stromboli, Filicudi and Alicudi. Remote (they are the product of volcanic activity in this, the deepest part of the Tyrrhenian Sea) and primitive (there is no electricity apart from that provided by private generators), the island are a haven of seclusion, and offer the visitor beaches of volcanic sand and clear blue waters, famed for their diving and fishing. Seafood is, not surprisingly, a specialty!"

Italy, text by Andy Gravette, Prentice Hall General Reference, Sun Tree Publishing 1993, Simon & Schuster, NY, NY, (ISBN 0-671-87903-0) Pages 254-255

"If you are looking for a real adventure holiday in a world lost to time, face to face with nature, these seven islands with their endless beaches, bays, grottoes, inlets and rocks, and the incomparable variety and richness of the sea-bed are certainly made for you. The natural beauty together with the many geological and volcanic aspects of seven-thousand years of history which you will discover when you visit the prehistorical villages and the archeological museum of Lipari contribute to making the archipelago with its modern tourist organization a real dream holiday spot all year round."

Isole Eolie tourist pamphlet, printed by the Local Tourist Office of the Aeolian Islands, Telefono (090) 9880095

"In terms of natural vegetation this island to have protected its environment with a nature reserve, the *Riserva Naturale die Monti Fossa delle Felcie dei Porri*. These are the names of the twin volcanoes that inspired the Greeks to name the island Didyme (twins). The Monte Fossa delle Felci (968 m.) is the highest peak of all the small islands and the second highest peak of all Italian islands. Another crater which is still visible and lies just above sea level contains the village of Pollara. The sea has covered one side of the crater, and one can swim quite peacefully in a place that was once spewing forth fire and brimstone!
Salina has three autonomous municipal authorities. S. Marina on the eastern coast, Malfa to the north and Leni to the south west. From Leni down towards the sea is the village of Rinella. An interesting feature of the island is the Salt Lake at Lingua where at one time salt was produced, hence the name Salina."

Salina, Turistic Map and Nautic Chart, Pubbi dee, Grafiche Santocono-Rosolini

The Other Aeolian Islands

(Some of this information taken from the brochure "IsoleEolie")

Lipari

Lipari is almost 38 square kilometers in size and has the largest population. It is the administrative center of six of the seven islands and is the major tourist stop. Visit the castle of Lipari with its archeological park and museum, among the most important in Europe. Tour the island, stopping at Quattrocchi, Quattropani-Chiesa Vecchia, Terme di S. Calogero, Acquacalda, the pumice and obsidian quarries, Canneto. Excursions to Monte Guardia, Monte S. Angelo, Cappero-Semaforo and Pirrera-Forgia Vecchia. Boat trips to the Fataglioni (large rocks protruding out of the sea) and Pietra del Bagno.

Vulcano

Vulcano is the southern most of the islands. Although Vulcano is not well known to the world, its name is. It is here that all volcanoes the world over got their name. Visit the Allume grotto; Valcanello; Cape Grillo; Grotta del Cavallo and the whole area of Baia di Levante with its exceptionally therapeutic hot-water sea-bed springs and natural mud baths.

Panarea

Penarea is the small, above water section, of a much larger submarine complex. You can visit the prehistoric village of Capo Milazzese and Calajunco; the smaller islands of Basiluzzo, Dattilo and Lisca Bianca. The exceptional clear water and the richness of the sea-bed make Panarea especially suitable for underwater exploration.

Stromboli

Northern most of the islands, Stromboli is famous for having one of the few volcanoes that erupt virtually continuously and is the most active of all Mediterranean volcanoes. Many tourist visit at night and climb, by way of a guide, to the crater.

Filicudi

The main tourist attraction of Filicudi is Capo Graziano, a small prehistoric village from the Bronze Age. While there visit the Grotta del Bue Marino (Cave of Sea Ox); La Canna high rocks, the small islands of Elefante & Montenassari; and the Fortuna Cliffs.

Alicudi

Alicudi is on the western end of the chain and is the most remote of the Aeolian Islands. It still retains most of its "savage" character that all the islands once had. Many visitors take "round-the-island" boat trips, stopping at Scoglio della Galera rocks and Timpone delle Ffemmine.

An old attractive map of Italy, Sicily and the Aeolian Islands

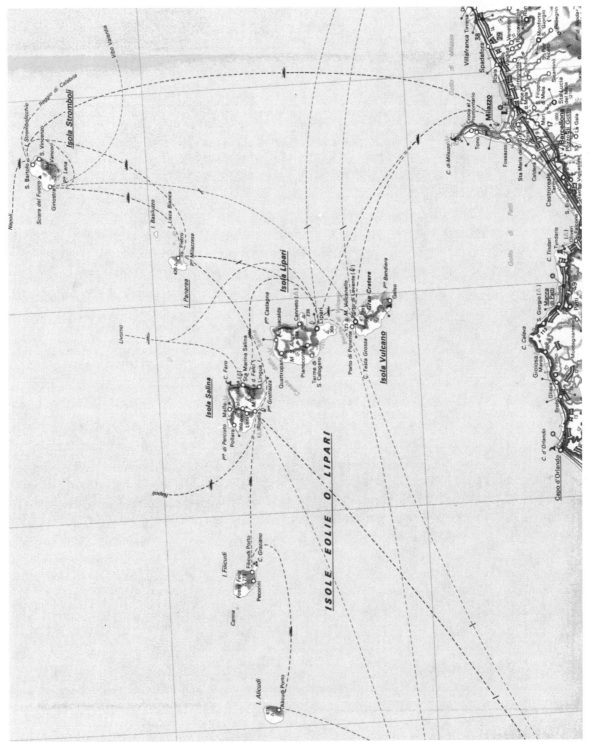

Close-up map of the Aeolian Islands

37

West side of Salina with the town of Leni with its port, Rinella, just to its south.

East side of Salina with the village of Lingua to the south and the town of S. Marina Salina to the east.

Story of the Blessed Mother
Maria S.S. Del Terzito

Written by Mary Goldrick as told to her by her father, Domenico Serra,
in 1980, the year before he died.

Statue of Maria S.S. Del Terzito and Domenico Serra

In the Mediterranean Sea there are seven small islands off the coast of Sicily, which is the largest island off the coast of the mainland of Italy. These seven small islands are called the Eolian islands. The most important island is called Lipari, which at the time of this happening was well populated. However, there was not much land on Lipari for good farming and because of this people had to seek work elsewhere.

In the Year of 1622 Alfonso Mereorella, his son and four other working men went with a row boat to the next island called Salina. This island has two big mountains and stands directly in front of the active volcano Stromboli. The men landed in a small town named Rinellao. They walked up to the middle of the two mountains to 'Val di Chiesa." There everything grew wild and they started to work clearing the brush and chopping down the trees. They worked for three days and had made good progress. Mereorella told the men to tie up the wood in bundles and carry them back to the beach, so they could load up the boat and take them back home to use for fire wood. While the men were away Mereorella remained alone working.

40

After a while he heard the sound of a bell tinkling, but he did not pay too much attention to it. After another little while he heard a second tinkling of a bell. He looked around to see where the sound was coming from. While he was looking he heard a third sound of the bell tinkling and at the same time he saw a beautiful woman wearing a veil and dressed in blue holding a bell in her right hand. She then disappeared. Meanwhile the other men came back and Mereorella told them what saw. The men were all astonished and they all started to look around and found what appeared to be the ruins of an old church. Inside the church they found a painting of the Blessed Mother, just as she appeared to Alfonso Mereorelia who had seen her. They cleaned up the painting and went back to the boat and went home to tell their families and neighbors what they saw on the other island.

The next day more people went to the island to see the beautiful painting of the Blessed Mother. It soon became a shrine where many people, sick, blind, and crippled visited to see the Blessed Mother. They asked and obtained the grace to be cured of their afflictions. Many, many miracles were performed there. People traveled from all over the mainland of Italy to pray to the Blessed Mother. The Emperor of Constantinople, Constante, also went to the island and had the church enlarged and made a Sanctuary of it. Many people came to make their residence on the island to be close to the Blessed Mother. They all worked and farmed the land producing for their families and everyone prospered. In 1914 one of the Cardinals made the coronation making the Blessed Mother "Maria S.S. Del Terzito, Queen of the Eolian Islands".

At the beginning of the 1900's some of the descendents of those people immigrated to the United Sates of America and established themselves In New York City. So great was their devotion to the Blessed Mother Maria S.S. Del Tersito that they founded the Congregation of the Blessed Mother Maria S.S. Del Terzito to honor her here in the United States. Three of the men were sent to Italy to have a replica of the statue of the Blessed Mother made and had it sent to America after obtaining permission from the Church to put it in the church of The Blessed Mother Mary Our Lady Help of Christians at 440 East 12th Street, New York City.

When the statue arrived at the dock in New York it was misplaced in an out of the way warehouse and could not be found for many months. One day a man with a speech impediment, (severe stuttering) came to the church at 12th street and told the priest that he had a dream telling him where the statue could be found. At first they sent him away. The man however, returned again and again to the priest and said he had the same dream of where to find the lost statue. To the great joy of all, the priest went with the man and found the statue, safe in the warehouse. They took it to the church Our Lady Help of Christians in New York City, where it still stands today, and can be seen at any time. After that the man's speech impediment was miraculously cured.

Each year on July 23rd the Congregation celebrates the Feast of our Blessed Mother Maria S.S. Del Terzito, of which Domenico Serra was secretary for sixty-seven years.

Valdichiesa - Santuario Madonna del Terzito

Madonna Del Terzito

Madonna Del Terzito

50TH

Annual Celebration

WILL BE HELD ON

Sunday. July 27th. 1958 at 11 A. M.

IN THE

CHURCH AT 440 EAST 12TH STREET

NEW YORK CITY

CONGREGA MARIA SS. DEL TERZITO
ANNESSA ALLA CHIESA DI MARY HELP OF CHRISTIANS

Particular notice to the families of the departed members: on Monday, July 28th at 9.00 o'clock, there will be a requem Mass for the deceased members.

COMMITTEE

FRANK COSTA, Patrono
JOSEPH GALLETTA, Presidente
LUIGI DI STEFANO Presidente Onorario a vita
DOMENICO SERRA, Segretario
GIUSEPPE VERGONA, Segretario di Finanza

MEMBERS

DOMENICO VILLANTE   ANTONINO SABATO
PIETRO DE FINA   JOSEPH PICONE
MATTEO SALVO   JOHN SCHEPIS

FRANK EMANUELE, Presidente della Congrega

Announcement for the 50th New York City Celebration

SANTUARIO MARIA SS. DEL TERZITO
98050 VALDICHIESA - LENI - ISOLE EOLIE

Vergine Benedetta del Terzito, venerando la Tua Icona nella verdeggiante "Oasi" di Valdichiesa, vogliamo rinvigorire la fede in Gesù, Maestro e Redentore.

Il tintinnio del mistico campanello, invita tutti noi a sintonizzarci sulla stessa lunghezza d'onda della Voce di Dio.

Aiutaci, "Benedetta tra le donne", a fare della vita un Cantico di lode e di adorazione al Padre.

Sostienici, "Piena di Grazia", in mezzo alle inevitabili prove che incontriamo lungo il Cammino.

Rivolgici, "Beata che hai creduto", il Tuo materno invito con la stessa intensità di Cana: "Fate quello che vi dirà!"

Ponendoci in ascolto della voce di Gesù Maestro ed edificando la "casa della nostra vita" sulla Roccia immutabile del Suo Amore, sarà possibile sperimentare ogni giorno "la Luce vera, quella che illumina ogni uomo".

Il suono del campanello ci farà percepire tanta gioia. Ci richiamerà la dolce melodia delle Campane di Pasqua, della cui gloria sei già partecipe.

E noi, con i riflessi del Risorto negli occhi, guidati dal soffio dello Spirito, contemplando Te, "Segno di Consolazione e di sicura Speranza", affretteremo il passo nel Pellegrinaggio verso il Padre. Amen.

Sac. Giuseppe Mirabito
Parroco

Card from Salina

My memories of Salina

Written by Christopher Obert, Francine DiGrandi and Jerry Eggleston
Photos supplied by the Eggleston Family the DiGrandi Family

Francine and her daughter Gina

I was going though some old e-mails and came across a very nice one sent to me from Francine DiGrandi. I had e-mailed her some photos of Salina and she sent me an e-mail back. The following is a copy of that e-mail and it gives us an excellent description of the island.

Hi Chris,

While I'm waiting for this one meg file to download I will start my response. I don't know what is in this document you are sending but I assume there are a lot of photos for it to be so large. I've been to the island of Salina. I was in the house, if you want to call it a house, where our grandparents were born. It was two rooms. I went 30 years ago when I was a teenager, so I don't know how clear my memory is. But I swear... I never touched the beautiful poppies that were growing all over the island. I vividly remember the dirt floor of the house and it seems that there were two rooms upstairs that had never finished construction. The two rooms downstairs were empty but one appeared to be the kitchen area and the other must have been where they all slept. I don't remember an interior stairway or an interior door between the rooms just a large oven in the one room. My Uncle Angelo had visited there a year or two before us and had taken the last of the remaining items. He had gotten a book of home remedies hand written in Italian that I remember everyone talking about. I'm sure it is still in his family's possession. I do remember taking some small glass bottles that I have since lost track of. Does anyone know who owns that land now?

My Uncle John and Aunt Olga had taken me there with my cousins Cheryl and Alex, their children. (I'm copying this to Cheryl to see she remembers the trip as I do.) We stayed only one night in an inn that was next door to a church with a bell and a rooster. Need I say more on that subject? The sheets were so filthy we didn't dare take our clothes off and the shared bathroom down the hall had towels I wouldn't use on my dogs. But the boat ride out there was so long and we were all so sea sick that we couldn't go back to Sicily that night. The inn was the lesser of 2 evils until Uncle John was robbed. He left some money and valuables in his room and they were gone when we got back that evening. I remember my uncle talking quite loud in Italian with the innkeeper that night.

Ah... the download is complete.... let me go look. Ah yes... I remember the island looking just like that as we approached it on the boat. In fact, all the islands we passed looked like that. It was like something out of Jason and the Argonauts. These islands were larger than life. Your picture does not do the size justice. I remember clearly passing one particular island that was entirely white as if it was covered with snow. It was white pumice I remember being told by someone. I may have lifted my dizzy head off the boat bench long enough to take a picture. I don't have any of my pictures of that trip. I gave them to Aunt Olga to develop years ago and I never retrieved them. I'm sure she has them and I visit her often. I'll get some before the reunion. Do you know of any other family members that have been there?

Eggleston photo of Lipari, that "White" island

I asked the Eggleston's to tell me more about their photo. This is Jerry's response:

"That picture was taken on the island of Lipari which is just south of the island of Salina. Marge's mother was born here. The picture shows a working pumice mine (really a hill) located on the north-east coast of the island. Marge has relatives that work there. The pumice was formed when a volcano erupted (centuries ago) and the heat of the eruption turned marble rock into very porous pumice stone. The stone is ground down to a fine powder and used as an abrasive... it's even used in tooth powder! We have a sample of the black marble which was not affected by the volcano heat and a sample of the pumice. Next time your here be sure to remind us to show them to you, it's quite remarkable."

The Genesis:
(My travels to the beginning: The Serra's Salina Story)

Written and photos by Christine di Grandi Jones

Last year (2002), I had the good fortune to visit the birth land of my four Italian grandparents. In the past, I had visited the mountain town of Turania, where my maternal Grandfather, Giovanni Clemenzi, grew up. Our cousins there have always been incredibly warm and hospitable. I had also visited the Island of Salina where my maternal grandmother, Concetta Serra Clemenzi, was born but could not find any relatives. I learned that all but my great grandfather, Battista, migrated to the United States. However, this time, I was bound and determined to learn more about their home and research family records.

Before leaving the States, I used the Internet to search for sir names from the four cities in which my grandparents were born. I found several names for Clemenzi in Rome and the outskirts, many for di Grandi in Ragusa and Lusco in Cefalu but nothing for Serra in Salina. I did, however, have the names and birth dates provided by Mary Serra Goldrick.

The grandeur of Rome and the incomparable beauty of the spectacular Amalfi Coast was only an appetizer to the delicious experience I was about to encounter-Two whole weeks in Sicily! From Rome, and a few days stay on the cliffs of the Amalfi Drive, my friends Colin, Arlene, Joe, and I headed south to the boot to cross on a short Ferry ride to Reggio a port in Sicily. Excitement, pride, and a feeling of ancestor's nationalism stirred within me, as the boat got closer to the main island.

Sicily embodies all that is Italian plus its own distinctive rich culture. She has been referred to as the playground of Europe and more classically said to be a melting pot of civilizations. There are influences of Arabs, Norman, Romans, Phoenicians, Greeks, French, Byzantines, Lombards, Spanish, and even Bavarian heritages. Historically rich and an incredibly gorgeous island; Sicily has sweeping views of mountains, oceans, and the dominant Mount Etna.

After soaking up the sun and landscape of gorgeous Taormina and Giardina Naxos, guided through the ruins in Syracusa, shopping, chatting with leisure fishermen, exploring, and eating everywhere, we headed north along the east coast of Sicily towards my main destination.

Milazzo is the port of embarkation for the Island of Salina. My Italian leaves a lot to be desired but I was able to figure out which ship would transport us to the place of my origins. It was suggested to leave the car at the dock and go via the faster hydro-foil "aliscafi," but since one cannot rent a car on Salina and knowing the exploring which I intended to do, I opted to transport it. (I later learned that there is a public bus that makes the rounds to the three municipalities of Salina). We drove up the ramp as you do on most all ferries and made our way up to where we had the choice of enclosed area where some relaxed and slept for the duration of the passage. Or, the bow or the stern was available for a windy suntan. I did a little of each. I had to be on the deck to see Salina come into view. Salina was the third stop. It was enjoyable seeing the trucks or produce and supplies being delivered to the islands and many islanders walk on and off board.

The Archipelago pokes up from the white sea foam to expose the presence of all the primordial volcanic forces of nature. Lipari boast of thermal hot spring and takes prides in the splendid Mycenaean grotto. Vulcano delights in sulfur muds and springs. Our Salina has the sharp contrast of the black sands and the bright green of the capers and the nectar of Malvasia wine. Salina is second place in the archipelago for population and first in the archipelago for its fertility of soil.

The drive from the port at San Marina to Malfa was about 30 minutes along the eastern shoreline. The narrow street steadily inclined and meandered. There were lots of trucks, which were narrow but BIG carrying a variety of products playing leapfrog with the numerous mopeds as they made their ascent. Giant geranium plants, cascading purple flowers, cactus flowers, and wonderful caper flowers, lined the way making the journey to the sea level town more interesting and beautiful. Some turns on the road were nearly 360 degrees—the roller coaster ride in Disney world had nothing on this approach! I had to stop filming because

46

the twists in the road were causing me carsickness. I always find it ironically amusing that whenever I would ask for directions, the response was inevitably: "Sempre directo" (always direct). "AGIP" gas stations were the only ones I ever saw. Gas is sold by the liter and, as you might imagine, more expensive on the island.

Salina consists of two volcanoes, inspiring the Greeks to name the island "Didyme" meaning twins. No matter where I traveled, they were always part of the vistas. They have not erupted in 13,000 years so, that seemed safe and cool.

The entrance to Malfa was bright and colorful with a large mural painted on the side of a building on Via Roma. We pulled into the center by San Lorenzo church whose courtyard is the center for meetings-especially in the evening. There was lots of activity. Many were walking around talking on cell phones, scaffolds supporting men applying a fresh cover of stucco to a building, and mopeds buzzing around the residents. Their popularity is understandable as it is nearly impossible to find parking and negotiate the roads, which better resembled alleyways. Straight ahead of me was a sign "Internet Café"! Wow-How progressive! I was impressed with the modern name and service. We passed through the doorway draped, as most are, with long strands of beads, to the local bar. Off in the corner, was the computer. Need I say, that they did not have a wideband connection. Given my Internet addiction, I had to send an email to the family to let them know of our arrival and to see if there were any other souvenir requests.

The little "corner stores" are called "Alementari". There was no diet coke to be found in Italy, it is called Coca Cola Light and did not have the sweetness to which I am accustomed! You could buy just about anything there. "Gelato", Ice cream is a big favorite throughout all of Italy. My eye was already searching the little shops for the list my cousins provided. A bottle of Malvasia wine, a newspaper, a flag, photos of people, a poster of Salina, a rock from our grandparents home, and of course T-shirts and hats bearing the name Salina were big on the list.

Salina logo on baseball hat.
(Chris Obert photo)

The Serra family was in search of their roots. Chris Obert was compiling the genealogy of the Serras and asked me to find out the birth and death dates of our "Bisnonni" (Great grandparents). I thought the cemetery was a good place to start my search for this information. There, I met Triola Palermo, the grounds keeper. He said there was no evidence that there were any Serras who were buried in Malfa. My further questioning resulted in him showing me the mausoleum of the Angelina and Francesca Carfarella sisters who were given permission by our great grandmother to use and cultivate the family property in exchange for caring for the land and paying the taxes. My mother, Mary di Grandi, had told me about the existence of such a written agreement. Word got out quickly that an American was asking about this property.

When I asked for directions from a frail aged man, he became rejuvenated! Francesco, who proudly declared he was 89 years old, hopped on his little motorcycle and led me to the Serra property. With a big grin, dancing eyes, and an expanded chest, he proudly told me how he dated Concetta Serra and that he once took her to Naples. I was really getting excited at the thoughts that this man knew my grandmother. I was doing some quick math in my head...my grandmother died at age 97 and that was about 15 years ago... hmmm... but when he was so certain that Concetta's sister Lena had a wooden leg, and that her family all moved to Australia, I knew there was a mix-up. Yet, he correctly named all the siblings in the Serra family. I was equipped with our family tree in hand and after a challenging mental and lingual exercise, I came to understand that our great grand father and his brother gave all their children the same names! Can you imagine the confusion since they all shared a humble abode?

After the death of our great grandfather, Battista Serra, our great grandmother, Bartolomea Lazzaro Serra, (my granddaughter, Bettina, is named after her) came to America with her son Domenico. Finally she would join her children who Domenico had previously brought across. Battista's brother and his children stayed in Salina for several years before migrating to Australia. Thus, the reason no one there remembers our branch of the family. Some day, I will seek them out.

The car had to be parked up the hill from the house since the path was much too narrow. The one story structure which was hand constructed of stone and mortar by our ancestors, now sits humbly it is a deteriorated state. It is located down the hill from the town and about a half-mile up from the seashore. The small house was divided into two sections for the two families. There was a big hole in one of the exterior walls and part was secured with a padlock. Though the structure was little more than rubble, the view of the Tyrrhenuan Sea was inviting and gorgeous! Turn 45 degrees and you have another breath taking view of a volcano. There were abundant grapevines embracing the property. I snapped a zillion photos of what was once our ancestors' home

The old house, with the volcano in the background

About 50 feet from where I stood at the property, I saw a rosy-cheeked teenage girl who lived in the neighboring house. She invited me to meet her grandparents, Mr. & Mrs. Lorenzo Lopez. Mr. Lopez explained that our grandfather, with the help of his brother, was building the two-story house across the walkway on the ocean side of our family's house. The façade of this house was newer with a smoother stucco finish. It had never been occupied. Battista died before the roof was installed and thus construction ceased.

The "new" unfinished house

Mr. Lopez was a wealth of information and gave me the inside scoop of how Lorenzo, the son of Francesca Carfarella, took all the property before 1979. It seems that one of his relatives uses the property to occasionally house her animals. I left a note on my calling card at the home of Giovana Virgona requesting the keys to this property. Mr. Lopez was eager to help me regain control of this land for my family by offering his attorney's name and phone number in Messina. I used my cell phone (which I bought in Rome and used a lot!) to call Aunt Sophia Villanti so the intricate details would be clearly understood. (They are six hours ahead of New York Eastern Standard Time.)

This helpful neighbor pointed out the boundary lines of the several tiny parcels of land which comprise this one area and which Serra family member owned each. The total of the parcels do not add up to half an acre. Senor Lopez also pointed out the bountiful grapes that are being cultivated on the Serra land. These are the unique grapes that make Malvasia wine which has a sweet aroma and high in alcohol. Salina is the largest producer of Malvasia wine. It is said that Julius Caesar came and fetched Malvasia wine by boats to drink it in Roma! We enjoyed a couple of bottles of the sweet and delicious wine at the Serra reunion, which followed a few weeks later. The other islands abandoned the culture of growing grapes due to a lack of labor. One of the greatest exports is its labor population that is still extensively emigrating towards the new world.

Green plants everywhere

49

For the first time, I saw how that wonderful caper grows in a white flowering plant, which is their major export. The Lopez property had the many of these beautiful flowering plants. He and his wife were most hospitable. I bought my cases of capers and wine from his store and delighted the young girl with the likes of American dollars. He also showed me his bakery and welcomed any American cigarettes we would send.

One of my goals was to get the birth certificate of my Nonna Concetta. I had learned that it was possible to get an Italian passport and citizenship if you met certain requirements. The next morning, I went to the "commune" to research the property ownership and get copies of the birth certificates of my grandmother and her brothers and sisters. Mr. Nando, with whom I had been corresponding, (commune.Malfa@tiscalinet.it) was most kind in trying to assist me. He printed out the tax map and identified the ownerships of the Serra properties.

All the birth entries were beautifully hand written in a calligraphy style in large books. Italians tend to write in a very fancy scroll type that can be challenging to read. Serra was a frequent entry. Holding this book with all our ancestors' names in it kicked up feelings. It was not the simplest to understand. Besides the sharing of names by the two families, there was a double entry for Caterina Serra born to the same parents. We finally figured out that one child had died and later also named another daughter Caterina. One of the kind town employees spent a good length of time to hand write a copy of each birth certificate for me-some in long form. I copied them (using a simpler method) and gave them out to the respective children and grandchildren at the reunion of 2002.

The records of Bartolomea and Battista Serra are in the archives in Messina on the main Island of Sicily. According to the records in Malfa, the land was still in the names Battista Serra and his brother, Guiseppe Serra. It was suggested that I take a boat to Lipari, the legal seat, where the high school for Salina is, and where documents are recorded in the Pretura. I did as suggested and searched records in the basement where the filing system consisted of towers of stacked books. Shame on me, but I couldn't resist taking a photo of this helpful man who became the soft landing for a few heaps of books. No petitions for adverse possession were found. Hope for our family to reclaim this land! I have been subsequently asked how I would get all the cousins agree on what to do with the land. My reply: If we do not save the property, the question is moot!

Via the Internet, I was able to make reservations. Hotel Signum on Via Scalo was well tucked away down footpaths and behind other masonry buildings. Parking was impossible and portaging the baggage was a Herculean event! But oh, how peaceful and fragrant set amidst, flowers and vineyards and the vista was magnificent! All dining experiences were on terraces with splendid ocean views. For the most part, restaurants were limited to the hotels' terraces. (Malfa has about 4-5 hotels).

The patroness, Clara, of this first class establishment contact a hotel owner in Malfa who was also helpful to me in connecting with the Town Hall and the Town's Historian, Antonio Brundu with whom she is very involved in the immigration museum. Senor Brundu, who is not only the librarian and responsible for most every photo you will ever seen published of Salina, but also the energy behind the creation and construction of the emigration Museum which gives tribute to those who have migrated from this dear Aeolian homeland. I found the library on the second floor of a building tucked behind the church of S. Lorenzo. Antonio Brundu was most welcoming and interested in our family history. He would love to have some artifacts from us for the museum. He gave me an extensive tour of the museum which temporary resides in a home of a philanthropist. Brundu showed me the site that they are trying to buy which will need total reconstruction at a cost of 80.000.000 milioni di lira.

As the Serra reunion was being planned for June 2002, it was suggested by my sister, Patty, that we do something for the hometown of our ancestors-Perhaps a plague to commemorate our family and pay tribute to the town of Malfa. We decided to raise money at the reunion to fund such a cause and learn what the town peoples might appreciate. We held a raffle and auction where many cousins, and aunts and uncles donated handmade gifts and artworks, dinners, and even a boat cruise! Over $1,300 was raised. The museum was the answer to the tribute we wanted to make!

Our cousin Angela told me of Uncle Domenico's devotion to Santa Maria del Terzito and asked me to take a photo of the church. Setting off on its own was this quiet church in Leni. As I was giving prayers of thanks giving, I was distracted other visitors. In the middle of the work day, two young men about 20 years of age dressed in their labor work clothes took off their hats and stood for some time in front of the statue of Our Lady. It was a simple but moving moment. Needless to say, I took more than one photo and have most everything on video.

Leni was also the home of my cousin's Villanti family. Just below is the town of lovely Rinella. From this tiny port, the aliscafi express boats for passengers only for to other islands in the archipelago. This time I enjoyed a great lunch under a trellis with the soft cool breeze of the ocean. There is a great little out doors restaurant we found near the port for lunch. I turned to my right and was elated to discover the hotel in which I stayed on my first trip. It is a very old and charming hotel on the water I stayed on my first trip- L'Ariana via Rotabile, 11, Rinella-Salina 98050 Isole Eolie. It was not until I retuned home that my mother told me that owns land here in this sweet ocean town that richly produces olives.

Pollara, another town is one of the most beautiful places I have seen in this world! On the Western side is a big crater lying just above sea level. The bottom combines to make an inclined plateau from 50 to 100 meters on which the built-up area of Pollara is situated. Beautiful stone stairs lined with terraced flowering caper plants down to the ocean. Dare I tell you that our family owned grape vineyards in this little paradise! <sigh>

Pollara

My time ended in Santa Marina, the largest port on the island. Last minute shopping was possible in a few shops, which sported a nice selection of colorful pottery made in Salina and even T-shits and hats! In an attempt to bring home something for everyone, I did my fair share to contribute to the welfare of Salina!

As I was making my way down to the port, there was a man with a table of bright colorful beaded jewelry. He was teaching his young son the skill of the trade of making a variety of delicate and colorful pieces. Needless to say, I bought several necklaces and took a photo of the Entrepreneurs! Just before my foot hit the boat, I was tempted by a refreshing specialty of the islands "Granita," a mixture of ice, flavoring and sugar. For centuries, nobles in Naples and Sicily marketed snow that was collected from the mountains. I squeezed and savored every second possible out of my Salina experience and literally ran to the ship. I sat at the stern and with appreciation, pride, and a tear, watched the verdant mountainous island disappear in the ship's wake.

Good-bye to the beautiful island

Upon reaching the main island of Sicily, we drove along the northern cost to the incredibly beautiful resort town of Cefalu. En route, I pulled out my trusty cell phone and called a few phone numbers of Lusco from my Internet search. I struck gold when I reached Lina Lusco. She made plans to meet me at a gas station. She arrived with her mother and brother-in-law and we followed them to their family compound. They were vivacious, warm and familial! Soon, her sister, brother, children and their husbands, and their children arrived. I was treated like the long lost relative! We ate, drank, laughed, and looked at family photos and their family history book. We could not go back beyond knowledge of our grandparents to see if we were at all related!! What a loving joyous experience with absolute strangers! We made promises to keep in touch and they would come to visit me in New York and I would one day return! These, my dear family, are Sicilians-perhaps not related by blood, but familial warmth that flows beyond. This incredible embracing hospitality is exactly what my Aunt Sophia would do if she got a call from strangers who said they were from Italy-they need not be relatives. My English companion was blown away with the receptions we received throughout Italy. Ah, to be Italian! It is delicious on many levels!

I wanted to bring home a treasure something indigenous to Sicily. I tend to be pragmatic and appreciate handmade goods and art and since I really like ceramics, the choice was easy. As I headed to the airport in Catania, I drove inland to the high mountain town of Caltagirone, once the location of a Saracen fortress and famous for ceramic art. Sicilians refer to the "Caltagirone style" in ceramic pottery, characterized by ornate traditional motifs using a limited palette. I now have such a creation gracing my entrance foyer of my home. Transporting my large uniquely designed and exquisitely painted vase is a story in itself. Let me just say, that the airport security had all the careful packing removed to be sure it was not a bomb. It flew on a first class seat to NYC (while I sat in coach) and pushing the large box and lugging, all the goodies and gifts from Salina inclusive of a large Sicilian flag pushing and pulling all my digs. I looked like a one-man parade.

Now, back home and on my laptop writing to you, I recall this all with the burning desire to return for a longer visit. Salina does not cater to the jet set but she embraces all that is rich in beauty and warmth. The rounded shape of the island with its tall volcanic peeks reminds me of a mother whose arms are encircling – embracing all who were birthed within and their descendants. Such a rich inheritance we have. Plan a vacation that includes a trip back to your ancestry's roots. Visit the museum to which we have financially contributed that honors those who migrated about one hundred years ago. More than the climate was idyllic! I am proud of my Italian heritage and even more fortunate to be not only Sicilian but also an Aeolian from Salina!

Thank you for reading this-I hope you have learned a bit more of your personal history.
Christine di Grandi Jones great granddaughter of Battista and Bartolomea Serra
July 2003

Salina in the Movies
Written by Christopher Obert

If you want to go on a tour of Salina without ever leaving your living room, I suggest renting the 1994 movie "The Postman" (Il Postino). Most of the movie's outdoor scenes were filmed on the Island of Salina. The movie (not to be confused with the 1997 Kevin Costner movie of the same name) is the story of the renowned Chilean diplomat and poet, Pablo Neruda (played by Philippe Noiret), who was forced into exile and granted sanctuary by the Italian government. The movie was nominated for 5 Academy Awards and won Best Original Score 1995. The movie is 116 minutes long and is in Italian with English subtitles.

"Il Postino" a 1995 Miramax Films release

Salina Web Pages

While I was doing research on Salina I visited many different WebPages. Two internet sites (Travel-Italy.com and The Treasuries of Italy) were very helpful. These two sites are devoted to the tourist trade. Travel-Italy is a travel agency specializing in Italy. You can check out the hotels, tourist destinations, local weather reports and plan trips from their web site. The Treasuries of Italy site will give you information on renting houses and villas on Salina. If you get the chance, please visit their sites and see if a trip to Salina is in your future. Both sites gave me permission to use information and photos from their sites. The following few pages contain material from those two websites. I hope you enjoy it.

Aeolian Islands - Salina

Sabrina Friedman, Staff Writer, Travel-Italy.com

With a name derived from the ancient Didyme (meaning twin), it's not hard to identify Salina solely from its shape: two reliefs separated by a saddle-like hump. Its present name, however, originated from a coastal lake that was once used as a salt pan. Salina is divided into three communes: Santa Marina Salina, Malfa and Leni. To the East, you'll find Fossa delle Felci and Rivi, which are connected to Monte dei Porri by the saddle. The saddle also acts as a connecting point with Malfa and the valley of Gavite to the North and Rinella the Vallonazzo in the South. The center of the islands offers the N-S depression of Valdichiesa, which separates the two mountain ranges and serves as an inhabited tourist attraction for its spectacular views and beautiful flora.

Phrasing and geography aside, a visit to Salina will confirm previous travelers' assents: A gorgeous island filled with culinary luxuries like aromatic, highly alcoholic red and white wines and plump, delicious capers, a wide variety of flora and fauna and a people, warm and welcoming, like no other.

The tall slopes of the island are covered by poplars, ilexes and chestnut trees. In addition to these species (particular to Salina in the Aeolian Islands,) you'll find the bush typical of the Mediterranean, such as myrtle, broom and a rather fragrant set of strawberry trees. The terraced lower slopes are sprinkled with both caper bushes and the prickly pear (frequent among smaller Aeolian Islands) and orchards, olive groves and the vineyards that produce the sweet white wine (called Malvasia) and concentrated reds that serve, along with capers, as the islands greatest export for much of the 20th century.

Interestingly, Salina is the largest producer of Malvasia in the Aeolian Islands; in fact, in other islands this practice has been all but obliterated, making the white wine that comes from Salina a rare and special treat. The Malvasia is not actually white, but a strong golden yellow color, reminiscent of apple juice, that emits a strong aroma.

If it's wine you're looking for, Salina's the place, but if you're looking for natural beauty and an island offering a warm welcome to its frequent tourists, well - Salina is the place for that, too.

Geographically, Salina is situated along the Lingua point; you'll find the action on this island (outside of the center N-S strip) to the West. Along this portion of the island, you'll find a series of ideal spots to enjoy a gourmet picnic complete with native wine and spectacular views. (Be sure to bring food from Lipari or whatever your initial destination may be. Get wine on the island, grab a spot amongst the bluffs overlooking the water and exhale.) I guarantee it will be the most relaxing, romantic picnic you can imagine. If you manage to catch the sunset, even better. Sunsets off Salina are absolutely breathtaking. Local legend holds that non-Italians who conceive on the island are destined to have a baby girl who will grow into the most irresistible of heartbreakers.

If you're more athletic than amorous, Salina can accommodate you, too. Water sports off the Salina coast are extremely popular. If you're so inclined, grab a jet ski or wave runner while in Lipari (there are plenty, trust me) and take off on your own private journey. You'll find a great deal of Italian teens zipping between islands on personal watercraft, so tourists who run into problems on the water generally find someone to help them out. Thus, if you've never tried jet skiing and want your first time to be memorable, check it out. It's a beautiful way to see the island. (Just be sure to lay off the Malvasia before taking off. While you won't find many alcohol-related watercraft accidents, you won't want to cause one of them.) Also note that strong marine currents circle the island, formed by directional waters that cross the channel between Salina and Lipari. If you can't swim, make the 24-square-mile jaunt around the island by boat.

http://www.travel-italy.com

Travel-Italy.com

Group Travel Enterprises, Inc. (d.b.a. Travel-Italy.com) was formed in 1992. Our first website appeared in 1995 and has continued to grow. Presently, Travel-Italy.com offers nearly 200 hotels in various Italian regions, over 2,300 vacation rental properties, sightseeing tour programs, great deals on auto rentals, and a selection of 225 city, provincial and regional maps. The company also makes available to web site users regular news and weather updates, a wealth of factual and creative travel information, and a regularly sent email newsletter keeping prospective clients informed about news events in Italy.

Christopher Group

cgroup@travel-italy.com
Direct: 1-573-256-6106 x800

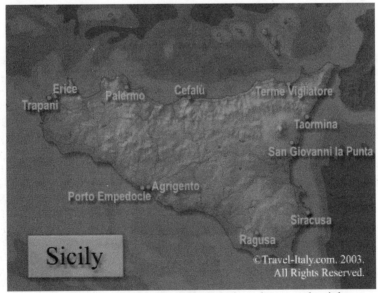

Map of Sicily, the Aeolian Island are just above on the right

Salina

I Tesori d'Italia - Case per vacanze

Salina

L'isola di Salina, seconda per estensione dell'arcipelago Eoliano con una superficie di 26 Kmq, è costituita interamente da rocce vulcaniche che rappresentano la parte emersa di un complesso vulcanico che si estende al di sotto del livello del mare fino a una profondità di 1500 m. Ancora facilmente individuabili sono i 2 crateri, il Monte Fossa delle Felci (mt 962) e il Monte Porri (mt860), simili tra loro e che danno all'isola una forma caratteristica da cui ha avuto origine l'antico nome di Dydyme (gemella).

Delle sette isole eoliane, Didyme-Salina è stata l'unica ad avere il più prezioso dei doni: l'acqua, che permise così la nascita e la crescita d'una vegetazione abbondante, eccezionale per un'isola vulcanica. Ci sono fitti boschi di felci, pini, castagni, querce; è abbondante la macchia mediterranea con i vermigli corbezzoli, i mirti, le ginestre; sparsi dappettutto sono i cespugli di capperi, una delle preziose risorse dell'isola, i fichi d'India, e vaste sono le zone dedicate ai vigneti, ai frutteti agli uliveti. Qui nasce, si produce la Malvasia, vino singolare dall'intenso aroma e dal sapore delicatamente dolce, che ha contribuito al rilancio economico dell'isola di Salina.

L'isola è divisa in tre comuni: Santa Marina, che è il porto e il paese principale dell'isola, con la sua frazione Lingua (a circa 2 km); Malfa è invece il comune più grande, sia come estensione che come abitanti (circa 1000 residenti), e comprende nel suo comune le frazioni di Pollara e Capo Faro; Leni è invece un pò più rialzato e comprende le frazioni di Rinella (altro porto dell'isola) e Valdichiesa.

Come detto Santa Marina Salina èe' il paese principale, dove fanno approdo tutte le navi e aliscafi.
Il paese e' ben distribuito e diviso principalmente in due parti: la parte del porto, con la Via Risorgimento, la via principale del paese, ove ci sono tutti i principali negozi, tutte le boutique, e dove c'e'è anche la nostra agenzia.

La parte alta e' quella dove vi sono la maggior parte delle case che compongono il paese. E' molto piu' fresca del centro, grazie soprattutto alle brezze di mare e di terra, che fanno in modo che tutte le case siano ventilate durante il giorno.

Del comune di Santa Marina fa anche parte Lingua, un piccolo paesino a circa 2 km, dove e' possibile fare una bella passeggiata attorno al laghetto di acqua salata ove anticamente vi erano delle saline (da qui prende il nome l'isola).

Malfa e' il comune piu' grande (1000 residenti). E' posizionata su un altopiano, quindi per scendere a mare (la spiaggia di Punta Scario) bisogna percorrere una piacevole discesa in scalini. Del comune di Malfa fa parte la zona più bella dell'isola, quella di Pollara.

Pollara, un piccolo paesino a 5 km da Malfa, è il luogo dell'isola rimasto più selvaggio: non ci sono ne mini-market, ne bar ne negozi, ma si gode di una spiaggia, di una vista e soprattutto di un tramonto che non si possono dimenticare. Pollara, come molti altri posti dell'isola e' un nido per innamorati, ove si puo' stare la sera ad osservare i mille colori del sole che tramonta accanto Filicudi e Alicudi. A Pollara da non perdere è anche il Perciato, un grande arco in pietra vulcanica, frutto dell'erosione marina e del vento.

Del comune di Malfa fa anche parte la zona di Capo Faro, un altro piccolo paesino tra Santa Marina e Malfa, dove si gode di una vista suggestiva di una tranquillità fantastica.

Leni e' il terzo dei comuni, situato in un altopiano, di cui fanno parte le frazioni di Valdichiesa e Rinella. Valdichiesa e' una zona bellissima dell'isola, a un passo dalla riserva naturale e dove si sente il profumo della montagna e della sua vegetazione, restando pur sempre a pochi km (circa 4) dal mare. Rinella e' la frazione sul mare, ove vi e' l'altro porto di Salina. Molto carina la spiaggia di Pra' Venezia, anche se un piu'òdifficile da raggiungere. A Rinella vi e' l'unica spiaggia con sabbia dell'isola (le altre sono quasi tutte con ciottoli).

Consigliabile è l'ascesa del Monte Fossa delle Felci ove girando su se stessi si possono osservare tutte e sette le isole Eolie, la costa calabra e quella sicula con l'imponente Monte Etna.

Mare incontaminato, clima secco e fresco, tramonti suggestivi, silenzi irreali caratterizzano questo spettacolare scenario dal fascino primitivo che esercita un'attrazione magnetica sul visitatore generando un prepotente desiderio di ritornare.

Salina e' l'isola degli innamorati, dei soggiorni romantici, delle passeggiate al chiaro di luna.

Sull'isola si possono noleggiare gommoni, motorini, barche. Non ci sono discoteche. Se si ha voglia di una serata in discoteca è possibile andare a Panarea, Lipari o Vulcano con una delle barche che offrono questo servizio di trasporto notturno.

Le case che noi offriamo sono dislocate in tutti i comuni e in tutte le frazioni dell'isola, a due passi dal mare o un pò più distanti, a seconda delle necessità.

http://www.itesoriditalia.com/index/index.htm

Photos of Salina
I Tesori d'Italia - Case per vacanze

Laghetto di Lingua con Lipari sullo sfondo

Faro di Lingua

Pollara - Perciato

Capo Faro

Baia di Pollara

Tipica spiaggia di Salina

I Tesori d'Italia - Case per vacanze
The Treasuries of Italy - Houses for vacations

Arcangelo Nicotra

tel. +39 090 9843436 (April-November)
tel. +39 090 9222200 (November-April)
fax +39 090 9843600
cell. +39 338 6262734
info@itesoriditalia.it
arcangelo@itesoriditalia.it

Santa Marina vista del mare

Next Stop: America!

Aeolian and Salina Notes:

*The subject of history
is the life of peoples and of humanity.*

--Leo Tolstoy, *War and Peace*

America,
Land of Opportunities

A Preface to Immigration and Ellis Island

The Economics of America vs. Italy

Written by Christopher Obert

The economics of the Aeolian Islands and the rest of Sicily and Italy were not very good

The Economics of Italy

There were many economic pressures compelling huge numbers of Italians to leave their homeland around the turn of the century. From 1870 to 1900 there was a decline in per capita income throughout Italy, and there was a slowdown in production in most foodstuffs. Malnutrition became widespread. Italians consumed mostly fruits and greens, while meats were beyond the reach of most families.

Over 80% of the people of Italy depended on agriculture for their livelihood. Most were still farming using the same implements and methods used by the Romans. The farmers were also victims of a land system which offered little hope for improvement. They were bound with "Shackles of Poverty" with little chance for advancement. Unemployment was high with workers always exceeding the demand for labor because of Italy's growing population.

After the turn of the century there was a small economic recovery and an increase in food production, not enough to correct the living conditions but just enough to pay for a boat ticket to America. Many people bought that ticket.

America offered the chance to obtain a better standard of living

The Economics of America

Numerous opportunities and dreams of unknown pleasures beckoned the Italians (and many other people) to America. For most urban amenities, such as running water, indoor bathing and toilet facilities and central heating, were attractions enough. Better economic, social, cultural and educational status was the icing on the cake.

Wages were pitiful in Italy when compared to the United States. A person in America doing the same job as someone in Italy could make twice as much money, have better living conditions and have access to better food and health care. The choice was simple America was the place to be.

Many thousands came to America, found jobs and started their lives over. Many of these people saved their money and sent some back home to Italy. It was this money from America that helped to improve the conditions in Italy. The newly arrived cash stimulated the economy and created new growth. The Italian government saw the benefit of this situation and encouraged more Italians to move to America, but also reminded them to send money home.

Signs of wealth were all around them, such as the Empire State Building

Ellis Island

Written by Christopher Obert
Photos by Nova Development Corp. and the National Park Service: Statue of Liberty National Monument

The Statue of Liberty, the symbol of a new life

"Give me your tired, your poor,
Your huddled masses, yearning to breathe free,
The wretched refuse of your teeming shore,
Send these, the homeless, tempest-tost, to me:
I lift my lamp beside the golden door."

-- Emma Lazarus, The New Colossus
(Inscription at the base of the Statue of Liberty)

Ellis Island

In 1892 the Federal Immigration and Naturalization Service (INS) moved its New York headquarters to Ellis Island. This was the beginning of a part of American history that still affects us today. Ellis Island was the port of entry for many millions of people into the United States. It was for many the symbol of hope and a cause of anxiety, for it was in it's halls that their future was to be written. Were they to stay and start a new life or were they to be sent back?

Because of the great number of people passing through Ellis the opportunity for exploitation was apparent. In the early years of Ellis Island corruption was so wide spread that President Theodore Roosevelt fired the top staff and ordered a major cleanup in 1901. It was in this new cleaned up Ellis Island that Domenico and thousands of others entered into America.

The number of immigrants coming into America was incredible. By 1903 two more islands were connected to Ellis (using soil obtained from the new IRT subway in New York) to help with the crowds.

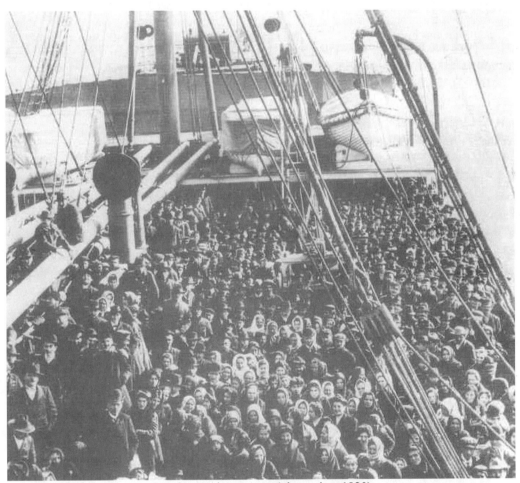
Immigrants in steerage (photo circa 1920)

<u>Inspection</u>

The cornerstone of federal immigration policy was to see that no immigrant became "Liable to become a public charge." In other words, all immigrants were not sick, too poor or incapable of taking care of themselves.

Processing began as steamships entered New York Harbor. Boarding Inspectors and doctors met the ship and examined the first and second class passengers aboard the ships. Most of these passengers were spared the visit to Ellis Island because of their status and wealth.

Most of the immigration passengers traveled in steerage or third class. They were all required to go to Ellis Island for processing. Most ships docked at a west side Manhattan pier. The steerage passengers were placed aboard a ferry and shuttled to Ellis Island. Each person was tagged with their name and the name of the ship they came from. The men were then separated from the woman and children. Children traveling alone were always held until a male relative came for them.

They all had to pass a medical examination. If the doctors found a problem or had any questions, the immigrant would be marked with chalk on their chest. They were then sent to a medical detention area for additional treatment and evaluation. If the people were found to be in good health, they were next sent to the Registry Room. There they were asked questions by an immigration inspector, a clerk and an interpreter. The typical interrogation was a list of 32 questions, such as "How much money do you have?" Immigrants had to show they had some money to prove that they were not paupers. If the inspector felt it was necessary, he could ask additional questions. If there were any problems, the person was held in detention. Medical and legal examinations lasted three to five hours. If a person was held in detention for medical or other reasons they could be forced to stay there for as short as a few hours, days, or weeks or they could be detained for many months. Up until 1909 it was up to the inspectors' discretion whether a person was detained. After that, immigrants had to have at least transportation tickets to their destination or $25.00. The railroad and steamships were common forms of transportation, especially in New England and the Southern states, and tickets could be bought on Ellis Island.

The Registry Room (photo circa 1905)

70

<u>A New Life</u>

From January 1, 1892 to November 12, 1954, 12 million people went through processing or detention. For some, it was the start of a new life. For others it was a heartbreaking experience. Either way, their lives and the lives of their family would never be the same.

For those lucky ones that made it through Ellis Island, the future was bright and happy. There would be lots of challenges and hard work ahead of them but the opportunities were well worth it. As they left Ellis Island to confront these challenges, they, America and the world would forever be altered.

Immigrants leaving Ellis Island for freedom (photo circa 1907)

They Came Off the Boat

Written by Christopher Obert

Some of you may not know that the original title of this book was going to be "They Came Off the Boat". But some people did not like that title. They thought that it did not sound right; others thought the title was an insult that people used to say to immigrants. I liked the title. I thought the one line said so much. It relayed the truthful facts of their journey. Our forefathers did come over by boat and they did have to deal with insults and hardships. Trying to please everyone, I decided to try and find another name that I liked even better. I was hoping that when I heard the title I would know it. One day, while I was making a list of people I wanted to remember to thank in the "acknowledgement" section, I was listening to the music CD I made for the Serra reunion. The CD had songs by Dean Martin, Frank Sinatra and Gene Kelly. As I worked and listened, one song started. It was a song sung by Bob Hope and Shirley Ross. The song was, "Thanks for the Memories." I said "That's It!" It was perfect. I wanted to thank people for all the memories that they were sending me, I wanted to thank my grandparents for their story and I wanted the book to show how grateful we all were. As I listened to the song, it seemed to me to be about the memories between a man and a woman. Not exactly what I was working on, but a very close tie in, so I was happy.

A few months later I found that that song was even better than I first thought. While I was doing research for this section, I found a great book on immigration called, "Ellis Island – Interviews in their own words" by Peter Morton Coan. Some of the information in this section came from that book. I highly recommend this book; it would be a great title to have on your bookshelf next to this one. I cannot tell you how surprised I was when I found out that Bob Hope was an immigrant that came through Ellis Island himself in 1908. His real name was Leslie Townes and he was born in England. In this book Hope states:

> "We were only at Ellis Island for a few hours. But I do remember standing with my mother and five brothers on the boat as it entered New York Harbor for the first time, and seeing the lights and the Statue of Liberty… I remember looking up at my mother after we passed through inspection. We smiled and kissed and hugged each other because we had achieved this great thing, this right of passage… Years later… I was doing some sort of publicity thing in New York-down near the harbor. I just remember staring out over the water to Ellis Island and the statue, and remember feeling very grateful, very lucky, and saying to myself, "Thank you." Thanks for the memory. That was the first song I sang in the movies with Shirley Ross and it was such a hit, I just kept on doing it. But emotionally, when I hear it, I think of that day we arrived at Ellis Island. I don't think, in all my years, I ever told anyone that…"

Sadly during the writing of this book, Bob Hope passed away. So, as you can see, the title is special. I hope that as you read it you are filled with love and happiness. Oh yes, and one more time, I want to thank everyone for their help with this book… Thanks for the memories!

Statue of Liberty completed in 1886 (photo circa 1894)

By the Numbers

Figures and names found in
"Ellis Island – Interviews in their own Words" by Peter Morton Coan and
"The Italians in America" by Ronald P. Grossman

Some famous Ellis Island immigrants:

Isaac Asimov	Author
Irving Berlin	Composer
Max Factor	Cosmetician
Edward Flanagan	Priest/Founder Boys-Town
Al Jolson	Actor/Singer
Bela Lugosi	Actor
Edward G. Robinson.	Actor

Other famous Ellis Island immigrants from Italy:

Charles Atlas	Body Builder
Frank Capra	Director
Enrico Caruso	Tenor
Enrico Fermi	Physicist
Vincent Impellitteri	NYC Mayor
Attilio Piccirilli	Sculptor
Arturo Tosanini	Conductor/Musician
Rudolph Valentino	Actor

Italian Immigration by the decade:

1831-1840	2,000
1841-1850	2,000
1851-1860	9,000
1861-1870	12,000
1871-1880	56,000
1881-1890	307,000
1891-1900	652,000
1901-1910	2,046,000
1911-1920	1,110,000
1921-1930	455,000
1931-1940	68,000
1941-1950	57,000

Ellis Island main building and ferries (photo circa 1905)

The ferries in the foreground were used to transfer immigrants to and from ships and the mainland.

The American Immigrant Wall of Honor

Written by Christopher Obert

Back in 1988 my wife Nancy found a story advertising a monument that was to be built to honor all the immigrants that came to the United States. She saved the clipping and gave it to me. I then sent the story to my Aunt Mary in New Jersey. The following is an excerpt from the letter she sent back to me:

Dear Chris and Nancy,

Hi. How are all of you doing? I hope everyone is feeing well now after the chicken pox! We all loved the pictures you sent to us. Jason got so big & Shari too, I can't believe how fast they are growing.

I am so happy that you sent me that little magazine article Chris. It's a great way to honor Nonna & Nonno! I have collected all the money from here. We need $100.00 for each name. So the 20 grandchildren can chip in $5.00 each & the 4 children can put in $25.00 each. I called 800 number & they sent me the pamphlet. I copied it to send to you. It explains just what to do. We even get certificates back. I can hardly wait to go & see it – (with the help of God.)

I called my brother & his son Johnny. They also thought it was a great thing to do for Nonna & Nonno. Thank God Nancy saw that article & remembered to save it for me. Aunt Bea loved the idea also… Let your brother and sisters read the pamphlet O.K.

Wishing you a great Merry Christmas & the Happiest New Year ever.

All my love & kisses,
Aunt Mary & Uncle Frank, Kathleen & Mike
(I'll always be grateful to you Nancy, Thanks so much!)

My Aunt Mary was true to her word; she collected all the money and filled out all the forms needed. By the end of the 1980's all of the construction and repairs at the museum, were completed and my grandparents had their names engraved at Ellis Island. Years later, I brought my family to visit Ellis Island and the Statue of Liberty. I took the photo of the names (shown next page). The photo did not turn out too well but the moment is burned into my memory. I am very proud and grateful to Domenico and Maria Concetta. It is because of them (and the help of this island) that my family and I are here in the United States of America, land that I love!

America Forever!

Ellis Island: Gateway to the New World

Photo of the wall where the names are engraved.

But the story does not end here. We were not the only people that thought of having our ancestors names recorded on the Wall of Honor. The families of Maria Concetta (Serra) Clemenzi, Giovanni Virgilio Clemenzi, Salvatore Serra and Maria Lazzaro also followed the directions to include their names on that special wall. I do not know the stories behind their quest to have those names included, but I am sure that it was just as ours was… full of love, respect and gratitude!

77

**The Statue of Liberty-
Ellis Island Foundation, Inc.**
52 Vanderbilt Avenue
New York, NY 10017-3808
212-883-1986

ELLIS ISLAND
— 1892–1992 —
TM © 1987 SL/EIF, INC

Lee A. Iacocca
Chairman Emeritus

December 27, 1988

Marie A. Goldrick

Dear Friend:

On behalf of The Statue of Liberty-Ellis Island Foundation, Inc. I am proud to present you with the Official Certificate of Registration in The American Immigrant Wall of Honor for:

DOMENICO SERRA from ITALY
MARIA CONCETTA COSTA SERRA from ITALY

All names registered will soon appear on public display at Ellis Island as a testament to the heroism and triumphs your family experienced in coming to America for the first time.

The many thousands of visitors who will come to Ellis Island each year will recognize and respect your family's role in fulfilling the American dream of hope, freedom and opportunity for all.

I also would like to thank you for the $200.00 contribution you sent to help us finish our restoration work on Ellis Island.

Since the Statue's completion, many Americans don't realize that we still have a long way to go before the buildings are restored and the museum can be opened to the public. Your financial support is greatly appreciated.

Ellis Island holds a very special place in my heart and I can tell it does for you, too. Thanks again for all your help.

Sincerely,

Lee Iacocca

Lee Iacocca

LIBERTY
1886·1986
"Dedicated to the Restoration and Preservation
of the Statue of Liberty and Ellis Island"

Letter sent to Marie Goldrick from the Ellis Island Foundation

78

1954 postcard of Ellis Island

Ellis Island

Ellis Island stands as a constant reminder of our nation's immigrant saga. Located just a few hundred yards north of the Statue of Liberty in New York Harbor, Ellis Island is a monument to the great traditions of freedom and opportunity in America.

Ellis Island was the major federal immigration facility in America. Between 1892 and 1954, 17 million immigrants were processed at Ellis Island. Today more than 40 percent, or over 100 million, of all living Americans can trace their roots to an ancestor who came through Ellis Island.

The restoration of Ellis Island, which began in 1984, will cost $140 million and is the largest restoration project of its kind in American history. Work is scheduled to be completed in 1989, when Ellis Island will reopen and once again receive millions of visitors from around the world.

The Ellis Island Immigration Museum

The new Ellis Island Immigration Museum, currently under construction and scheduled to open in 1989, will tell the inspiring story of the largest human migration in modern history.

The museum will be located in the 200,000-square-foot Main Building—the most historically significant structure on Ellis Island. It was here, in various rooms of the building, where new arrivals—many fearful of rejection—were processed and inspected and ultimately granted permission to enter the country. It will offer visitors a fascinating, complete look at the total immigrant experience, using innovative displays that feature historic artifacts and photos, interactive devices, computers and taped reminiscences of the immigrants themselves.

The American Immigrant Wall Of Honor

You are invited to place the name of an immigrant ancestor, individual or family name on display, for posterity, at the only national museum built to honor them.

Prominently located in the museum, this unique exhibit will be devoted solely to the display of thousands of names of immigrants, representing individual family heritages central to the peopling of America during the last four centuries. Each name will be an individual gift of remembrance and devotion. The names will remain for posterity in the shadow of the Statue of Liberty, recording forever the people you wish to honor.

Whether your ancestors first set foot on American soil at Ellis Island or entered through another gateway, The American Immigrant Wall of Honor will be a marvelous opportunity for every American to honor their family. In years to come, children who visit the museum will be proud to find the name of their grandparent or great-grandparent recorded with others who came and built America.

When you make a $100 tax-deductible contribution to restore Ellis Island, the name you designate will be permanently placed on the newly created American Immigrant Wall of Honor. You will receive a handsome Certificate, personalized with the name and country of the individual you choose to honor. This official document will take its place alongside your family's most precious heirlooms. Contributions of $1,000, $5,000 and $10,000 will receive special places of honor.

In addition, all names will be entered, together with a country of origin and the name of the donor, in a computer register located in the same room.

Please send your registration form today. By acting now, you will assure that the Ellis Island Immigration Museum will be a monument to your heritage, as well as to the great American traditions of freedom, hope and opportunity.

Pamphlet for Ellis Island and the Wall of Honor

The Statue of Liberty-Ellis Island Foundation, Inc.

proudly presents this

Official Certificate of Registration

in

THE AMERICAN IMMIGRANT WALL OF HONOR

to officially certify that

DOMENICO SERRA

who came to America from

ITALY

is among those courageous men and women who came to this country in search of personal
freedom, economic opportunity and a future of hope for their families.

Lee A. Iacocca
The Statue of Liberty-Ellis Island
Foundation, Inc.

Domenico Serra Certificate (Panel 400)

The Statue of Liberty-Ellis Island Foundation, Inc.

proudly presents this

Official Certificate of Registration

in

THE AMERICAN IMMIGRANT WALL OF HONOR

to officially certify that

MARIA CONCETTA COSTA SERRA

who came to America from

ITALY

is among those courageous men and women who came to this country in search of personal
freedom, economic opportunity and a future of hope for their families.

Lee A. Iacocca
The Statue of Liberty-Ellis Island
Foundation, Inc.

Maria Concetta (Costa) Serra Certificate (Panel 400)

The Statue of Liberty-Ellis Island Foundation, Inc.

proudly presents this

Official Certificate of Registration

in

THE AMERICAN IMMIGRANT WALL OF HONOR

to officially certify that

Maria Concetta Serra Clemenzi

came to the United States of America from

Salina, Sicily, Italy

joining those courageous men and women who came to this country in search of personal
freedom, economic opportunity and a future of hope for their families.

Lee A. Iacocca
The Statue of Liberty-Ellis Island
Foundation, Inc.

Maria Concetta (Serra) Clemenzi Certificate (Panel 082)

The Statue of Liberty-Ellis Island Foundation, Inc.

proudly presents this

Official Certificate of Registration

in

THE AMERICAN IMMIGRANT WALL OF HONOR

to officially certify that

Giovanni Virgilio Clemenzi

came to the United States of America from

Turania, Roma, Italy

joining those courageous men and women who came to this country in search of personal
freedom, economic opportunity and a future of hope for their families.

Lee A. Iacocca
The Statue of Liberty-Ellis Island
Foundation, Inc.

Giovanni Virgilio Clemenzi Certificate (Panel 082)

The Statue of Liberty-Ellis Island Foundation, Inc.

proudly presents this

Official Certificate of Registration

in

THE AMERICAN IMMIGRANT WALL OF HONOR

to officially certify that

Salvatore Serra

came to the United States of America from

Italy

joining those courageous men and women who came to this country in search of personal
freedom, economic opportunity and a future of hope for their families.

Lee A. Iacocca
The Statue of Liberty-Ellis Island
Foundation, Inc.

Salvatore Serra Certificate (Panel 400)

The Statue of Liberty-Ellis Island Foundation, Inc.

proudly presents this

Official Certificate of Registration

in

THE AMERICAN IMMIGRANT WALL OF HONOR

to officially certify that

Maria Lozero

came to the United States of America from

Italy

joining those courageous men and women who came to this country in search of personal
freedom, economic opportunity and a future of hope for their families.

Lee A. Iacocca
The Statue of Liberty-Ellis Island
Foundation, Inc.

Maria Lazzaro Certificate (Panel 262)

America Immigration Notes:

History is a pact between the dead,
the living, and the yet unborn.

--Edmund Burke

A Family's Dream, and a Boy's Journey

An Aeolian Family's Story

Giovani Battista Serra (1848 to circa 1910)

Bartolomeo (Lazzaro) Serra (1852 to 1948)

A Boy Charged with his Family's Destiny

Written by Christopher Obert
Photos and images supplied by many different sources

One of my main areas of interest, while I was working on the Serra Family Tree, was the story behind our ancestors' trip to America. The following is the short write up that I included on the invitation to the 2002 Serra Family reunion.

"Domenico Serra was the first of our Serra ancestors to come to America. He immigrated to America from the port of Naples, Italy for the first time as a boy of 12 in 1901. The ship was named the Liguria. He made the trip with several friends from his village. It was a long hard crossing in steerage, but they were determined to get to America, because there was no work in Italy. It took at least five years of residency before one could apply for citizenship papers. Domenico became a full citizen on May 27, 1912.

America offered many opportunities, so Dominic saved his money so he could bring the rest of his family to America. In 1907 he went back to Italy to get his brothers and sisters. He brought Joseph, Angelina, Anthony and Maria Concetta first. The second trip he intended to get his parents and the rest of the family. Unfortunately, his father, John Battista, got sick and died in 1910, or 1911, before he returned to Italy. So he went back to get his mother Bartolomea, his brother Salvatore, and sisters Catherine and Caroline. In 1912, Dominico made his third and last trip back to Italy. While there, he married his cousin Maria Concetta Costa. After the wedding, the two of them returned to America.

Today, we honor the memory and spirit of these people. It is because of their courage that we are here today."

I was hoping that I could gather so much more information on the reason for coming over from Salina, information surrounding the different trips over by boat, and stories of the experience of passing through Ellis Island. Unfortunately, I did not receive that much information on these topics. I am afraid that these tales are now lost to history. This is the reason I have included so much information throughout this book on Salina, Ellis Island and any facts I could find on that time period. I am hoping that they will spark a memory that someone in the family could record for future generations. This miscellaneous information, I hope, will also paint a picture of the world that our relatives lived in.

In addition to the general information, I have included some information supplied by other family members. You may notice that some of the information in the different stories, at times, does not match. This is because different people remember events differently. I will leave it up to the next family researcher to determine which information is correct.

In the following few paragraphs, I will discuss some of the information I have found, some of the problems I have discovered, and list some of the missing material. As you read the different stories throughout this book, see if you can find clues that can solve some of these questions!

<u>Why Domenico?</u>
One of the stories I heard was that "Bartolomeo sent her son, Domenico, to America to help their living conditions improve. Italy was very, very poor, especially the villages on the smaller islands where they lived. If it was not for her foresight back in 1901, all this would not have been possible. She chose Domenico because he was the best choice of her sons. He had courage, daring and enough intelligence to make the trip and be successful in securing jobs to save the money he would use for their family to get to America. Also, he obeyed his mother's orders implicitly. Her dreams for their future rested on a 12 year old's shoulders..." I am sure that there is so much more to this story that has not been told. My dream is that more of this story will be forthcoming as people read and react to this book...

Bartolomeo and her son, Domenico, no longer a 12 year old boy!

Not a direct crossing!
One of the things I have discovered was the Serra family left Salina by way of the port of Rinella. It was from this small port that they took small boats to get to larger ports, such as Naples, so they could board a larger ship to take them to America.

Rinella, Leni's port, was the jumping off point that took them to Naples
(Photo is from the front of a postcard sent to the Goldrick's from the Galleeta's)

What is the story behind the "New House?"
One question I have is "Why was the Serra Family building a new house on Salina, if the family was planning to leave Salina?" There could be many reasons for this… 1) Even though the family was leaving, life does go on, and if the old house was inadequate, they would need a new house even if they were leaving the island. 2) To leave (or sell) to other family members. 3) They could sell it for cash or keep it in the family.

Photo of the old house.

What happened to Anthonio Serra?
One of the mysteries of the Serra Family is "What happened to Anthonio Serra?" I have heard many different stories and theories. 1) He died in the war, but which war? 2) He moved to Florida. Some say he lived on a Native American (Indian) reservation. 3) He moved from Florida to Australia. 4) He moved to Argentina.
I do not know which story (if any of them) is true...

Back Row: Giuseppe, Domenico & Anthonio Serra
Front Row: Angelina & Concetta Serra

Who were Domenico's friends that he traveled with?
I had heard the Domenico Serra immigrated to America with several friends from his village, one of whom was called Antonio Cincotta. 'Nino' had some relatives living in Salem, Mass. at the time, but I have not been able to prove that this is true. The passenger list from the Liguria does not list anyone named Antonio Cincotta. An Antonio Cincotta does appear in the records on another trip. There were many people listed on the manifest from Salina, but how do you figure out who knew who?

The "Liguria", the ship Domenico came over on in 1901

Are there better records?

As I looked up the records of the different ships and the different trips that our relatives made to America, I found only a few matches. One of the few matches I did make was on the second trip that Domenico made. I found that the name of the ship was called the "Princess Irene". He brought Joseph, Angelina, Anthony and Maria Concetta on this trip. Other than this, I have had a very difficult time checking the information on the different trips.

The "Princess Irene", the ship used by the Serra Family on the second trip.

How did they get from here to there?

I found that our relative's destination, after passing through Ellis Island, was Salem, Mass. I have been told that they took both an electric trolley and a boat to get to Salem. I believe that they boarded a boat in New York Harbor to the Port of Boston. Then they took the electric trolley to Salem. I have found lots of supporting information that shows this is the most likely route.

Photo of a Massachusetts trolley (circa 1892)

What took so long?

It took at least five years of residency before one could apply for citizenship papers. Domenico became a full citizen on May 27, 1912, 11 years after he arrived. I am not sure why it took him so long to obtain citizenship. I would like to compare how long it took other family members to get their citizenship. This delay could be normal because of the vast numbers of immigrants.

What it was all about, citizenship!

What information do we have already?

As you can see we still have a lot of unanswered questions! But luckily, many people have sent in stories and information, so we do have a starting point to gather more information. The following pages are some of this material that has been collected. It also contains some memories that the family has about the early days. I hope that it helps with the next step in our search for answers…

1938 Class Project

Written by Marie Serra (Age 10)

Public School #3, Bright Street, Jersey City, NJ
(Some parts of this paper were added later)

I, Maria Serra was born on October 30, 1928 of Italian parentage. My paternal grandfather, John Battista Serra, was born in 1848 on the island of Salina, Province of Messina, Italy. He spent most of his life in Italy cultivating his own farmlands. He loved the sea and spent much time traveling up and down the Mediterranean Sea.

In 1880 he married Bartolomea (Lazzaro) and they settled in Canneto, Italy. They spent many happy years there and had eleven children. The first three children died when they were very young. They were daughters Maria, Catherine and Maria Terzito.

Then Angelina was born on Feb. 17, 1885 (died June 14, 1972)
Joseph was born on Oct. 14, 1886 (died Sept. 26, 1966)
Domenico was born Sept. 3, 1888 (died April 14, 1981)
Maria Concetta was born on April 13, 1890 (died Jan. 16, 1987)
Anthony was born in 1892
Catherine was born on Feb. 13, 1894 (died March 31, 1984)
Salvatore was born April 4, 1896 (August 7, 1978)
Maria Carolina, the youngest, was born Nov. 16, 1898 (died Oct. 26, 1980).

My paternal grandfather, John Battista Serra, died in Salina in 1910 or 1911, just before my father was to bring him to America. A short time later my father went back to Italy and got his mother, Bartolomea and his sisters Catherine and Caroline and youngest brother, Salvatore. My grandmother is now living in Beverly, Mass at the age of 86 with her youngest daughter Caroline De Lorenzo, at 41 Roundy Street.

My maternal grandfather, Philip Costa, was born in 1845 on the island of Salina, Province of Messina, to Angela (Vergona) and Philip Costa.
He served as a sailor in the Italian Navy and served in the War of Lissa. After his release he went to South America where he spent four years. When he returned to Italy he married my grandmother, Giovanna Lazzaro, born in 1850, to parents Catherina (Pitorina) and Domenico Lazzaro.
They had seven children altogether. The oldest son Joseph then four daughters Angela, Giovanna, Catherine and Maria Concetta, who is my mother. The two youngest boys, Philip and Gaetano, died when they were very young. My grandmother was so depressed over their deaths that she became very sick and did not get well for a long time because she grieved for her sons so much. It was feared that she would die of a broken heart. It wasn't until she sought outside help and talked to her parish priest that she became consoled and finally resigned herself to the loss of her children.

My father, Domenico Serra, was born on Sept. 3, 1888, in Malfa on the island of Salina, Province of Messina, Italy. At the age of six he started school and completed a four year course. At the age of 12 he came to America with friends from his village. One friend called "Nino" Cincotta had an Uncle living in Newton Center, Massachusetts, called Joseph Cafarella. My father worked there for a short time on a farm, then went to Everett, Mass and worked in a grocery store for about 3 years. From there he went to Beverly, Mass and obtained a job at the United Shoe Co. where he worked for several years.

He was able to save enough money to return to Italy three times to get his mother, brothers and sisters. On the last trip in 1912, he married my mother, Maria Concetta Costa.

The newlyweds came to New York City to live where my father got a job working for the Western Electric Co. When WE Co. moved to Illinois, they asked my father to move out to Chicago so he could remain with the company, but he refused the offer and moved to Harrison, NJ where he worked for the Hyatt Roller Bearing Co. for 13 years as a screw machine operator. They then moved to Jersey City and bought a small grocery store and the house which is our present residence, 267 York Street. They lived at this address for 45 Years.

My mother, Maria Concetta, was born on Dec. 13, 1891, in Leni, Province of Messina, Italy.

When she was six she started school and completed a five year course. After graduating, the nuns taught the girls to hand loom flax into linen cloth to make sheets, tablecloths and towels. They were also taught to knit, crochet and embroider. My mother was very skillful, more so than some of the other girls and was paid very well for some of her crocheted articles. She crocheted many doilies, tablecloths and in later years she crocheted each of us children a beautiful bedspread for our hope chests which we still use and treasure.

My mother married my father in 1912 in Italy and they took the boat to come to America.

My mother recalls the boat trip across the Atlantic Ocean very vividly. The sea was often rough and she spent most of the voyage in the cabin being seasick, and unable to hold down food. This was a difficult time for her because she was not accustomed to the boat travel and she was also very homesick for her parents, and the rest of the family she had left behind in Italy. She was consoled by the fact that she would be seeing her older sister Giovanna who was already living in New York City, with her husband Gaetano Maltese.

At first Domenico and Maria Concetta lived in Salem, Mass, were my father had a job working in a grocery store. My mother learned how to cook and keep house. Everything was going well when my father came down with Typhoid fever and he was very sick for about two months. My mother nursed him back to health. She was very religious and prayed to the Blesses Mother Del Terzito, every day for him to regain his good health. The doctor came to the house often to see him. The high fever would cause my father to act irrationally, spitting out his medicine and not even recognizing my mother at times. He came very close to dying, but with the help of God, the doctor and the love and patience of my mother he survived the illness.

Sometime later, after he got well, they moved to Manhattan on Ave. A, in New York City. My mother was reunited with both her sisters, who were also living there. Her sister, Giovanna, married to Gaetano Maltese who had come to America before my mother did, and Catherina, who came to America shortly after my mother did, who was married to Dominick Villanti.

My mother remembers how happy she was living in the same house and being reunited with at least part of her family. A short while later, her sister Giovanna and husband went back to Italy. About three years later, both my mother and her sister Catherine moved to Harrison, New Jersey, where my father got an excellent job working for the Hyatt Roller Bearing Company, as a screw machine operator.

After being married for nine years, my mother became pregnant. She named her first born Bartolomea after my father's mother as was the custom in those days. They had four children all together. Bartolomea and Giovannina were born in Harrison, N.J. A few years later they moved to Jersey City and lived on Gregory Street, where their son John Battista was born. Being the first son he was named after my father's father. My mother miscarried a son before moving to 241 York Street where I was born, their youngest daughter Maria. 267 York Street was a three family house with a store on the bottom floor.

On York Street my father went into business with his brother Salvatore as it was their mothers wish for Domenico to help his younger brother in the grocery business. Domenico always obeyed his mother's wishes.

This is a copy of a letter sent to Battista and Olga before the August 2, 1986 Serra Reunion.
They needed the information for the newspaper article…

Dear Battista and Olga,   July 8, 1986

Our paternal grandmother Bartolomea Lazzaro, daughter of
Domenico Lazzaro and Catherina Pittorina, was born in Canneto,
Province of Messina, Italy, in the year 1852.

Our paternal grandfather, John Battista Serra was born in
the year 1848 in Salina, Province of Messina, Italy. He was
the son of Joseph Serra and Maria (Lazzaro ?) There seems to be
some question as to her maiden name, wish I could verify it.
Maybe Aunt Grace remembers it. I must remember to ask her. *(Never did)*

John Battista and Bartolomea were married in the year 1880
in Salina, Province of Messina, and they had eleven children
born to them.

The first three daughters Maria, Catherine and Maria Terzito
died as infants. Of the surviving children the first was;

(DeAngelis) Angelina--born on February 17, 1885. She died June 14, 1972.
Joseph--born on October 14, 1886. He died Sept. 26, 1966.
Domenico --born September 3, 1888. He died April 14, 1981.
(Clemenzi) - Maria Concetta--Born on April 13, 1890--living at this writing.
Anthony--born in 1892, we think. *Went Australia, never heard from again.*
(Costa) - Catherine was born February 13, 1894. She died March 31, 1984.
Salvatore--born on April 4, 1896. He died August 7, 1978.
(DeLorenzo) - Maria Carolina--born November 16, 1898. She died October 26, 1980.

Domenico Serra emmigrated to America from the Port of Naples,
Italy, for the first time as a boy of 12, in 1901. The boat was
named the 'Liguria'. He made the trip with several friends from
his village, one of whom was called Antonio Cincotta. 'Nino'
had some relatives living in Salem, Mass. at the time.
It was a long hard crossing in steerage, but they were determined to get to America, because there was no work in Italy
and they could not earn a living there.

Domenico and his friends worked their way across on the ship. After landing in New York, everyone was taken to Ellis Island, where they were processed for entry into the United States. They all passed the entry physical and were permitted to continue to their destination which was Salem, Mass. They took the electric trolley car from New York to Boston, because that was the only means of transportation on land. They took it to get to the boat which would take them to Boston, and eventually to Salem, Mass.

Domenico's first job was on a farm in Salem. He said it was a good paying job because many people were out of work at that time. He then obtained a job working as a clerk in a grocery store also in Salem. He worked 10 hours a day for fifty cents a day and earned three dollars a week. He was a hard and dilligent worker and obtained several other jobs as well. He liked the new country and learned to speak English as he progressed, with the intention of obtaining his citizenship papers.

It took at least five years of residency before one could apply for citizenship papers. Domenico became a full citizen on May 27, 1912.

He realized the opportunities that America had to offer and saved his money so he could bring the rest of his family to America.

In approximately 1907 he went back to Italy to get his older brothers and sisters. He brought Joseph, Angelina, Anthony and Maria Concetta first.

The second trip he intended to get his parents and the rest of the family. Unfortunately his father, John Battista, got sick and died in 1910 or 11 before he returned to Italy. So he went back to get his mother Bartolomea, his brother Salvatore and sisters Catherine and Caroline.

In 1912, Domenico made his third and last trip back to Italy and married my mother Maria Concetta Costa, on August 11,1912, in Leni, Italy. Maria Concetta and Domenico were first cousins. Their mothers Giovanna and Bartolomea were sisters.

The Serra children married and proceeded to raise their families. Most of them settled in Massachusetts. Anthony traveled to Florida and then to Australia and to our knowledge was never heard from by any member of his family again.

Domenico and Salvatore lived for a time in Mass., then moved to N.Y.City and finally settled in Jersey City.

Bartolomea Serra, when she died in Beverly, Mass. on April 17, 1948, was 96 years old and was survived by eight children, thirty eight grandchildren and as close as I can figure about 15 great grandchildren.

The families in Mass. were among the first to get married and have children. Maybe we can determine the number at the reunion next month. It will be held at 11 Hart Street, Beverly, Mass., the residence of our late first cousin Angelo Clemenzi, who is survived by his wife, Lucia and seven children. Several of which are now married with children of their own.

With the exception of Anthony Serra, all of Bartolomea and John Battista Serra's children lived a good long life and all were able to enjoy seeing their children, grandchildren and also their great grandchildren. Not many families can boast of that achievment.

Hoping this letter finds you, Battista and Olga, and all your family feeling well, especially your dear mother. Please give her and my Aunt Catherine Villanti and also Aunt Grace Serra, when you see her, my love and warmest regards. I have been thinking of all of them this past Fourth of July and 100th Anniversary of the Statue of Liberty, and what they all had to endure when they left their native land to make a new life here in America.

Being the sons and daughters of immigrants, I feel we all owe a debt of gratitude to our parents if they are alive, or to their memories. As for me I am particularly very proud of my mother and father and all our ancestors and the heritage they left to us. After all, if not for their sacrificies, where would we be today????

With our love and best regards to all from all,
Your cousin, Mary (Serra) Goldrick

Mary

America: Land of Dreams and Opportunity

Written by Giovannina (Serra) Obert and Christopher Obert

Mama Barthy and Papa John raised their children to pray morning and night. They had a strong and lively Catholic faith. The children learned to love God the Father, Jesus, and Mary before they could walk. God was always with them to love and protect them. They kissed the holy cards and the small statue of Jesus and Mary on the kitchen table. Mama Barthy prayed the rosary while she rocked the babies to sleep and the girls also prayed the rosary silently. Sunday was the day for Mass at the town church. They all attended together.

There were some people from the village who were getting ready to go to America soon. When they heard this news, the idea came to them that they would send Domenico with them. He could get a job and send money back home and that would keep them from losing everything. If things went well, maybe he could even bring the entire family to America!

The problem remained, where would they get the money he'd need in time for the trip? They had to find out how much the trip would cost and what kind of clothes he would need and how much money he would need for eating and lodging. They also wanted to know how long it would take to cross the ocean. After gathering all of this information, they decided to use some of the "seed money" (money saved for new seeds and other family needs) to pay for the trip.

Domenico's parents said to him, "You are the hope of the family. You are to go to America, work hard and save your money so that you can bring your brothers and sisters over." They asked Domenico, "What do you think of this idea?" He was sad, thinking of leaving his parents and family, but he knew what had to be done. Domenico learned very early in his young life that sacrifice and self-determination were what made dreams come true. Hard work gave you the coins that turned into the dollars that were necessary for life. He told them "I shall pray and save for the time when we could all be together again." Dominick said, "It was a very good idea."

On his first trip, the first thing he learned was to say his name in American - Dominick Serra. He listened attentively and wanted to talk as Americans did. He always had this on his mind, that he must be an American first. It was fortunate that he had a sharp mind and good memory. In order to become an American, he had to get citizenship papers that stated he was a citizen of the United States. He knew that he had to do that first. He was helpful and cheerful with his new friends. They liked him and helped him by telling him the things he needed to know in this new country. The REASON he came to this new country never left his mind. The letters that he wrote from America were always encouraging. He did not want them to worry. Work was plentiful and he was busy and happy.

While Domenico was in America life still had to go on back on Salina. The whole family worked together, just as they always did to keep the family strong. Mama Barthy took good care of them whenever they got sick. She knew all the good remedies and how to make them comfortable so they could sleep and rest to get well fast.

Papa John's death was a shocking blow for everyone. Mama's care and attention was to no avail. The doctor said Papa John's lungs were very weak and damaged. There was no cure available for his sickness. Papa John died and was buried. This was an especially sad event because Domenico was working hard in America and was bringing his family over a few at a time. He was going to bring his parents over just before that his father died.

Memories of Bartolomea Serra

Written by Angela Villanti as told to her by her mother
Sophie (Clemenzi) Villanti.
Photos supplied by Giovannina (Serra) Obert

Bartolomea Serra

My grandmother, Bartolomea Serra came to Beverly in 1914, the year I was born. The most frightening experience of her life took place that year, the Great Salem Fire of June; 1914. Bartolomea was living in Salem with her son, Domenico and his wife at the time, near St. Joseph's Church. Much of the city of Salem was destroyed and people had to be relocated. The Serras moved to Beverly after the fire.

L to R: Angelina (Serra) DeAngelis, Bartolomeo (Lazzaro) Serra,
Domenico Serra, Caroline (Serra) DeLorenzo

My grandmother made the best cookies in the world. They were on the idea of ladyfingers, very light, but hers were better than any you can find today, but nobody has her recipe, and of course she didn't measure!

Bartolomea knew how to take care of many ailments. She could set bones and then apply whipped egg whites rather than a cast to hold it in place. She learned her medical skills from her uncle in Italy who was a doctor.

I (Sophie) remember my grandmother sending me to the Red Star pharmacy in Boston to get leeches from Mr. Caffarella, the pharmacist, who also came from Salina. She used the leeches on herself to draw out some blood in order to relieve the discomfort of high blood pressure.

While my grandmother lived with the DeLorenzo family she always did the mending for the family. One day she asked me to take her to the eye doctor because she was having difficulty seeing. The doctor examined her, and then recommended she get either two pair of glasses, one for close up and one for distances, or a pair of bifocals. She thought about it, and responded "I only need one pair so I can do the mending. When I get old I'll come back and get the other pair." The doctor asked how old she was -75! She never did return for a second pair of glasses.

Thoughts of my Nonna

By Mary (Serra) Goldrick
Photo supplied by Janice Charowsky

Bartolomea (Lazzaro) Serra and one of the Vandi twins

My grandmother lived in Beverly, MA with her daughter Caroline De Lorenzo and family on 41 Roundy St. My father Domenico liked to visit his mother in the summer-time. My mother and I accompanied him on the train or by Greyhound Bus where someone in the family would pick us up at the station and drive us to the house where Nonna waited for us.

I remember how small Nonna was and how happy she was to see us all, especially my father. She had an unusually distinctive voice and I loved hearing her speak in Italian to us. She always gave us her sweet Italian cookies to eat. She baked huge batches of the cookies and kept them in a large tin to keep fresh. I remember vividly how delicious they tasted to me. I've never tasted anything like them since.

My aunts and uncles always stopped by to see us while we were in Beverly. We spent many enjoyable visits with them, had meals, picnics and family gatherings. I loved listening to all the adults talking and laughing and enjoying themselves while they played their Italian card games. They were *so serious* about winning a game and they only played for points, *never* money!

When my Nonna died in 1948, I was 20 years old. I accompanied my father and mother to Beverly for the wake and funeral. As was the custom in those days, Nonna was waked in the parlor on Roundy St. She lived to the age of 96. All the relatives were there and it was a sad time for us all. I knelt at her coffin and led the family in the recitation of the Holy Rosary. As we all prayed, I looked at this diminutive woman laying there in front of me.

I could not help but marvel at the courage she displayed so many years before when she made the decision to send her 12 year old son, Domenico, alone across the ocean to a place and language unknown to him. The bravery of her decision changed the lives of each one of her children and of each one of their descendents. How truly fortunate we all are to be living in America today. I believe God truly blessed our Nonna. May she now be peacefully resting in His Loving Care.

World Civilizations II   a.k.a. "Who has a letter?"

Written by Christopher Obert

During the time I was compiling this book, I was also a full time college student. As I told you earlier, I took many computer courses. Another of the courses I took was World Civilizations II. On one particular test, there was a question on immigration. As you will see, my mind was on more than just answering the question. It was on trying to understand the amazing thing our ancestors did for us.

Focus Question: Discuss the role that migration played in the expansion of the United States. Why did migrants come to the United States? What awaited them? What were the benefits and difficulties of migration?

My Answer: I chose this question because it has been on my mind a lot lately. You see, I am currently writing a book on my family's immigration to America. My grandfather Domenico Serra came to America in 1901, when he was 12 years old. He worked here, saved his money and made three trips back home to the island of Salina (a small island north of Sicily) to bring his family back to America. He brought his brothers, sisters and mother back. On his last trip he married his cousin and brought her back also. The book I am writing is about the family's trip over and as many family stories as I can gather. It has been a huge task, and it has been both fun and exhausting, but I have learned a lot about the people of that time, well at least my family. Two words that kept coming up in my research were "opportunity" and "hardship". Both were a way of life for the immigrant. But I did not once find anyone say that the hardships outweighed the opportunities. Although one of my relatives did go back home to be with family, she took much more than she brought. All agreed that it was worth the risks. As I sit here and try to list the items that awaited them, I find myself dwelling on all the bad things that could have happened. If I was to leave all the people and things I know, then go off into the world, it would be much easier to imagine what could go wrong than right. It must have taken a lot of guts to pack up and go. Thank God they did or I would not be here.

I think there are just as many reasons why people came to America as people that came. Jobs, persecution, gold, careers, health, family, and for some immigrants, they had no choice. These were just some of the reasons. What awaited them? It was an entirely new society, full of a mix of new, wonderful, cruel and strange people and ideas waiting to embrace them. The benefits were many: more jobs, better pay, increased health care, better housing and an incredible and diverse world of entertainment and luxury. The difficulties were things like discrimination, crime and home sickness.

I remember one story my grandfather told me. When immigrants went looking for work they were often asked if they had a letter. This letter was given to the immigrant from a previous American person stating that "This guy is ok, he has worked for me and he is ok". If you had a letter you got picked first. Many times if you had no letter, you had no job. The problem was, how do you get your fist job without a letter? My grandfather told me that he wrote his own letter. He stated that "he was an honest person and that he would work hard for anyone willing to give him a chance". At the next job posting they asked "who has a letter?'. My grandfather raised his hand and was asked in. They looked at the letter and smiled. He got the job. Now I do not know if this story ever really happened. Was my grandfather telling me a story that simplified the entire job process, or was he telling me the story as it happened? I do not know. I am not even sure that I remember the story correctly (he told me this story so long ago I cannot remember how old I was). But it does show what the immigrants had to go through, the hope, the sadness, the loneliness, the fear and finally the joy. This story reminds me of what I hear today… "No experience, no job" but "how do I get experience without a job". It makes me realize that just because it took place 100 years ago, it does not mean that the process was any easier.

By the way, as I sit here and type this I am unemployed myself; would you like to see my letter?

Journey to America Notes:

*There would be no great ones
if there were no little ones.*

--George Herbert (1593-1633)

One Dream that Grew Into a Family Tree

Serra Family Tree

The Serra Family Tree

Salina

Maria SS Del Terzito

SS Liguria

Serra Family Tree collage

How to Read the Serra Family Tree

Anyone that has ever worked on a family tree knows that starting out is easy but after you start getting more and more names it becomes very difficult to keep track of everyone and maintain order. I used the computer software "Family Tree Maker" (version 9) to record the Serra Family Tree. I also have the Obert Family Tree, the Blanchette Family Tree and the Fitzgerald Family Tree in this data base. Currently there are over 900 names in the entire tree. This section contains the Serra Family tree starting with **Giovani Battista Serra** and **Bartolomea Lazzaro**. They are the parents of the Serra children that came over to the United States in the early years of the 20th Century.

I used the Family Tree Maker software to print this section of the book. The software uses established Genealogy markings to help you move through the tree. To some people these markings make the tree more difficult to understand. Therefore, we will review the meanings behind the marks. Boy, do I hope I get them all right!

When you look at the family tree you will notice that it is divided into sections... "Generation No. 1", "Generation No. 2", and so on. Each of these sections shows the children (descendents) of the main person, or persons, in that family group. For example: Generation No. 1 shows the children of Giovani Battista Serra and Bartolomea Lazzaro. Generation No. 2 shows the children of Giovani and Bartolomea's children, in other words the grandchildren. These grandkids are shown under their parents. Generation No. 3 is made up of the grandchildren's children, in other words the great grandchildren. Once again, the children are shown under their parents. This is called a descending family tree. As you can see, each section (Generation) gets larger as we go forward in time (or move down the family tree). There is another way to print your family tree, called an ascending family tree. It starts with a person then moves backward in time. The family tree gets larger and larger as you move back. We will just use the descending family tree in this book. Maybe one of you out there will write the next Serra book working on the ascending family tree!

Descendants of Giovani Battista Serra

Generation No. 1

1. Giovani Battista² Serra (Giuseppe¹) was born 1848 in Salina, Messina, Sicily, and died 1910 in Salina, Messina, Sicily. He married **Bartolomeo Lazzaro** 1880 in Salina, Messina, Sicily, daughter of Domenico Lazzaro and Catherina Pittorina. She was born 1852 in Canneto, Messina, Sicily, and died April 17, 1948.

Children of Giovani Serra and Bartolomeo Lazzaro are:

	2	i.	Maria Terzito³ Serra.
	3	ii.	Maria Serra, born May 10, 1882.
	4	iii.	Caterina Serra, born May 04, 1883.
+	5	iv.	Angelina Serra, born February 17, 1885 in Malfa, Salina, Sicily; died June 14, 1972.
+	6	v.	Giuseppe Serra, born October 15, 1886 in Malfa, Salina, Sicily; died September 26, 1966.
+	7	vi.	Domenico Serra, born September 03, 1888 in Malfa, Salina, Sicily; died April 14, 1981 in Middletown, NJ.
+	8	vii.	MariaConcetta Serra, born April 13, 1890 in Malfa, Salina, Sicily; died January 16, 1987.
	9	viii.	Antonio Serra, born February 14, 1892 in Malfa, Salina, Sicily.
+	10	ix.	Caterina Serra, born February 14, 1894 in Malfa, Salina, Sicily; died March 31, 1984.
+	11	x.	Salvatore Serra, born April 03, 1896 in Malfa, Salina, Sicily; died August 07, 1978.
+	12	xi.	Maria Carolina Serra, born November 16, 1898 in Malfa, Salina, Sicily; died October 26, 1980.

You may have noticed that in each section, and in each family, there is a set of numbers, plus signs (+) and lower case letters associated with them. These markings help you to quickly gain information from the tree. Let's start with the numbers. Since this is the "Descendants of Giovani Battista Serra" family tree, he is given the number "1". His children are then each given a number, as are their children, as are the grandchildren. This numbering continues all the way down the family tree. You may have noticed that his wife Bartolomea does not receive a number. That is because she is not his descendant, she is his wife. Also notice that the wives and husbands of the children and grandchildren all the way down do not receive numbers. This is for the same reason they are not descendants. When printing this type of family tree it does not mater if you start with a woman or a man. Whoever you chose to start with gets the first number and their descendents get the following numbers. For example, if we chose Bartolomea to start with, she would be number 1 and Giovani would not have a number. Other than that, the family tree would look exactly the same as Giovani's. That is because all of his descendents are also her descendents.

So what can we tell from these numbers? Well, if you go to the end of the tree and look for the highest number, you will instantly know how many descendents the first person (Giovani, in this tree) has. Remember, this does not tell you how many people are in the tree, because his wife and the other spouses are missing. Another thing you can use these numbers for is to follow a family down through the generations. For example, Giovani and Bartolomea have a daughter named Angelina. Her number is 5. If you look at the beginning of Generation No. 2 you will see her listed as the first person in that section, her number 5 still next to her name. This is true for everyone that gets a number; it follows them throughout the tree. You will see that Angelina had children of her own. By looking at their numbers you can quickly find their families farther down in the family tree. You can use this use of numbers for each family. You may have noticed that when the person is listed as a child in one group, the number is in normal print, but when the person is listed as the parent in the group, the number is bold. For example Angelina, daughter of Giovani, is number "5" but Angelina, mother of Rose, is number "**5**". Same person, same number, just different type to help you find her family.

Generation No. 2

5. Angelina³ **Serra** (Giovani Battista², Giuseppe¹) was born February 17, 1885 in Malfa, Salina, Sicily, and died June 14, 1972. She married **Colombo De Angelis**.

Children of Angelina Serra and Colombo De Angelis are:
+ 13   i.   Adelgisa Theresa⁴ De Angelis, born August 13, 1915; died February 12, 1971.
+ 14   ii. Rose De Angelis, born August 01, 1923.

What if you do not know if the person in one group has children or not of their own. Do you have to go looking through the tree to try to find if they have a family or not? The answer is no. You do not have to go looking for that person's number, in bold print, farther down the tree to know if they have any children. When you look at the list of children in each family you will notice that some children have a "+" sign next to their number. This sign (+) means that this person has children of their own. You should now go down the family tree until you come across their number again. For example, Giovani and Bartolomea's son Domenico has children, he has a plus sign (+), but Maria Terzito does not have children, she has no sign.

---

2   i.   Maria Terzito³ Serra.

+ 7   vi. Domenico Serra, born September 03, 1888 in Malfa, Salina, Sicily; died April 14, 1981 in Middletown, NJ.

Now just because someone does not have children does not mean that they are not married. If a person is married and has no children, the software lists the spouse's name next to theirs in the person's family group.

Now what if you just want to know how many kids were in a family. What do we do? The numbers are used to count the total descendents, not each family. The family tree software uses another counting method. Next to each child's name in each family section there are lower case Roman numerals. For example, i, ii, iii, iv. These are used to count the number of children in each family. So, using these Roman numerals, you will see that Giovani and Bartolomea had 11 children.

Children of Giovani Serra and Bartolomeo Lazzaro are:			
	2	i.	Maria Terzito^3 Serra.
	3	ii.	Maria Serra, born May 10, 1882.
	4	iii.	Caterina Serra, born May 04, 1883.
+	5	iv.	Angelina Serra, born February 17, 1885 in Malfa, Salina, Sicily; died June 14, 1972.
+	6	v.	Giuseppe Serra, born October 15, 1886 in Malfa, Salina, Sicily; died September 26, 1966.
+	7	vi.	Domenico Serra, born September 03, 1888 in Malfa, Salina, Sicily; died April 14, 1981 in Middletown, NJ.
+	8	vii.	MariaConcetta Serra, born April 13, 1890 in Malfa, Salina, Sicily; died January 16, 1987.
	9	viii.	Antonio Serra, born February 14, 1892 in Malfa, Salina, Sicily.
+	10	ix.	Caterina Serra, born February 14, 1894 in Malfa, Salina, Sicily; died March 31, 1984.
+	11	x.	Salvatore Serra, born April 03, 1896 in Malfa, Salina, Sicily; died August 07, 1978.
+	12	xi.	Maria Carolina Serra, born November 16, 1898 in Malfa, Salina, Sicily; died October 26, 1980.

The last marking we will cover is the names listed in parentheses with little numbers listed next to them, for example (Giuseppe^1). As you see, each family section starts with the parent (that is the descendent of Giovani) in bold type. Next to their name are the names of their ancestors going back to Giovani's father Giuseppe. For example next to my name, Christopher Obert, in my families section is (Giovannina^4 Serra, Domenico^3, Giovani Battista^2, Giuseppe^1). My mother is Giovannina Serra her father is Domenico, his father is Giovania Battista and his father is Giuseppe.

86. Christopher Paul^5 Obert (Giovannina^4 Serra, Domenico^3, Giovani Battista^2, Giuseppe^1) was born July 09, 1962 in Amesbury Hospital, Amesbury, MA. He married **Nancy Sue Blanchette** December 20, 1981 in Red Tavern, Methuen, MA, daughter of Herve Blanchette and Mary Fitzgerald. She was born June 19, 1963 in Bon Secoeurs Hospital, Methuen, MA.			
Children of Christopher Obert and Nancy Blanchette are:			
209	i.	Shari Lyn^6 Obert, born April 29, 1982 in Lawrence General Hospital, Lawrence, MA.	
210	ii.	Jason Edward Obert, born May 31, 1985 in Lawrence General Hospital, Lawrence, MA.	

Ok, did you understand all of that? Don't worry if it takes some time to figure it out.
One last thing, you may notice that some people have lots of information associated with them: date and location of birth, date and location of death, spouse's name, spouse's date of birth, date and location of marriage and other information. Others have little information. This is not a mistake; it is because I do not have that information for everyone. This family tree is not complete and still needs a lot of work.

Descendants of Giovani Battista Serra

Generation No. 1

1. Giovani Battista² Serra (Giuseppe¹) was born 1848 in Salina, Messina, Sicily, and died 1910 in Salina, Messina, Sicily. He married **Bartolomea Lazzaro** 1880 in Salina, Messina, Sicily, daughter of Domenico Lazzaro and Catherina Pittorina. She was born 1852 in Canneto, Lipari, Messina, Sicily, and died April 17, 1948.

Children of Giovani Serra and Bartolomea Lazzaro are:

	2	i.	Maria Terzito³ Serra, died as an infant.
	3	ii.	Maria Serra, born May 10, 1882, died as an infant.
	4	iii.	Caterina Serra, born May 04, 1883, died as an infant.
+	5	iv.	Angelina Serra, born February 17, 1885 in Malfa, Salina, Sicily; died June 14, 1972.
+	6	v.	Giuseppe Serra, born October 15, 1886 in Malfa, Salina, Sicily; died September 26, 1966.
+	7	vi.	Domenico Serra, born September 03, 1888 in Malfa, Salina, Sicily; died April 14, 1981 in Middletown, NJ.
+	8	vii.	MariaConcetta Serra, born April 13, 1890 in Malfa, Salina, Sicily; died January 16, 1987.
	9	viii.	Antonio Serra, born February 14, 1892 in Malfa, Salina, Sicily.
+	10	ix.	Caterina Serra, born February 13, 1894 in Malfa, Salina, Sicily; died March 31, 1984 in Beverly, MA.
+	11	x.	Salvatore Serra, born April 03, 1896 in Malfa, Salina, Sicily; died August 07, 1978.
+	12	xi.	Maria Carolina Serra, born November 16, 1898 in Malfa, Salina, Sicily; died October 26, 1980.

Generation No. 2

5. Angelina³ Serra (Giovani Battista², Giuseppe¹) was born February 17, 1885 in Malfa, Salina, Sicily, and died June 14, 1972. She married **Colombo De Angelis**.

Children of Angelina Serra and Colombo De Angelis are:

+	13	i.	Adelgisa Theresa⁴ De Angelis, born August 13, 1915; died February 12, 1971.
+	14	ii.	Rose De Angelis, born August 01, 1923; died July 26, 2003.

6. Giuseppe³ Serra (Giovani Battista², Giuseppe¹) was born October 15, 1886 in Malfa, Salina, Sicily, and died September 26, 1966. He married **Grazia Lazzaro** June 20, 1920 in Jersey City, daughter of Christopher Lazzaro and Santina Merlino. She was born May 25, 1900 in Conneto, Lipori, Sicily, and died April 21, 1987.

Children of Giuseppe Serra and Grazia Lazzaro are:

+	15	i.	Bettina⁴ Serra, died August 09, 1973.
+	16	ii.	Santina Serra, died August 27, 1991.
	17	iii.	Caroline Serra, born June 07, 1924; died July 21, 2001.
+	18	iv.	Maria Rose Serra, born April 29, 1927.
	19	v.	John Battista Serra, born June 11, 1929. He married Mary Smythe May 16, 1971; born December 08, 1919.
+	20	vi.	Margherita Serra, born August 21, 1932.

7. Domenico[3] **Serra** (Giovani Battista[2], Giuseppe[1]) was born September 03, 1888 in Malfa, Salina, Sicily, and died April 14, 1981 in Middletown, NJ. He married **Maria Concetta Costa** August 11, 1912 in St. Guiseppe's Church, Leni, Sicily, daughter of Phillipo Costa and Giovanna Lazzaro. She was born December 13, 1891 in Leni, Salina, Sicily, and died May 21, 1984 in Middletown, NJ.

Children of Domenico Serra and Maria Costa are:

+	21	i.	Bartolomea[4] Serra, born September 07, 1921 in Harrison, NJ; died July 19, 1996 in Secaucus, NJ.
+	22	ii.	Giovannina Serra, born September 20, 1923 in 105 South 4th St., Harrison, NJ.
+	23	iii.	Giovanni Battista Serra, born September 24, 1926 in Gregory St., Jersey City, NJ.
+	24	iv.	Maria Antoinette Serra, born October 30, 1928 in 241 York St. Jersey City, NJ.

8. MariaConcetta[3] **Serra** (Giovani Battista[2], Giuseppe[1]) was born April 13, 1890 in Malfa, Salina, Sicily, and died January 16, 1987. She married **Giovanni Clemenzi** February 25, 1912 in Sacred Heart Church, Boston, MA, son of Dominico Clemenzi and Sofia Marapodi. He was born February 27, 1885 in Turania, di Reiti.

Children of MariaConcetta Serra and Giovanni Clemenzi are:

+	25	i.	Sophia[4] Clemenzi, born August 14, 1914.
+	26	ii.	Marietta Stephanie Clemenzi, born June 08, 1916 in Beverly, MA.
+	27	iii.	Emma Clemenzi, born March 11, 1918.
+	28	iv.	Dominick Clemenzi, born January 11, 1920.
+	29	v.	John Battista Clemenzi, born October 15, 1922.
+	30	vi.	Peter Clemenzi, born October 03, 1924.
+	31	vii.	Angelo Clemenzi, born July 02, 1927.

10. Caterina[3] **Serra** (Giovani Battista[2], Giuseppe[1]) was born February 13, 1894 in Malfa, Salina, Sicily, and died March 31, 1984 in Beverly, MA. She married **Giovanni Costa** March 12, 1912, son of Orazio Costa and Nancy Calapai. He was born January 08, 1888 in Italy, and died March 12, 1952 in Beverly, MA.

Children of Caterina Serra and Giovanni Costa are:

	32	i.	Nancy[4] Costa, born November 21, 1912; died August 24, 1955. She married Thomas Stewart.
+	33	ii.	Orazio Oscar Costa, born May 23, 1914 in Beverly, MA; died October 02, 1993 in Beverly, MA.
	34	iii.	Battista Costa, born July 17, 1916; died February 11, 1947. He married Margret Cassese.
+	35	iv.	Josephine Costa, born July 12, 1918 in Beverly, MA.
+	36	v.	Maria Concetta Costa, born March 03, 1921 in Beverly, MA.
+	37	vi.	Santa Costa, born May 31, 1923 in Beverly, MA; died February 23, 2003 in Massachusetts.
+	38	vii.	Frank Costa, born September 21, 1925.
	39	viii.	Bobby Costa, born November 22, 1931.

11. Salvatore[3] **Serra** (Giovani Battista[2], Giuseppe[1]) was born April 03, 1896 in Malfa, Salina, Sicily, and died August 07, 1978. He married **Maria Lazzaro**, daughter of Christopher Lazzaro. She died November 23, 1974 in Jersey City, NJ.

Children of Salvatore Serra and Maria Lazzaro are:

	40	i.	Bartolomea[4] Serra, born September 02, 1921. She married Thomas Fanto May 07, 1950.
+	41	ii.	John Battista Christopher Serra, born May 20, 1925; died May 16, 1994.
+	42	iii.	Angelina Serra, born June 06, 1931.
+	43	iv.	Santina Serra, born August 13, 1927; died July 20, 1976.

12. Maria Carolina[3] **Serra** (Giovani Battista[2], Giuseppe[1]) was born November 16, 1898 in Malfa, Salina, Sicily, and died October 26, 1980. She married **Gaetano De Lorenzo** April 23, 1916. He was born December 06, 1894, and died November 13, 1983.

Children of Maria Serra and Gaetano De Lorenzo are:
+   44   i.   Catherine Jenni[4] De Lorenzo, born April 12, 1917.
+   45   ii.   Maria Concetta De Lorenzo, born January 25, 1919.
+   46   iii. Antonio De Lorenzo, born March 01, 1921.
+   47   iv.   John Battista De Lorenzo, born September 21, 1923.
+   48   v.   Beatrice De Lorenzo, born October 20, 1925.
+   49   vi.   Joseph De Lorenzo, born November 20, 1927.
+   50   vii. Rose Marie De Lorenzo, born December 16, 1929.

Generation No. 3

13. Adelgisa Theresa[4] **De Angelis** (Angelina[3] Serra, Giovani Battista[2], Giuseppe[1]) was born August 13, 1915, and died February 12, 1971. She married **Enrico Miranda** December 28, 1947 in Saco Salerno Italy. He was born November 13, 1911, and died May 22, 1985.

Children of Adelgisa De Angelis and Enrico Miranda are:
+   51   i.   Michael[5] Miranda, born October 30, 1948.
+   52   ii.   John Miranda, born July 02, 1950.
+   53   iii. Dominic Miranda, born October 07, 1951.
     54   iv.   Josephine Miranda, born September 25, 1952; died July 14, 1953.
+   55   v.   Josephine Miranda, born March 18, 1954.
+   56   vi.   Anthony Miranda, born March 30, 1955.
+   57   vii. Angelo Miranda, born June 10, 1956.
+   58   viii. Bettina Miranda, born August 1959.
+   59   ix.   Lucia Miranda, born April 19, 1961.

14. Rose[4] **De Angelis** (Angelina[3] Serra, Giovani Battista[2], Giuseppe[1]) was born August 01, 1923, and died July 26, 2003. She married **Mario Vandi** April 25, 1943 in Beverly, MA. He was born August 25, 1920 in Rimini, Italy, and died July 02, 1974.

Children of Rose De Angelis and Mario Vandi are:
+   60   i.   Carolyn[5] Vandi, born November 25, 1943 in Beverly, MA.
+   61   ii.   Marilyn Vandi, born November 25, 1943 in Beverly, MA.
+   62   iii. Dennis Vandi, born December 16, 1946 in Beverly, MA.
+   63   iv.   Gene Scott Vandi, born September 02, 1950 in Beverly, MA.
+   64   v.   Sharon Faith Vandi, born May 03, 1956 in Beverly, MA.

15. Bettina[4] **Serra** (Giuseppe[3], Giovani Battista[2], Giuseppe[1]) died August 09, 1973. She married **Victor Sienkiewicz**. He died May 1999.

Children of Bettina Serra and Victor Sienkiewicz are:
+   65   i.   Peter[5] Sienkiewicz, born May 23, 1949.
+   66   ii.   Paul Sienkiewicz, born June 02, 1952.
+   67   iii. Catherine Sienkiewicz, born January 21, 1958.

16. Santina[4] **Serra** (Giuseppe[3], Giovani Battista[2], Giuseppe[1]) died August 27, 1991. She married **Harold Jones**.

Child of Santina Serra and Harold Jones is:
    68   i.   Richard[5] Jones.

18. Maria Rose[4] **Serra** (Giuseppe[3], Giovani Battista[2], Giuseppe[1]) was born April 29, 1927. She married **Joseph F. Bonaiuto** October 19, 1947. He was born June 08, 1921.

Children of Maria Serra and Joseph Bonaiuto are:
    69   i.   Maria Grace[5] Bonaiuto, born September 04, 1951.
    70   ii. Frank Joseph Bonaiuto, born October 17, 1953.
    71   iii. Betty Ann Bonaiuto, born April 28, 1955.
+ 72   iv. Joseph John Bonaiuto, born October 29, 1958.
    73   v. Steven Anthony Bonaiuto, born June 06, 1963.

20. Margherita[4] **Serra** (Giuseppe[3], Giovani Battista[2], Giuseppe[1]) was born August 21, 1932. She married **Gerard D. Eggleston**.

Children of Margherita Serra and Gerard Eggleston are:
+ 74   i.   Sharon Ann[5] Eggleston, born June 14, 1956.
+ 75   ii. Theresa Grace Eggleston, born August 03, 1959.
+ 76   iii. William Joseph Eggleston, born May 30, 1962.

21. Bartolomea[4] **Serra** (Domenico[3], Giovani Battista[2], Giuseppe[1]) was born September 07, 1921 in Harrison, NJ, and died July 19, 1996 in Secaucus, NJ. She married **Michael Charowsky** in St. Peter's Church, Jersey City, NJ. He was born October 18, 1917, and died February 26, 1993 in NJ.

Children of Bartolomea Serra and Michael Charowsky are:
    77   i.   Michael Jude[5] Charowsky, born November 16, 1948 in Margaret Hague Hospital, Jersey City, NJ. He married Elena Mercante October 18, 1981 in St. Aloysius Church, Jersey City, NJ; born October 19, 1947.
+ 78   ii. Dominick Charowsky, born August 01, 1952 in Margaret Hague Hospital, Jersey City, NJ.
+ 79   iii. Robert Charowsky, born March 28, 1955 in Margaret Hague Hospital, Jersey City, NJ.
    80   iv. Janice Maria Charowsky, born February 28, 1956 in Margaret Hague Hospital, Jersey City, NJ.
+ 81   v. Maria Concetta Charowsky, born December 15, 1958 in Margaret Hague Hospital, Jersey City, NJ.

22. Giovannina[4] **Serra** (Domenico[3], Giovani Battista[2], Giuseppe[1]) was born September 20, 1923 in 105 South 4th St., Harrison, NJ. She married **Norman Joseph Edward Obert** September 29, 1946 in St. Peter's Church, Jersey City, NJ, son of Edward Obert and Nellie Schambier. He was born January 13, 1924 in Berlin, NH.

Children of Giovannina Serra and Norman Obert are:
+ 82   i.   Mary Nellie[5] Obert, born September 13, 1951 in Amesbury Hospital, Amesbury, MA.
+ 83   ii. Norma Jean Obert, born September 27, 1953 in Amesbury Hospital, Amesbury, MA.
+ 84   iii. Edward Norman Obert, born November 17, 1955 in Amesbury Hospital, Amesbury, MA.
+ 85   iv. Patricia Ann Obert, born September 24, 1957 in Amesbury Hospital, Amesbury, MA.
+ 86   v. Christopher Paul Obert, born July 09, 1962 in Amesbury Hospital, Amesbury, MA.

23. Giovanni Battista⁴ Serra (Domenico³, Giovani Battista², Giuseppe¹) was born September 24, 1926 in Gregory St., Jersey City, NJ. He married **Charlotte Simms** October 12, 1952 in Church of St. Peter, Jersey City, NJ, daughter of William Simms and Anna Cordes. She was born October 18, 1931 in Brooklyn, NY.

Children of Giovanni Serra and Charlotte Simms are:
+ 87   i.   Dominick⁵ Serra, born January 09, 1955 in Jersey City, NJ.
+ 88   ii.   Donna Marie Serra, born December 31, 1955.
+ 89   iii. John Phillip Serra, born June 03, 1957.
+ 90   iv.   Mary Lynn Serra, born February 20, 1960.
  91   v.   Jacqueline Susan Serra, born August 16, 1962.
+ 92   vi.   Carol Ann Serra, born August 01, 1965.
  93   vii. Antonio Charles Serra, born August 16, 1968 in Margret Hague Hospital, Jersey City.
  94   viii. Joseph Kevin Serra, born April 11, 1972.

24. Maria Antoinette⁴ Serra (Domenico³, Giovani Battista², Giuseppe¹) was born October 30, 1928 in 241 York St. Jersey City, NJ. She married **Francis Patrick Goldrick** May 29, 1960 in St. Bridget's Church, Montgomery St., Jersey City, NJ, son of Francis Goldrick and Mildred McElroy. He was born October 15, 1933.

Children of Maria Serra and Francis Goldrick are:
+ 95   i.   Kathleen Mary⁵ Goldrick, born April 23, 1966 in Baltimore, MD.
  96   ii.   Michael Patrick Goldrick, born October 16, 1967 in Jersey City, NJ. He married Pamela Ryan November 16, 1996 in St. Patrick's Church, Bayshore, Long Island, NY; born November 24, 1966.

25. Sophia⁴ Clemenzi (MariaConcetta³ Serra, Giovani Battista², Giuseppe¹) was born August 14, 1914. She married **Dominick Villanti** August 25, 1940, son of Dominick Villanti and Catherina Costa. He was born April 11, 1914 in New York City, NY, and died April 26, 1987.

Children of Sophia Clemenzi and Dominick Villanti are:
+ 97   i.   Catherine⁵ Villanti, born September 08, 1947.
  98   ii.   Maria Villanti, born May 12, 1951. She married Dennis Parent August 11, 1984.
  99   iii. Angela Villanti, born March 29, 1957.

26. Marietta Stephanie⁴ Clemenzi (MariaConcetta³ Serra, Giovani Battista², Giuseppe¹) was born June 08, 1916 in Beverly, MA. She married **George Di Grandi** October 29, 1944 in Beverly, MA, son of Pasquale Di Grandi and Rose Lusco.

Children of Marietta Clemenzi and George Di Grandi are:
  100   i.   Diana⁵ Di Grandi, born February 15, 1945.
+ 101   ii.   Ronald Di Grandi, born March 03, 1946.
+ 102   iii. Christine Di Grandi, born March 13, 1949.
+ 103   iv.   Patricia Di Grandi, born October 12, 1953 in Beverly Hospital, Beverly, MA.
+ 104   v.   Francine Di Grandi, born October 22, 1954 in Beverly Hospital, Beverly, MA.

27. Emma⁴ Clemenzi (MariaConcetta³ Serra, Giovani Battista², Giuseppe¹) was born March 11, 1918. She married **Phillip Villanti** October 12, 1940, son of Dominick Villanti and Catherina Costa. He was born 1917 in Harrison, N.J..

Children of Emma Clemenzi and Phillip Villanti are:
+ 105   i.   Roberta⁵ Villanti, born October 04, 1941.
  106   ii.   Phillip Villanti, born June 1947. He married Connie Howard.

28. Dominick[4] Clemenzi (MariaConcetta[3] Serra, Giovani Battista[2], Giuseppe[1]) was born January 11, 1920. He married **Helen Virginia Carper** May 06, 1943. She was born September 03, 1924.

Children of Dominick Clemenzi and Helen Carper are:

	107	i.	Robert[5] Clemenzi, born April 21, 1944; died August 1977.
+	108	ii.	Richard Clemenzi, born April 21, 1944.
+	109	iii.	Dorothy Clemenzi, born October 11, 1946.
+	110	iv.	David Clemenzi, born May 10, 1949.
+	111	v.	Mary Catherine Clemenzi, born October 01, 1953.

29. John Battista[4] Clemenzi (MariaConcetta[3] Serra, Giovani Battista[2], Giuseppe[1]) was born October 15, 1922. He married **Olga Vandi** April 23, 1950.

Children of John Clemenzi and Olga Vandi are:

+	112	i.	Marie C.[5] Clemenzi, born April 1951.
+	113	ii.	John T. Clemenzi, born May 13, 1953.
+	114	iii.	Cheryl Ann Clemenzi, born August 14, 1955.
	115	iv.	Alex J. Clemenzi, born August 20, 1959.

30. Peter[4] Clemenzi (MariaConcetta[3] Serra, Giovani Battista[2], Giuseppe[1]) was born October 03, 1924. He married **Rose Nardella** July 06, 1952 in St. Mary's Church, Beverly, MA. She died 1996.

Children of Peter Clemenzi and Rose Nardella are:

	116	i.	Peter James[5] Clemenzi, born February 23, 1954.
+	117	ii.	John Anthony Clemenzi, born March 11, 1955.
+	118	iii.	Robert Michael Clemenzi, born July 22, 1956.
+	119	iv.	Gary Steven Clemenzi, born October 28, 1959.
+	120	v.	Donald Clemenzi, born April 10, 1963.

31. Angelo[4] Clemenzi (MariaConcetta[3] Serra, Giovani Battista[2], Giuseppe[1]) was born July 02, 1927. He married **Lucia Anselmo** September 02, 1950.

Children of Angelo Clemenzi and Lucia Anselmo are:

+	121	i.	John A.[5] Clemenzi.
	122	ii.	Mark Clemenzi.
	123	iii.	Elizabeth Clemenzi. She married Anthony Garreffi.
	124	iv.	Susan Clemenzi. She married Wayne Wendell.
	125	v.	Ann Clemenzi, born 1955. She married David Ferris.
	126	vi.	Joan Clemenzi, born August 1957; died April 1999.
	127	vii.	Paul Clemenzi, born 1960. He married Christine Mizioch February 14, 1981.

33. Orazio Oscar[4] Costa (Caterina[3] Serra, Giovani Battista[2], Giuseppe[1]) was born May 23, 1914 in Beverly, MA, and died October 02, 1993 in Beverly, MA. He married **Rose Theresa Femino** December 01, 1945 in St. Mary's Church, Beverly, MA, daughter of Lawrence Femino and Dominica Parisi. She was born January 27, 1916 in Salem, MA, and died November 20, 1981 in Danvers, MA.

Children of Orazio Costa and Rose Femino are:

+	128	i.	Concetto Joseph Anthony[5] Costa, born September 10, 1946 in Beverly, MA.
+	129	ii.	John Lawrence Costa, born November 10, 1948.
+	130	iii.	Marieann Frances Costa, born June 09, 1953 in Beverly, MA.
+	131	iv.	Nancy Rita Costa, born February 17, 1958 in Beverly, MA.

35. Josephine[4] Costa (Caterina[3] Serra, Giovani Battista[2], Giuseppe[1]) was born July 12, 1918 in Beverly, MA. She married **Silvio Scaglairini** November 24, 1945 in Beverly, MA. He was born October 04, 1916 in Springfield, MA.

Children of Josephine Costa and Silvio Scaglairini are:
+   132   i.   John Anthony[5] Scaglairini, born April 19, 1947.
     133   ii.   Paul Joseph Scaglairini, born January 18, 1951. He married Cindy M; born August 31, 1959.
+   134   iii. Theresa Ann Scaglairini, born April 23, 1956.

36. Maria Concetta[4] Costa (Caterina[3] Serra, Giovani Battista[2], Giuseppe[1]) was born March 03, 1921 in Beverly, MA. She married **(1) Ray Linwood Brown** November 25, 1944 in St. Mary's Star of the Sea Church, Beverly, MA. He was born April 20, 1918 in Union, North Carolina, and died October 28, 1977 in Richmond, VA. She married **(2) Edward Thomas Copeland** June 08, 1984 in St. Augustine Church, Richmond, VA. He was born June 24, 1931.

Children of Maria Costa and Ray Brown are:
     135   i.   Ray Linwood[5] Brown III, born October 12, 1945. He married Susan Eyler Morris March 31, 1977; born April 11, 1949.
+   136   ii.   Thomas Edward Brown, born June 24, 1947.
+   137   iii. Donia Kathleen Brown, born September 10, 1949 in C&O RR Hospital, Huntington, West Virginia.

37. Santa[4] Costa (Caterina[3] Serra, Giovani Battista[2], Giuseppe[1]) was born May 31, 1923 in Beverly, MA, and died February 23, 2003 in Massachusetts. She married **(1) Henry Weislik** January 1946 in St. Mary's Church. He died 1967. She married **(2) Leo Krauskus** 1970. She married **(3) Lawrence Augustus** 1977.

Children of Santa Costa and Henry Weislik are:
+   138   i.   Judy[5] Weislik, born January 23, 1947.
     139   ii.   Dennis Weislik, born March 05, 1952.

38. Frank[4] Costa (Caterina[3] Serra, Giovani Battista[2], Giuseppe[1]) was born September 21, 1925. He married **Norma Blake** 1943.

Children of Frank Costa and Norma Blake are:
     140   i.   Frank[5] Costa, born March 05, 1944.
     141   ii.   Richard Costa, born November 10, 1947.
+   142   iii. John Costa, born July 07, 1950.
     143   iv.   Beth Ann Costa, born June 13, 1961.

41. John Battista Christopher[4] Serra (Salvatore[3], Giovani Battista[2], Giuseppe[1]) was born May 20, 1925, and died May 16, 1994. He married **Jennie Didamo** September 03, 1955. She died 2000.

Children of John Serra and Jennie Didamo are:
+   144   i.   Maria[5] Serra.
     145   ii.   Christopher Serra.

116

42. Angelina[4] **Serra** (Salvatore[3], Giovani Battista[2], Giuseppe[1]) was born June 06, 1931. She married **Joseph Scibetta** September 02, 1951.

Children of Angelina Serra and Joseph Scibetta are:
+ 146   i.   Barbara Jo[5] Scibetta, born March 12, 1953.
+ 147   ii.   Betty Ann Scibetta, born June 22, 1958.
+ 148   iii.   Joseph Scibetta, born March 10, 1960.

43. Santina[4] **Serra** (Salvatore[3], Giovani Battista[2], Giuseppe[1]) was born August 13, 1927, and died July 20, 1976. She married **Dominick Galletta** 1949.

Children of Santina Serra and Dominick Galletta are:
149   i.   Josephine[5] Galletta.
150   ii.   Dominick Galletta.

44. Catherine Jenni[4] **De Lorenzo** (Maria Carolina[3] Serra, Giovani Battista[2], Giuseppe[1]) was born April 12, 1917. She married **Kenneth Stone**.

Child of Catherine De Lorenzo and Kenneth Stone is:
+ 151   i.   Carol Ann[5] Stone.

45. Maria Concetta[4] **De Lorenzo** (Maria Carolina[3] Serra, Giovani Battista[2], Giuseppe[1]) was born January 25, 1919. She married **Anthony Carmada**.

Children of Maria De Lorenzo and Anthony Carmada are:
152   i.   Steven[5] Carmada.
153   ii.   Tommy Carmada.
154   iii.   Joanne Carmada. She married Ray Whiteman.

46. Antonio[4] **De Lorenzo** (Maria Carolina[3] Serra, Giovani Battista[2], Giuseppe[1]) was born March 01, 1921. He married **Muriel McIntyre**.

Children of Antonio De Lorenzo and Muriel McIntyre are:
155   i.   Anthony[5] De Lorenzo.
156   ii.   Muriel De Lorenzo.

47. John Battista[4] **De Lorenzo** (Maria Carolina[3] Serra, Giovani Battista[2], Giuseppe[1]) was born September 21, 1923. He married **Anita Trembly**.

Children of John De Lorenzo and Anita Trembly are:
157   i.   Jeanne[5] De Lorenzo.
158   ii.   Jacqueline De Lorenzo.
159   iii.   Debra De Lorenzo.
160   iv.   John De Lorenzo.

48. Beatrice[4] **De Lorenzo** (Maria Carolina[3] Serra, Giovani Battista[2], Giuseppe[1]) was born October 20, 1925. She married **Philip Elwood Chenery**.

Children of Beatrice De Lorenzo and Philip Chenery are:

+	161	i.	Linda Mae[5] Chenery.
+	162	ii.	Joanne Marie Chenery.
+	163	iii.	Kenneth Guy Chenery.
+	164	iv.	Elaine Kay Chenery.
	165	v.	Philip Augustin Chenery, born 1951; died 1986.

49. Joseph[4] **De Lorenzo** (Maria Carolina[3] Serra, Giovani Battista[2], Giuseppe[1]) was born November 20, 1927. He married **Barbara Brotchie**.

Children of Joseph De Lorenzo and Barbara Brotchie are:

166	i.	Janice[5] De Lorenzo.
167	ii.	Nancy De Lorenzo.
168	iii.	Larry De Lorenzo.
169	iv.	Daniel De Lorenzo.
170	v.	Paul De Lorenzo.
171	vi.	Keven De Lorenzo.

50. Rose Marie[4] **De Lorenzo** (Maria Carolina[3] Serra, Giovani Battista[2], Giuseppe[1]) was born December 16, 1929. She married **Fred Czarnecki**.

Children of Rose De Lorenzo and Fred Czarnecki are:

	172	i.	Ronald[5] Czarnecki.
+	173	ii.	Joseph Czarnecki.
	174	iii.	Michael Czarnecki.

Generation No. 4

51. Michael[5] **Miranda** (Adelgisa Theresa[4] De Angelis, Angelina[3] Serra, Giovani Battista[2], Giuseppe[1]) was born October 30, 1948. He married **Marjoriel Panorelli** November 1982. She was born August 21, 1952.

Children of Michael Miranda and Marjoriel Panorelli are:

175	i.	Michael Paul[6] Miranda, born January 13, 1987.
176	ii.	Matthew Miranda, born July 06, 1988.

52. John[5] **Miranda** (Adelgisa Theresa[4] De Angelis, Angelina[3] Serra, Giovani Battista[2], Giuseppe[1]) was born July 02, 1950. He married **Sheila Gorman** in Lowell, MA. She was born November 29, 1951.

Children of John Miranda and Sheila Gorman are:

177	i.	Karen[6] Miranda, born August 26, 1982.
178	ii.	John Miranda, born March 25, 1984.
179	iii.	Leah Miranda, born April 02, 1987.

53. Dominic[5] **Miranda** (Adelgisa Theresa[4] De Angelis, Angelina[3] Serra, Giovani Battista[2], Giuseppe[1]) was born October 07, 1951. He married **Christine Wawzyniecki** November 29, 1975 in Athol, MA. She was born April 11, 1950.

Children of Dominic Miranda and Christine Wawzyniecki are:
- 180   i.   Lisa[6] Miranda, born April 22, 1982.
- 181   ii. Emily Miranda, born October 26, 1984.

55. Josephine[5] **Miranda** (Adelgisa Theresa[4] De Angelis, Angelina[3] Serra, Giovani Battista[2], Giuseppe[1]) was born March 18, 1954. She married **Gavin Keenan** June 03, 1979 in St. Mary's Star of the Sea Church, Beverly, MA. He was born October 16, 1955.

Children of Josephine Miranda and Gavin Keenan are:
- 182   i.   Sarah[6] Keenan, born May 03, 1981.
- 183   ii. Patrick Keenan, born March 05, 1984.

56. Anthony[5] **Miranda** (Adelgisa Theresa[4] De Angelis, Angelina[3] Serra, Giovani Battista[2], Giuseppe[1]) was born March 30, 1955. He married **Angela Ali** May 22, 1988 in St. Mary's Star of the Sea Church, Beverly, MA. She was born January 27, 1960.

Children of Anthony Miranda and Angela Ali are:
- 184   i.   Erica[6] Miranda, born February 01, 1990.
- 185   ii. Marc Miranda, born July 21, 1992.

57. Angelo[5] **Miranda** (Adelgisa Theresa[4] De Angelis, Angelina[3] Serra, Giovani Battista[2], Giuseppe[1]) was born June 10, 1956. He married **Diane Brooks** June 1981. She was born October 01, 1956.

Children of Angelo Miranda and Diane Brooks are:
- 186   i.   Ashley[6] Miranda, born July 17, 1989.
- 187   ii. Lauren Miranda, born April 04, 1993.

58. Bettina[5] **Miranda** (Adelgisa Theresa[4] De Angelis, Angelina[3] Serra, Giovani Battista[2], Giuseppe[1]) was born August 1959. She married **Dan Moriarty** September 11, 1988 in St. Mary's Star of the Sea Church, Beverly, MA. He was born April 1957.

Children of Bettina Miranda and Dan Moriarty are:
- 188   i.   Katherine[6] Moriarty, born July 1992.
- 189   ii. Rebecca Moriarty, born May 1994.
- 190   iii. Emma Moriarty, born November 1996.

59. Lucia[5] **Miranda** (Adelgisa Theresa[4] De Angelis, Angelina[3] Serra, Giovani Battista[2], Giuseppe[1]) was born April 19, 1961. She married **Dean Darr** June 26, 1988 in St. Mary's Star of the Sea Church, Beverly, MA. He was born January 06, 1963.

Children of Lucia Miranda and Dean Darr are:
- 191   i.   Gregory[6] Darr, born June 03, 1991.
- 192   ii. Jessica Darr, born May 06, 1993.

60. Carolyn[5] **Vandi** (Rose[4] De Angelis, Angelina[3] Serra, Giovani Battista[2], Giuseppe[1]) was born November 25, 1943 in Beverly, MA. She married **John Marletta** July 24, 1966. He was born January 01, 1943 in Beverly, MA.

Children of Carolyn Vandi and John Marletta are:

     193   i.   John David[6] Marletta, born August 05, 1970 in Beverly, MA. He married Tiffany Nadeau September 01, 2001.

\+   194   ii.   Lisa Marie Marletta, born April 19, 1973 in Gloucester, MA.

     195   iii. Sarah Ann Marletta, born February 22, 1976 in Gloucester, MA.

61. Marilyn[5] **Vandi** (Rose[4] De Angelis, Angelina[3] Serra, Giovani Battista[2], Giuseppe[1]) was born November 25, 1943 in Beverly, MA. She married **Emmanuel Kuntupis** June 26, 1970. He was born in Ikaria, Greece.

Children of Marilyn Vandi and Emmanuel Kuntupis are:

     196   i.   Kara Ann[6] Kuntupis, born October 16, 1973.

     197   ii.   Katie Amanda Kuntupis, born October 22, 1976.

62. Dennis[5] **Vandi** (Rose[4] De Angelis, Angelina[3] Serra, Giovani Battista[2], Giuseppe[1]) was born December 16, 1946 in Beverly, MA. He married **Mary Laura Young** October 26, 1974.

Child of Dennis Vandi and Mary Young is:

     198   i.   Dennis Scott[6] Vandi, born April 16, 1982 in Lowell, MA.

63. Gene Scott[5] **Vandi** (Rose[4] De Angelis, Angelina[3] Serra, Giovani Battista[2], Giuseppe[1]) was born September 02, 1950 in Beverly, MA. He married **(1) Laurie J. Colella** March 1974.   He married **(2) Tina J. Wagner** October 27, 1990. She was born March 16, 1962.

Child of Gene Vandi and Laurie Colella is:

     199   i.   Joelle Denise[6] Vandi, born October 13, 1975.

Children of Gene Vandi and Tina Wagner are:

     200   i.   Gene Scott[6] Vandi, born March 03, 1993 in Clearwater, FL.

     201   ii.   Nicholas Anthony Vandi, born November 07, 1994 in Clearwater, FL.

64. Sharon Faith[5] **Vandi** (Rose[4] De Angelis, Angelina[3] Serra, Giovani Battista[2], Giuseppe[1]) was born May 03, 1956 in Beverly, MA. She married **David H. D'Amato** April 16, 1978. He was born September 30, 1954.

Children of Sharon Vandi and David D'Amato are:

     202   i.   Emily Joan[6] D'Amato, born February 09, 1982 in Beverly, MA.

     203   ii.   David Samuel D'Amato, born December 17, 1984 in Beverly, MA.

     204   iii. Anna Rose D'Amato, born April 22, 1986 in Beverly, MA.

65. Peter^5 Sienkiewicz (Bettina^4 Serra, Giuseppe^3, Giovani Battista^2, Giuseppe^1) was born May 23, 1949. He married **Jane Masters** August 23, 1980.

Children of Peter Sienkiewicz and Jane Masters are:
205	i.	John^6 Sienkiewicz, born June 04, 1987.
206	ii.	Elizabeth Sienkiewicz, born October 16, 1988.
207	iii.	Joseph Sienkiewicz, born September 26, 1993.

66. Paul^5 Sienkiewicz (Bettina^4 Serra, Giuseppe^3, Giovani Battista^2, Giuseppe^1) was born June 02, 1952. He married **Faye Friedman** August 24, 1975. She was born May 01, 1952.

Children of Paul Sienkiewicz and Faye Friedman are:
208	i.	Matthew^6 Sienkiewicz, born September 21, 1980.
209	ii.	Emily Sienkiewicz, born July 14, 1983.

67. Catherine^5 Sienkiewicz (Bettina^4 Serra, Giuseppe^3, Giovani Battista^2, Giuseppe^1) was born January 21, 1958. She married **Jorn Balle** August 22.

Children of Catherine Sienkiewicz and Jorn Balle are:
210	i.	Bettina^6 Balle, born September 25, 1985.
211	ii.	Sophia Balle, born January 02, 1987.
212	iii.	Leif Balle, born November 27, 1989.
213	iv.	Asger Balle, born April 20, 2002.

72. Joseph John^5 Bonaiuto (Maria Rose^4 Serra, Giuseppe^3, Giovani Battista^2, Giuseppe^1) was born October 29, 1958. He married **Elaine M. Pelletier** September 08, 1984. She was born October 15, 1960.

Children of Joseph Bonaiuto and Elaine Pelletier are:
214	i.	Nathan Joseph^6 Bonaiuto, born August 13, 1988.
215	ii.	Grace Alice Bonaiuto, born May 06, 1992.

74. Sharon Ann^5 Eggleston (Margherita^4 Serra, Giuseppe^3, Giovani Battista^2, Giuseppe^1) was born June 14, 1956. She married **Richard Turcotte** August 11, 1979.

Child of Sharon Eggleston and Richard Turcotte is:
216	i.	Gregory^6 Turcotte, born October 03, 1980.

75. Theresa Grace^5 Eggleston (Margherita^4 Serra, Giuseppe^3, Giovani Battista^2, Giuseppe^1) was born August 03, 1959. She married **Stephen Smith** July 30, 1983.

Children of Theresa Eggleston and Stephen Smith are:
217	i.	Sean^6 Smith, born January 18, 1988.
218	ii.	Quinton Smith, born February 05, 1989.
219	iii.	Zackary Smith, born February 05, 1989.
220	iv.	Gabriella Smith, born September 17, 1990.

76. William Joseph[5] Eggleston (Margherita[4] Serra, Giuseppe[3], Giovani Battista[2], Giuseppe[1]) was born May 30, 1962. He married **Kim Kenyon** September 26, 1987.

Children of William Eggleston and Kim Kenyon are:
221	i.	Daniel[6] Eggleston, born July 14, 1992.
222	ii.	Michael Eggleston, born August 22, 1996.

78. Dominick[5] Charowsky (Bartolomea[4] Serra, Domenico[3], Giovani Battista[2], Giuseppe[1]) was born August 01, 1952 in Margaret Hague Hospital, Jersey City, NJ. He married **(1) Peir-Lian Tseng** July 14, 1977. She was born April 17, 1951 in Hualien, Taiwan. He married **(2) Catherine Buttner** April 19, 2001.

Children of Dominick Charowsky and Peir-Lian Tseng are:
223	i.	Lorraine[6] Charowsky, born July 13, 1978 in Fort Bragg Army Hospital, Fayetteville, NC.
224	ii.	Eileen Charowsky, born July 01, 1983.

79. Robert[5] Charowsky (Bartolomea[4] Serra, Domenico[3], Giovani Battista[2], Giuseppe[1]) was born March 28, 1955 in Margaret Hague Hospital, Jersey City, NJ. He married **Patricia Ferenc**, daughter of Alexander Ferenc and Josephine. She was born November 24, 1954 in Jersey City, NJ.

Children of Robert Charowsky and Patricia Ferenc are:
225	i.	Robert[6] Charowsky, born April 17, 1983 in Jersey City, NJ.
226	ii.	Heather Marie Charowsky, born February 08, 1985 in Secaucus, NJ.

81. Maria Concetta[5] Charowsky (Bartolomea[4] Serra, Domenico[3], Giovani Battista[2], Giuseppe[1]) was born December 15, 1958 in Margaret Hague Hospital, Jersey City, NJ. She married **William Dombrowski** June 12, 1982 in St. Aloysius Church, Jersey City, NJ.

Children of Maria Charowsky and William Dombrowski are:
227	i.	Christina[6] Dombrowski, born July 10, 1984.
228	ii.	Jennifer Dombrowski, born November 09, 1987.
229	iii.	Kimberly Dombrowski, born September 21, 1994.

82. Mary Nellie[5] Obert (Giovannina[4] Serra, Domenico[3], Giovani Battista[2], Giuseppe[1]) was born September 13, 1951 in Amesbury Hospital, Amesbury, MA. She met **(1) Earl Messer**. He was born October 29, 1922, and died May 19, 1992. She married **(2) Roger Fortin** April 29, 2000 in St. Elizabeth Church, Seabrook, NH, son of Desiree Fortin and Martha Marquis. He was born April 25, 1941 in St. Anne, Madawaska, Quebec, Canada.

Child of Mary Obert and Earl Messer is:
+ 230	i.	Michelle Elizabeth[6] Obert, born July 01, 1974 in Lawrence, MA.

83. Norma Jean[5] Obert (Giovannina[4] Serra, Domenico[3], Giovani Battista[2], Giuseppe[1]) was born September 27, 1953 in Amesbury Hospital, Amesbury, MA. She married **Lawrence John Ayers** in Rocky Hill Meeting House, Amesbury, MA. He was born July 21, 1949 in NY.

Children of Norma Obert and Lawrence Ayers are:
231	i.	Geremy Matthew[6] Ayers, born December 31, 1975.
232	ii.	Amy Marie Ayers, born May 18, 1983.

84. Edward Norman[5] **Obert** (Giovannina[4] Serra, Domenico[3], Giovani Battista[2], Giuseppe[1]) was born November 17, 1955 in Amesbury Hospital, Amesbury, MA. He married **Norma Jean Grandmont** June 20, 1980 in St. James Church, Haverhill, MA. She was born March 07, 1949 in Hale (old) Hospital, Haverhill, MA.

Child of Edward Obert and Norma Grandmont is:

+ 233   i.   Robert James[6] Obert, born August 02, 1970 in Hale (old) Hospital, Haverhill, MA.

85. Patricia Ann[5] **Obert** (Giovannina[4] Serra, Domenico[3], Giovani Battista[2], Giuseppe[1]) was born September 24, 1957 in Amesbury Hospital, Amesbury, MA. She married **Robert Ponticelli** December 31, 1981, son of Robert Ponticelli and Shirley. He was born June 03, 1960.

Children of Patricia Obert and Robert Ponticelli are:

234   i.   Ryan Robert[6] Ponticelli, born July 02, 1982 in Anna Jacques Hospital, Newburyport, MA.
235   ii.   Angela Marie Ponticelli, born January 20, 1988 in Anna Jacques Hospital, Newburyport, MA.

86. Christopher Paul[5] **Obert** (Giovannina[4] Serra, Domenico[3], Giovani Battista[2], Giuseppe[1]) was born July 09, 1962 in Amesbury Hospital, Amesbury, MA. He married **Nancy Sue Blanchette** December 20, 1981 in Red Tavern, Methuen, MA, daughter of Herve Blanchette and Mary Fitzgerald. She was born June 19, 1963 in Bon Secoeurs Hospital, Methuen, MA.

Children of Christopher Obert and Nancy Blanchette are:

236   i.   Shari Lyn[6] Obert, born April 29, 1982 in Lawrence General Hospital, Lawrence, MA.
237   ii.   Jason Edward Obert, born May 31, 1985 in Lawrence General Hospital, Lawrence, MA.

87. Dominick[5] **Serra** (Giovanni Battista[4], Domenico[3], Giovani Battista[2], Giuseppe[1]) was born January 09, 1955 in Jersey City, NJ. He married **Diane Marie McGuirl** November 19, 1977 in Holy Rosary Church, Jersey City, NJ. She was born January 20, 1953 in Jersey City, NJ.

Children of Dominick Serra and Diane McGuirl are:

238   i.   Danielle Marie[6] Serra, born July 13, 1981 in Englewood, NJ.
239   ii.   Dominick Anthony Serra, born December 22, 1983 in Englewood, NJ.
240   iii.   Daniel Matthew Serra, born August 14, 1986 in Englewood, NJ.

88. Donna Marie[5] **Serra** (Giovanni Battista[4], Domenico[3], Giovani Battista[2], Giuseppe[1]) was born December 31, 1955. She married **(1) Raul Lopez**. She married **(2) Harry Vincent Lorusso** November 21, 1987. He was born September 03, 1957.

Children of Donna Serra and Raul Lopez are:

241   i.   Steven Guy[6] Lorusso, born September 11, 1976.
242   ii.   Gina Marie Lorusso, born February 16, 1984.

89. John Phillip[5] **Serra** (Giovanni Battista[4], Domenico[3], Giovani Battista[2], Giuseppe[1]) was born June 03, 1957. He married **Donna Marie Gennace** August 20, 1983. She was born June 27, 1958.

Children of John Serra and Donna Gennace are:

243   i.   David John[6] Serra, born July 08, 1987.
244   ii.   Matthew Phillip Serra, born December 11, 1990.

90. Mary Lynn[5] Serra (Giovanni Battista[4], Domenico[3], Giovani Battista[2], Giuseppe[1]) was born February 20, 1960. She married **Roberto Gonzalez** June 03, 1993. He was born April 18, 1970.

Child of Mary Serra and Roberto Gonzalez is:
> 245   i.   Rebecca Lynn[6] Gonzalez, born November 14, 1993.

92. Carol Ann[5] Serra (Giovanni Battista[4], Domenico[3], Giovani Battista[2], Giuseppe[1]) was born August 01, 1965. She married **Daniel Joseph Downing** October 08, 1989. He was born September 08, 1959.

Children of Carol Serra and Daniel Downing are:
> 246   i.   Noelle Amanda[6] Downing, born December 19, 1990.
> 247   ii. Daniel Mark Downing, born May 15, 1993.

95. Kathleen Mary[5] Goldrick (Maria Antoinette[4] Serra, Domenico[3], Giovani Battista[2], Giuseppe[1]) was born April 23, 1966 in Baltimore, MD. She married **Robert W. Wilson** April 20, 1990 in St. Mary's Church, New Monmouth, NJ, son of John Wilson and Theresa Kelley. He was born October 24, 1965.

Children of Kathleen Goldrick and Robert Wilson are:
> 248   i.   Grace Marie Shan-Shan[6] Wilson, born July 20, 1997 in Yue Yang, Hunan Province China.
> 249   ii. Julia Margaret Yu-Fu Wilson, born July 21, 2001 in Nan Chung, Szechuan Province, China.

97. Catherine[5] Villanti (Sophia[4] Clemenzi, MariaConcetta[3] Serra, Giovani Battista[2], Giuseppe[1]) was born September 08, 1947. She married **George Constantelo** July 07, 1984.

Children of Catherine Villanti and George Constantelo are:
> + 250   i.   Kristen[6] Constantelo, born August 02, 1974.
>   251   ii. Alana Constantelo, born November 15, 1980.

101. Ronald[5] Di Grandi (Marietta Stephanie[4] Clemenzi, MariaConcetta[3] Serra, Giovani Battista[2], Giuseppe[1]) was born March 03, 1946. He married **Pao Lien Chen**.

Child of Ronald Di Grandi and Pao Chen is:
> 252   i.   Patricia[6] Di Grandi, born May 25, 1986 in Northern Dutchess Hospital, Rhinebeck, NY.

102. Christine[5] Di Grandi (Marietta Stephanie[4] Clemenzi, MariaConcetta[3] Serra, Giovani Battista[2], Giuseppe[1]) was born March 13, 1949. She married **Mace Earl Jones** June 08, 1968.

Children of Christine Di Grandi and Mace Jones are:
> 253   i.   Trisha[6] Jones, born December 20, 1970 in Vassar Hospital, Poughkeepsie, NY. She married Jonathan Freiermuth.
> 254   ii. Mace Jones, born March 22, 1978 in Northern Dutchess Hospital, Rhinebeck, NY; died March 27, 1993.
> + 255   iii. Deanna Jones, born September 06, 1979 in Northern Dutchess Hospital, Rhinebeck, NY.

103. Patricia⁵ Di Grandi (Marietta Stephanie⁴ Clemenzi, MariaConcetta³ Serra, Giovani Battista², Giuseppe¹) was born October 12, 1953 in Beverly Hospital, Beverly, MA. She married **John Hohmann** October 1988.

Children of Patricia Di Grandi and John Hohmann are:
- 256   i.   Stefanie⁶ Hohman, born October 1990.
- 257   ii.   Sarah Hohman, born March 1992.
- 258   iii.   Robert Hohman, born February 1996.

104. Francine⁵ Di Grandi (Marietta Stephanie⁴ Clemenzi, MariaConcetta³ Serra, Giovani Battista², Giuseppe¹) was born October 22, 1954 in Beverly Hospital, Beverly, MA.

Child of Francine Di Grandi is:
- 259   i.   Gina⁶ Di Grandi, born June 24, 1985 in Northern Dutchess Hospital, Rhinebeck, NY.

105. Roberta⁵ Villanti (Emma⁴ Clemenzi, MariaConcetta³ Serra, Giovani Battista², Giuseppe¹) was born October 04, 1941. She married **David Jaquith**.

Children of Roberta Villanti and David Jaquith are:
- 260   i.   Danielle⁶ Jaquith, born January 06, 1971.
- 261   ii.   Nicole Jaquith, born March 28, 1975.

108. Richard⁵ Clemenzi (Dominick⁴, MariaConcetta³ Serra, Giovani Battista², Giuseppe¹) was born April 21, 1944. He married **Kathleen Boyer**.

Children of Richard Clemenzi and Kathleen Boyer are:
- 262   i.   Anthony⁶ Clemenzi, born October 09, 1973.
- 263   ii.   Christopher Clemenzi, born October 26, 1979.

109. Dorothy⁵ Clemenzi (Dominick⁴, MariaConcetta³ Serra, Giovani Battista², Giuseppe¹) was born October 11, 1946. She married **Tim Blanchette**.

Children of Dorothy Clemenzi and Tim Blanchette are:
- 264   i.   Ethan⁶ Blanchette, born December 23, 1977.
- 265   ii.   Aaron Blanchette, born January 28, 1981.

110. David⁵ Clemenzi (Dominick⁴, MariaConcetta³ Serra, Giovani Battista², Giuseppe¹) was born May 10, 1949. He married **Charlene Irish**.

Children of David Clemenzi and Charlene Irish are:
- 266   i.   Eric⁶ Clemenzi, born March 06, 1979.
- 267   ii.   Tina Clemenzi, born February 06, 1981.

111. Mary Catherine⁵ Clemenzi (Dominick⁴, MariaConcetta³ Serra, Giovani Battista², Giuseppe¹) was born October 01, 1953. She married **Mostafa Khalil**.

Children of Mary Clemenzi and Mostafa Khalil are:
- 268   i.   Omar⁶ Khalil, born August 31, 1979.
- 269   ii.   Aisha Khalil, born May 28, 1985.
- 270   iii.   Sarah Khalil, born January 11, 1987.

112. Marie C.⁵ Clemenzi (John Battista⁴, MariaConcetta³ Serra, Giovani Battista², Giuseppe¹) was born April 1951. She married **Daniel Beane** June 03, 1972.

Children of Marie Clemenzi and Daniel Beane are:
 271 i. Carrie-Anne⁶ Beane, born January 17, 1975.
 272 ii. Mark Charles Beane, born March 28, 1978. He married Amanda Wolfe June 29, 2001.

113. John T.⁵ Clemenzi (John Battista⁴, MariaConcetta³ Serra, Giovani Battista², Giuseppe¹) was born May 13, 1953. He married **Christine Hoops** July 27, 1991.

Child of John Clemenzi and Christine Hoops is:
 273 i. Benjamin⁶ Clemenzi, born July 28, 1993.

114. Cheryl Ann⁵ Clemenzi (John Battista⁴, MariaConcetta³ Serra, Giovani Battista², Giuseppe¹) was born August 14, 1955. She married **Michael J. Comstock** August 18, 1979.

Children of Cheryl Clemenzi and Michael Comstock are:
 274 i. Jennifer Lynn⁶ Comstock, born November 22, 1980.
 275 ii. Amy Lee Comstock, born June 08, 1982.
 276 iii. James Michael Comstock, born November 04, 1985.

117. John Anthony⁵ Clemenzi (Peter⁴, MariaConcetta³ Serra, Giovani Battista², Giuseppe¹) was born March 11, 1955. He married **Kathy Lyman**.

Children of John Clemenzi and Kathy Lyman are:
 277 i. Brendan⁶ Clemenzi. He married Karen Ahern 2002.
 278 ii. Margaret Clemenzi.
 279 iii. Kiera Lee Clemenzi.
 280 iv. John David Clemenzi.

118. Robert Michael⁵ Clemenzi (Peter⁴, MariaConcetta³ Serra, Giovani Battista², Giuseppe¹) was born July 22, 1956. He married **Joyce Osgood**.

Child of Robert Clemenzi and Joyce Osgood is:
 281 i. Candice⁶ Clemenzi.

119. Gary Steven⁵ Clemenzi (Peter⁴, MariaConcetta³ Serra, Giovani Battista², Giuseppe¹) was born October 28, 1959. He married **Barbara**.

Child of Gary Clemenzi and Barbara is:
 282 i. Cristofer⁶ Clemenzi.

120. Donald⁵ Clemenzi (Peter⁴, MariaConcetta³ Serra, Giovani Battista², Giuseppe¹) was born April 10, 1963. He married **Gayle Johnson** 1990.

Children of Donald Clemenzi and Gayle Johnson are:
 283 i. Marissa Rose⁶ Clemenzi, born April 07, 1998.
 284 ii. Kendra Lynn Clemenzi, born April 07, 1998.
 285 iii. Jenna Marie Clemenzi, born April 07, 1998.

121. John A.[5] Clemenzi (Angelo[4], MariaConcetta[3] Serra, Giovani Battista[2], Giuseppe[1]) He married **Gail**.

Children of John Clemenzi and Gail are:
- 286   i.   Aaron[6] Clemenzi.
- 287   ii. Lara Clemenzi.

128. Concetto Joseph Anthony[5] Costa (Orazio Oscar[4], Caterina[3] Serra, Giovani Battista[2], Giuseppe[1]) was born September 10, 1946 in Beverly, MA. He met **(1) Karen Friberg**. She was born March 22, 1948. He married **(2) Barbara Steen** July 11, 1970 in St. Alphonsus Church, Danvers, MA. She was born March 16, 1952 in Danvers, MA.

Children of Concetto Costa and Barbara Steen are:
- + 288   i.   Concetto Joseph Anthony[6] Costa, born February 03, 1971.
- + 289   ii. Anita Marie Costa, born June 24, 1977.
- + 290   iii. Linda Diane Costa, born July 31, 1980.
-     291   iv. Joseph Andrew Costa, born August 17, 1986.

129. John Lawrence[5] Costa (Orazio Oscar[4], Caterina[3] Serra, Giovani Battista[2], Giuseppe[1]) was born November 10, 1948. He married **Marilyn Melanson** February 17, 1974 in St. Alphonsus Church, Danvers, MA, daughter of Charles Melanson and Dorothy. She was born February 16, 1951.

Children of John Costa and Marilyn Melanson are:
- 292   i.   John Ryan[6] Costa, born September 23, 1974.
- 293   ii. Matthew Costa, born July 01, 1977.

130. Marieann Frances[5] Costa (Orazio Oscar[4], Caterina[3] Serra, Giovani Battista[2], Giuseppe[1]) was born June 09, 1953 in Beverly, MA. She married **David Russell Calder** July 11, 1971 in St. Alphonsus Church, Danvers, MA. He was born September 30, 1946.

Children of Marieann Costa and David Calder are:
- 294   i.   David Russel[6] Calder, born January 25, 1972.
- 295   ii. Sharon Marie Calder, born April 15, 1973.
- 296   iii. Marc Andrew Calder, born April 27, 1975.
- 297   iv. RoseMarie Louise Calder, born March 21, 1983.

131. Nancy Rita[5] Costa (Orazio Oscar[4], Caterina[3] Serra, Giovani Battista[2], Giuseppe[1]) was born February 17, 1958 in Beverly, MA. She married **Keith Thomas Desmond** December 01, 1984 in St. Margaret's Church, Beverly Farms, son of Richard Desmond and Alice Bartnicki. He was born September 07, 1955.

Children of Nancy Costa and Keith Desmond are:
- 298   i.   Rose Theresa[6] Desmond, born October 01, 1986.
- 299   ii. Danielle Alison Desmond, born September 26, 1989.

132. John Anthony[5] **Scaglairini** (Josephine[4] Costa, Caterina[3] Serra, Giovani Battista[2], Giuseppe[1]) was born April 19, 1947. He married **Kathy Mastroranni** February 15, 1970 in Springfield, MA. She was born November 23, 1947 in Springfield, MA.

Children of John Scaglairini and Kathy Mastroranni are:
>   300   i.   Brian[6] Scaglairini, born March 13, 1973.
>   301   ii. Alison Scaglairini, born December 16, 1973.
>   302   iii. Jason Scaglairini, born October 31, 1983.

134. Theresa Ann[5] **Scaglairini** (Josephine[4] Costa, Caterina[3] Serra, Giovani Battista[2], Giuseppe[1]) was born April 23, 1956. She married **Stephen Haskins** October 22, 1983 in Springfield, MA. He was born November 21, 1955 in Long Meadow.

Child of Theresa Scaglairini and Stephen Haskins is:
>   303   i.   James[6] Haskins, born April 15, 1987.

136. Thomas Edward[5] **Brown** (Maria Concetta[4] Costa, Caterina[3] Serra, Giovani Battista[2], Giuseppe[1]) was born June 24, 1947. He married **Lenora Sears** August 30, 1969 in Carl, West Virginia. She was born March 09, 1950.

Children of Thomas Brown and Lenora Sears are:
> + 304   i.   Thomas Michael[6] Brown, born March 17, 1972.
> + 305   ii. David Ray Brown, born April 17, 1974.
>   306   iii. Jessica Maria Brown, born April 13, 1982.

137. Donia Kathleen[5] **Brown** (Maria Concetta[4] Costa, Caterina[3] Serra, Giovani Battista[2], Giuseppe[1]) was born September 10, 1949 in C&O RR Hospital, Huntington, West Virginia. She married **Robert Leon Blanton** June 22, 1968 in Sacred Heart Church, Richmond, Virginia. He was born November 16, 1949 in Richmond, VA.

Children of Donia Brown and Robert Blanton are:
> + 307   i.   Robert L.[6] Blanton III, born January 28, 1969 in Medical College of Virginia Hospital, Richmond, VA.
> + 308   ii. Donald Ray Blanton, born July 04, 1971 in St. Mary's Hospital, Richmond, VA.

138. Judy[5] **Weislik** (Santa[4] Costa, Caterina[3] Serra, Giovani Battista[2], Giuseppe[1]) was born January 23, 1947. She married **Jeffrey Day** June 29, 1969. He was born November 24, 1945.

Children of Judy Weislik and Jeffrey Day are:
> + 309   i.   Jennifer[6] Day, born December 27, 1969 in Lynn, MA.
>   310   ii. Nancy Day, born March 15, 1971 in Lynn, MA.

142. John[5] **Costa** (Frank[4], Caterina[3] Serra, Giovani Battista[2], Giuseppe[1]) was born July 07, 1950. He married **Ruth**.

Children of John Costa and Ruth are:
>   311   i.   John[6] Costa.
>   312   ii. Angela Costa.

144. Maria[5] **Serra** (John Battista Christopher[4], Salvatore[3], Giovani Battista[2], Giuseppe[1]) She married **John Hyla**.

Child of Maria Serra and John Hyla is:

    313   i.   Jenna[6] Hyla.

146. Barbara Jo[5] **Scibetta** (Angelina[4] Serra, Salvatore[3], Giovani Battista[2], Giuseppe[1]) was born March 12, 1953. She married **Emil D'Elia** September 13, 1975.

Children of Barbara Scibetta and Emil D'Elia are:

    314   i.   Lynette[6] D'Elia, born September 29, 1979.
    315   ii.   Michael D'Elia, born September 01, 1983.

147. Betty Ann[5] **Scibetta** (Angelina[4] Serra, Salvatore[3], Giovani Battista[2], Giuseppe[1]) was born June 22, 1958. She married **Michael Tagliarini** September 11, 1982.

Child of Betty Scibetta and Michael Tagliarini is:

    316   i.   Angela[6] Tagliarini, born May 21, 1989.

148. Joseph[5] **Scibetta** (Angelina[4] Serra, Salvatore[3], Giovani Battista[2], Giuseppe[1]) was born March 10, 1960. He married **Geraldine**.

Children of Joseph Scibetta and Geraldine are:

    317   i.   Amanda[6] Scibetta, born August 28, 1985.
    318   ii.   Brittany Scibetta, born July 14, 1987.

151. Carol Ann[5] **Stone** (Catherine Jenni[4] De Lorenzo, Maria Carolina[3] Serra, Giovani Battista[2], Giuseppe[1]) She married **Richard Kobierski**.

Children of Carol Stone and Richard Kobierski are:

    319   i.   Kenneth[6] Kobierski.
    320   ii.   Lisa Kobierski.
    321   iii.   Richard Kobierski.
    322   iv.   Adam Kobierski.
    323   v.   Catherine Kobierski.
    324   vi.   Nancy Kobierski.
    325   vii.   Bobby Kobierski.
    326   viii.   Dianna Kobierski.

161. Linda Mae[5] **Chenery** (Beatrice[4] De Lorenzo, Maria Carolina[3] Serra, Giovani Battista[2], Giuseppe[1]) She married **John Gilmartin**.

Children of Linda Chenery and John Gilmartin are:

+   327   i.   Tara[6] Gilmartin.
+   328   ii.   Shawn Philip Gilmartin.

162. Joanne Marie^5 Chenery (Beatrice^4 De Lorenzo, Maria Carolina^3 Serra, Giovani Battista^2, Giuseppe^1) She married **Richard Hartigan Buckley**.

Children of Joanne Chenery and Richard Buckley are:
- 329   i.   Janelle Marie^6 Buckley.
- 330   ii.   Meghan Anne Buckley.
- 331   iii.   Ryan Philip Buckley.
- 332   iv.   Shauna Rose Buckley.

163. Kenneth Guy^5 Chenery (Beatrice^4 De Lorenzo, Maria Carolina^3 Serra, Giovani Battista^2, Giuseppe^1) He married **Lorraine Malvitch**.

Children of Kenneth Chenery and Lorraine Malvitch are:
- 333   i.   Nicholos Guy^6 Chenery.
- 334   ii.   Dana Philip Chenery.
- 335   iii.   Kyle Michael Chenery.

164. Elaine Kay^5 Chenery (Beatrice^4 De Lorenzo, Maria Carolina^3 Serra, Giovani Battista^2, Giuseppe^1) She married **Michael Racki**.

Children of Elaine Chenery and Michael Racki are:
- \+ 336   i.   Kristan Mae^6 Racki.
- 337   ii.   Steven Michael Racki. He married Nicole K. Cheries.
- 338   iii.   Samantha Marie Racki.

173. Joseph^5 Czarnecki (Rose Marie^4 De Lorenzo, Maria Carolina^3 Serra, Giovani Battista^2, Giuseppe^1) He married **Kathi**.

Child of Joseph Czarnecki and Kathi is:
- 339   i.   Alyssa^6 Czarnecki.

Generation No. 5

194. Lisa Marie^6 Marletta (Carolyn^5 Vandi, Rose^4 De Angelis, Angelina^3 Serra, Giovani Battista^2, Giuseppe^1) was born April 19, 1973 in Gloucester, MA. She married **James Groleau** July 21, 2001.

Child of Lisa Marletta and James Groleau is:
- 340   i.   Sam Pado^7 Groleau, born November 03, 2002.

230. Michelle Elizabeth^6 Obert (Mary Nellie^5, Giovannina^4 Serra, Domenico^3, Giovani Battista^2, Giuseppe^1) was born July 01, 1974 in Lawrence, MA. She met **Stephen LaFrance**. He was born July.

Child of Michelle Obert and Stephen LaFrance is:
- 341   i.   Emma Rae^7 Obert, born March 25, 2002 in Portsmouth, NH.

233. Robert James[6] Obert (Edward Norman[5], Giovannina[4] Serra, Domenico[3], Giovani Battista[2], Giuseppe[1]) was born August 02, 1970 in Hale (old) Hospital, Haverhill, MA. He married **Cheryl Marie Laliberty** June 29, 1996 in St. Patrick's Church, Lawrence, MA, daughter of Bill Laliberty and Linda Maraylin. She was born January 14, 1972 in Lawrence, MA.

Children of Robert Obert and Cheryl Laliberty are:

342	i.	Katherine Marie[7] Obert, born April 24, 1993 in Methuen, MA.
343	ii.	Matthew Jason Obert, born August 07, 1997 in Holy Family Hospital, Methuen, MA.

250. Kristen[6] Constantelo (Catherine[5] Villanti, Sophia[4] Clemenzi, MariaConcetta[3] Serra, Giovani Battista[2], Giuseppe[1]) was born August 02, 1974.

Children of Kristen Constantelo are:

344	i.	Anthony Jordan[7] Constantelo, born December 25, 1995.
345	ii.	Kaitlyn Elizabeth Shairs, born January 15, 2000.
346	iii.	Jared Michael, born June 22, 2003 in Beverly Hospital.

255. Deanna[6] Jones (Christine[5] Di Grandi, Marietta Stephanie[4] Clemenzi, MariaConcetta[3] Serra, Giovani Battista[2], Giuseppe[1]) was born September 06, 1979 in Northern Dutchess Hospital, Rhinebeck, NY.

Child of Deanna Jones is:

347	i.	Bettina Pietra[7] Jones, born September 1999 in Northern Dutchess Hospital, Rhinebeck, NY.

288. Concetto Joseph Anthony[6] Costa (Concetto Joseph Anthony[5], Orazio Oscar[4], Caterina[3] Serra, Giovani Battista[2], Giuseppe[1]) was born February 03, 1971. He met **Cindy Fish**.

Child of Concetto Costa and Cindy Fish is:

348	i.	Sarina[7] Costa, born April 19, 1996.

289. Anita Marie[6] Costa (Concetto Joseph Anthony[5], Orazio Oscar[4], Caterina[3] Serra, Giovani Battista[2], Giuseppe[1]) was born June 24, 1977. She married **Jeff Mir**. He was born October 01, 1972.

Children of Anita Costa and Jeff Mir are:

349	i.	Tyler Jeffrey[7] Mir, born June 04, 1995.
350	ii.	Tori Jannelle Mir, born October 21, 1996.

290. Linda Diane[6] Costa (Concetto Joseph Anthony[5], Orazio Oscar[4], Caterina[3] Serra, Giovani Battista[2], Giuseppe[1]) was born July 31, 1980. She met **(1) Victor Nolasco**. She married **(2) Eudy Beltre** March 15, 2001. He was born November 10, 1976.

Children of Linda Costa and Victor Nolasco are:

351	i.	Mariah Mercedes[7] Nolasco, born December 01, 1995.
352	ii.	Anthony Jordan Nolasco, born July 18, 1997.
353	iii.	Jacob Manuel Nolasco, born July 08, 1999.

Child of Linda Costa and Eudy Beltre is:

354	i.	Kiarra Jasmine[7] Beltre, born May 07, 2002.

304. Thomas Michael[6] Brown (Thomas Edward[5], Maria Concetta[4] Costa, Caterina[3] Serra, Giovani Battista[2], Giuseppe[1]) was born March 17, 1972. He married **Penny Renee Gathright** June 03, 2000. She was born March 03, 1976.

Child of Thomas Brown and Penny Gathright is:
355 i. Sara Jane[7] Brown, born June 24, 2002.

305. David Ray[6] Brown (Thomas Edward[5], Maria Concetta[4] Costa, Caterina[3] Serra, Giovani Battista[2], Giuseppe[1]) was born April 17, 1974. He met **(1) Hick**. He married **(2) Deirdre Sue Craddock** April 04, 1998. She was born May 18, 1974.

Child of David Brown and Hick is:
356 i. Tyler R.[7] Brown, born November 20, 1995.

Children of David Brown and Deirdre Craddock are:
357 i. Sierra Suzanne[7] Brown, born October 23, 1998.
358 ii. Savannah Marie Brown, born December 16, 1999.
359 iii. David Shayne Brown, born February 18, 2001.
360 iv. Summer Grace Brown, born 2002.

307. Robert L.[6] Blanton III (Donia Kathleen[5] Brown, Maria Concetta[4] Costa, Caterina[3] Serra, Giovani Battista[2], Giuseppe[1]) was born January 28, 1969 in Medical College of Virginia Hospital, Richmond, VA. He married **Andrea Lynn Grim** August 12, 1995 in James Madison University. She was born September 08, 1969 in Winchester, VA.

Children of Robert Blanton and Andrea Grim are:
361 i. Jakob Robert[7] Blanton, born January 14, 1999 in Martha Jefferson Hospital, Charlottesville, VA.
362 ii. Ian Richard Blanton, born February 05, 2001 in Martha Jefferson Hospital, Charlottesville, VA.

308. Donald Ray[6] Blanton (Donia Kathleen[5] Brown, Maria Concetta[4] Costa, Caterina[3] Serra, Giovani Battista[2], Giuseppe[1]) was born July 04, 1971 in St. Mary's Hospital, Richmond, VA. He married **Adrienne Blair Thornton** November 16, 1996 in St. Augustine Church, Richmond, VA. She was born June 10, 1973.

Children of Donald Blanton and Adrienne Thornton are:
363 i. Dylan Ray[7] Blanton, born March 02, 2000 in Chippenham Hospital, Richmond, VA.
364 ii. Andrew Carter Blanton, born October 01, 2002 in Chippenham Hospital, Richmond, VA.

309. Jennifer[6] Day (Judy[5] Weislik, Santa[4] Costa, Caterina[3] Serra, Giovani Battista[2], Giuseppe[1]) was born December 27, 1969 in Lynn, MA. She married **Stephen Morgan** October 02, 1994 in Endicott College, Beverly, MA. He was born December 02, 1968 in Salem, MA.

Child of Jennifer Day and Stephen Morgan is:
365 i. Sean Patrick[7] Morgan, born March 16, 2002.

327. Tara[6] **Gilmartin** (Linda Mae[5] Chenery, Beatrice[4] De Lorenzo, Maria Carolina[3] Serra, Giovani Battista[2], Giuseppe[1]) She married **Jamie Fraser**.

Child of Tara Gilmartin and Jamie Fraser is:
    366   i.   Ella Cynthia[7] Fraser.

328. Shawn Philip[6] **Gilmartin** (Linda Mae[5] Chenery, Beatrice[4] De Lorenzo, Maria Carolina[3] Serra, Giovani Battista[2], Giuseppe[1]) He married **Tracy Green**.

Child of Shawn Gilmartin and Tracy Green is:
    367   i.   Madison[7] Gilmartin.

336. Kristan Mae[6] **Racki** (Elaine Kay[5] Chenery, Beatrice[4] De Lorenzo, Maria Carolina[3] Serra, Giovani Battista[2], Giuseppe[1]) She married **Michael Pellizzaro**.

Children of Kristan Racki and Michael Pellizzaro are:
    368   i.   Hannah Rose[7] Pellizzaro.
    369   ii.   Julia Elizabeth Pellizzaro.

Family Relationship Graph

Common Ancestor	Child	Grandchild	Great Grandchild	Great Great Grandchild	3rd Great Grandchild	4th Great Grandchild	5th Great Grandchild
Child	Brother/Sister	Nephew/Niece	Grand Nephew/Niece	Great Grand Nephew/Niece	Great Great Grand N/N	3rd Great Grand N/N	4th Great Grand N/N
Grandchild	Nephew/Niece	1st Cousin	1st Cousin 1 removed	1st Cousin 2 removed	1st Cousin 3 removed	1st Cousin 4 removed	1st Cousin 5 removed
Great Grandchild	Grand Nephew/Niece	1st Cousin 1 removed	2nd Cousin	2nd Cousin 1 removed	2nd Cousin 2 removed	2nd Cousin 3 removed	2nd Cousin 4 removed
Great Great Grandchild	Great Grand Nephew/Niece	1st Cousin 2 removed	2nd Cousin 1 removed	3rd Cousin	3rd Cousin 1 removed	3rd Cousin 2 removed	3rd Cousin 3 removed
3rd Great Grandchild	Great Great Grand N/N	1st Cousin 3 removed	2nd Cousin 2 removed	3rd Cousin 1 removed	4th Cousin	4th Cousin 1 removed	4th Cousin 2 removed
4th Great Grandchild	3rd Great Grand N/N	1st Cousin 4 removed	2nd Cousin 3 removed	3rd Cousin 2 removed	4th Cousin 1 removed	5th Cousin	5th Cousin 1 removed
5th Great Grandchild	4th Great Grand N/N	1st Cousin 5 removed	2nd Cousin 4 removed	3rd Cousin 3 removed	4th Cousin 2 removed	5th Cousin 1 removed	6th Cousin

Family Tree Notes:

Family Tree Notes:

Family Tree Notes:

Part Two

*To forget one's ancestors is to be a brook without a source,
a tree without a root.*

--Chinese Proverb

Angelina Serra and Colombo DeAngelis Family

Angelina Serra De Angelis

Written by Carolyn Marletta as told to her by her mom, Rose Vandi
Photos supplied by Lisa Marletta Groleaa

Angelina (Serra) De Angelis

Angelina (Serra) De Angelis was the oldest daughter of Bartalomea and Giovani. She attended school up to the second grade in Salina before she was considered old enough to pick capers and help tend the garden and olive groves. She said her teacher begged her to come back and visited her home to try to convince her parents that she should continue with her education, but they were poor.

Because of the education, she had learned how to read and write and became the "foreign correspondent" between the Italian & American contingents of the family as they, one by one, began to emigrate to the United States.

She and Maria Concetta (Serra) Clemenzi came to America together with their brother Domenico in 1906. Angelina was 22, Maria Concetta was 17. Maria Concetta met and married John Clemenzi. Eventually, they introduced her to her future husband, Columbo De Angelis. One of the reasons she found him appealing was that both he and her brother-in-law were from the same town, Turania, in Italy. She reasoned that if and when the families returned to Italy, she would at least be living in the same town as her sister.

Angelina (Serra) De Angelis and Columbo De Angelis

Domenico Serra was an annual summer visitor after he moved to Jersey City, NJ. Before his son John could drive, he would hire a car and chauffeur (Peter) to get him to Beverly, MA.

Angelina enjoyed his company and the families stayed close despite the distance between them. When Dominic came for his summer visit (from the 1930's to the 1970's) they spent hours playing Italian card games, "Scoba" and "Briscola".

Angelina (Serra) De Angelis and Columbo De Angelis
Wedding Day

Every summer she, Uncle Dominic and whoever they could round up made a pilgrimage to Wingaersheek Beach in Gloucester. The moon had to be in the right phase, the tide out as far as it could go, because their mission was to "clam". They went to the clam flats armed with mesh sacks and pitch forks. Most summers they hauled in sacks quite full of sea clams. The feast that night was always wonderful.

Home Remedies:

Angelina's mom Bartolomea was a physician's assistant in Italy. She had a great deal of knowledge in the area of "homeopathic" medicine. She taught her daughter Angelina the following treatments:

Salt water (ocean water) was beneficial for many kinds of skin problems including burns, swollen ankles, acne and lesions caused by injuries or cuts.

Olive oil warmed and soothingly applied to the stomach would cure a stomach ache. The same warmed olive oil dropped into the ear and rubbed carefully around the outer ear helped to ease an ear ache. These olive oil treatments were always accompanied by soothing chants.

A bread and wine "poultice" helped to heal bruises and also to minimize scarring. When Rose (De Angelis) Vandi was four she fell from her grandmother's Roundy Street (Beverly) 2nd floor porch. Her mother, Angelina and her grandmother Bartolomea, prepared a bread and wine poultice and applied it to her bruises. When Rose recovered she had no scars even though her face had been quite battered by the fall. Milk and bread was also used as a poultice.

A glass of homemade red wine warmed was used to help get rid of a fever and just about any ailment. Once Rose was given wine when she had the measles to encourage the spots to come out.

To stop a case of hiccups, Angelina repeated the following chant:

> Sequto mia, Sequto mia
> Si ni vini multo, multo
> Io non du volare,
> Its seguto, cen na via

> Loosely translated…

> My hiccups, my hiccups
> They came quietly, very quietly
> I did not want them
> The hiccups went away

Pequot Mills

Photos supplied by Lisa Marletta Groleaa

Angelina (Serra) De Angelis

Angelina Serra, circled at right, circa 1910

Enrico and Theresa (DeAngelis) Miranda and Family

Written by Josie Keenan
Photos supplied by Dean Darr & Josie Keenan

I am the oldest daughter of Angelina Serra's daughter Theresa DeAngelis Miranda. Sadly my mother died young and left 8 children.

In 1947 Theresa DeAngelis traveled to Italy by ship accompanied by her dear Uncle John Clemenzi. Theresa and Enrico had written letters to each other but never met. Theresa brought her wedding gown across the ocean but did not finalize her decision to marry Enrico until after they had a chance to meet and get to know each other.

Theresa DeAngelis and Enrico Miranda Wedding Day Dec. 28, 1947

Marrying Into the Family

Written by Gavin Keenan

This story is dedicated to the memory of my beloved Father in Law, Enrico Miranda, who gave to me his wonderful daughter Josephine, and a family of special people.

I met Josephine Miranda in September of 1973. We were both attending night school at North Shore Community College in Beverly MA. When we met, I was seventeen years old, Josie was eighteen. I remember her beautiful brown eyes and thinking how smart she was. We were attracted to each other right from the start. In retrospect, I would say that it was love at first sight.

I was a shy and awkward teenager at the time. Josie had her work cut out for her in drawing me out of my shell. She did a pretty good job of it I think. Love makes all the difference.

I grew up in Ipswich, a small town just North of Beverly where Josie lived. Our first dates were centered around having coffee after school, and going for drives and to the movies. After a while I began to pick her up for class. She would not let me come to her door to get her. She told me that she did not know what her father Enrico Miranda would make of me. Josie loved and admired her father very much. I remember thinking that he must be a strict old-world type of guy. The type that would chase me off of his property with a baseball bat in his hands. I could not have been more wrong.

We had been dating for a couple of months before Josie let me meet her father. I was understandably nervous and apprehensive. I had not yet met any other members of the family. It was in the evening after dinner. Enrico was at his kitchen table. He was tall, muscular, and deeply tanned. He looked like a man who made his living through hard work. He was a stone mason by trade, and projected a rugged appearance. He welcomed me into his home in a deep, strong voice, with a heavy Italian accent that I came to cherish.

Enrico's second wife Carmela (Josie's mother Theresa died in 1971) was busy at the kitchen counter slicing up a huge watermelon. When she was finished a plate filled with melon was put in front of me. Enrico told me to eat. I did what I was told. Josie disputes the chronology here – she doesn't think that watermelon would have been available at this time of year. I only know what I remember, and at any rate the watermelon was tasty. I believe that Enrico poured me a glass or two of Cribari Rosso Wine from a large gallon jug. I was impressed. I drank both glasses; the drinking age was eighteen then.

I remember feeling immediately accepted and welcomed at # 9 Russell Street. Enrico was a generous and gracious man. We talked; we laughed, and mostly just got to know each other. Various members of his family – my future brothers and sisters in law – would pass through the kitchen. Each and every one of them sat, talked, and looked me over. I think that a note on cultural differences is in order here. I grew up the youngest of three boys in an Irish / German / Catholic family. I did not have any sisters, and as the youngest of three was mostly treated as the "baby" of the family. The Irish are not as a rule known for an affinity to be spontaneous and embracing of others– at least not in my experience. So the Miranda family of 9 Russell Street – all ten of them – were quite a different take for me. And I loved every minute of it.

Through the lives of Josie's seven brothers and sisters, I was able to experience the ups and downs of family life on a more intense level than my former existence had allowed for. Hardly a day would go by without a new story of heartache, triumph, agony, and most of all laughter. Josie's sisters Bettina and Lucia – Tina and Chi as they are known throughout the world today – a pair of Beverly beauties. They broke more hearts in that city than any of us can remember. Her brothers Michael, John, Dominic, Anthony and Angelo were either scheming, working, going to school, or the dog track. In short, they were living life to the fullest, and I could only awe at what it must be like to be them.

Josie and I dated for five years before we became engaged. In that time we finished college, got jobs, attended several family weddings, and prepared for the future. We had a photograph taken for the engagement announcement. I still keep it both in my locker at work, and on my bureau at home. It is one of my favorite pictures, and will be with me always.

148

We were married on June 3, 1979 at Saint Mary's Star of the Sea Catholic Church in Beverly. We moved into a small apartment in Ipswich. We visited Enrico's home at least once a week. Josie needed to inhale Beverly air. I became a police officer in Ipswich in July of 1980. I went to the State Police Academy in Framingham during the winter of that year with Josie's brother Tony, who is a Beverly Policeman. We had to live at the academy then. Josie and I had bought a little "starter" home in Ipswich in October of that year. Number 9 Applewood Drive. We thought that the number 9 was a good omen. Enrico and Tony helped us move in. The girls helped decorate the place. Enrico and I built a chimney for our wood stove. The chimney is still there, and so are we.

When Tony and I graduated from the police academy, Enrico, Carmela, Josie, Tina, and Chi came to the ceremony. So did Sarah – albeit as part and parcel to Josie. When Sarah was born, Enrico was at the hospital with me. As Sarah was his first grandchild you can imagine the joy he took in her birth. When Sarah was a baby, Josie worked days at Beverly Hospital. I worked midnights as a cop. During those days Josie would bundle Sarah up at six-thirty in the morning and deliver her to Enrico's for the day so I could sleep. Josie would pick Sarah up after work, or I would go and join them in Beverly.

At Nonie Enrico's Sarah received love and attention from not only her grandfather and Carmela, but from her aunts and uncles. She also began to speak with an Italian accent – I kid you not! Tina was living at 9 Russell then and is Sarah's Godmother. Tina took this role very seriously and took it upon herself to "stimulate" Sarah for her own good. We attribute Sarah's intelligence to this nurture and give Tina all of the credit. Sarah and Tina remain close, and Sarah now reciprocates the love she received on her little cousins. Life comes full circle.

At Enrico's home Sarah took her first steps on Fathers Day, 1982. Our wonderful son Patrick was born in 1984. Enrico attended his birth as well. Enrico loved him like crazy, and although Enrico's health had begun to fail, he showered Patrick with affection and attention. By this time I was mostly off of midnights and could do more of the childcare. However, Sarah and Pat were still regular fixtures at Russell Street. After all of these years, I still remember and treasure these times.

In the early 1980's, mostly because we had children and lived close to Beverly, our home was often the site of family parties and gatherings. Our two kids spent their early years surrounded by boisterous happy people who enjoyed each others company as well as eating, drinking, and playing card games. In good weather we would have outdoor parties. Nights and bad weather events were held indoors. We would stuff everyone into our little six-room ranch house and let it roll. Clean up was always a horror, but usually there were no leftovers. I would get worked up over all the mess, the noise, etc. Josie however, loved these things. She loved having the family around, watching the nieces and nephews growing up, getting the latest gossip, and breathing the rarified air.

When Enrico passed away in 1985, a huge hole was left in our lives. Not only did his passing sadden us all, but to me it represented an end to an era. However, I think his legacy lives on in his sons and daughters, and in his eighteen – yes eighteen grandchildren. You see, this family means more to me than just a good story. They are all so much a part of me now that I can't imagine life without them. It sure would be a much duller and less interesting world. So for all of the good times and the even the bad times that we have shared, I will be eternally grateful to you all. Amore.

Colombo and Angelina (Serra) DeAngelis Wedding Day

Back Row: Josephine, John, Michael, Dominic
Front: Anthony, Enrico, Lucia, Theresa, Bettina, Angelo

Jessica and Gregory
Dean and Lucia (Miranda) Darr

Mario and Rose Vandi Wedding Day

Rose Vandi and the twins Carolyn and Marilyn

John and Carolyn Marletta's children: Lisa, John and Sarah

Anthony and Angela (Ali) Miranda Wedding

Sharon (Vandi) and David D'Amato

Angelina (Serra) De Angelis Family Notes:

Distance has the same effect on the mind
as on the eye.

--Samuel Johnson (1709-1784)

Giuseppe Serra and Grazia Lazzaro Family

Giuseppe Serra

Written by Margherita & Gerard Eggleston
Photos supplied by Margherita & Gerard Eggleston and Giovannina Obert

Giuseppe Serra (age 23)

Giuseppe Serra was born in Malfa on October 14, 1886. He immigrated to the United States in the early 1900's and married Gracia Lazzaro in Jersey City, NJ on June 20, 1920. The couple settled in Beverly Massachusetts. They lived on Roundy Street for a short while and eventually purchased a home at 24 west Dane street in Beverly where they lived the rest of their lives.

During his early days in the Beverly, Massachusetts area, Giuseppe along with a couple of brothers and brothers- in-law operated a fruit and vegetables store which also sold ice cream sodas. This store was located in Salem, Massachusetts. However the Great Salem Fire completely destroyed the store and the business was terminated.

Giuseppe Serra in the Salem store before the Great Salem Fire of 1914

For several years, Giuseppe worked as a machinist at the united shoe manufacturing company in Beverly which was close by their home on west Dane street. He left the united shoe company after several years to seek better employment in Jersey City, NJ but returned to Beverly after a short stay in New Jersey. He spent his remaining working years at leather tanneries in Peabody, Massachusetts.

Gracia (Lazzaro) and Giuseppe Serra (1962)

All of Gracia and Giuseppe's children were born in Beverly. They were: Bettina, Santina, Caroline, Maria Rose, John and Margherita.

159

Nunny

Written by Margherita & Gerard Eggleston
Photos supplied by Margherita & Gerard Eggleston

Grazia (Lazzaro) Serra

This story is about Grazia (Lazzaro) Serra "Nunny", mother of Margherita Serra. She was born May 25, 1900 and died on April 21, 1987

Nunny was born in the Sicilian Island of Lipari, one of the Aeolian Islands off the northern coast of Sicily. Her father was Figli Christopher Lazzaro and her mother was Santa Merlino. Christopher left Lipari without his wife and three children to establish himself in the Jersey City, NJ area. He eventually sent for his family who booked passage on a boat bound from Sicily to New York...Ellis Island. On their way from Messina to Naples, Nunny's mother met a cousin on the boat. They were both quite surprised and happy. They gave each other many hugs and kisses. During that night, nunny's mother, who was sleeping with nunny, had a heart attack and died...... perhaps from all the excitement. Nunny, who at this time was twelve years old, was the oldest of the three children. There was her sister Maria and her brother Thomas.

After their mother's death, they had to return back to Lipari for the funeral. After this sad experience, Nunny's father asked a friend of the family living on Lipari Island to pose as the mother of the three kids and accompany them on their second attempt to get to Ellis Island. We think this woman's name was Felica. When their boat arrived at Ellis Island, Christopher met them and took them to New Jersey. While living there, this woman, Felica, taught Nunny to cook and clean and in general run the apartment. Her father worked in the area and Nunny's brother and sister went to school. Nunny never did go to school in the United States. Her father was quite protective of nunny and would not let her go on the streets while he was at work. Nunny married Giuseppe Serra in Jersey City, NJ on June 20, 1920. She was 20 years old then.

Note: I have been told by a different source that Christopher Lazzaro's wife's name was Maria Merlino. Margherita & Gerard Eggleston told me that when they visited Salina in 1974 that they checked the name and believe that Santa is correct but are not positive. Another question is the name of the woman, who taught Nunny how to cook; her name could have been Josephine not Felica. These are the type of problems I have encountered doing research on the Serra Family. This is why it is so important that we get these stories recorded as soon as possible.

Bonaiuto Family Stories

Written by Joe Bonaiuto
Photos supplied by the Bonaiuto Family

The Bonaiuto Family at Grace's 1st Holy Communion

I think you know some of my background, but I'll start from the beginning. My grandmother and grandfather were Grazzia (Lazzaro) and Guisseppe Serra. My mother is Maria Rose (Serra) Bonaiuto. She is one of six children; Santina, Bettina, Caroline, Margie, and John are her siblings.

I am one of five children, my siblings are, Maria, Betty, Frank, and Steven. I am married to Elaine (Pelletier). We have two children: Nathan age 14 and Grace age 11.

Elaine and I met in 1981 and were married on Sept. 8, 1984. We bought a house in the Ryal side section of Beverly December 23rd 1985. I am a cabinetmaker. At the time Elaine was a Dietetic Assistant working at Salem Hospital. She is now a preschool teacher. I was with Jules A. Gourdeau an Architectural woodworking company located in Beverly. We worked hard to make that house our home. Over the years we added on three rooms and one bathroom. Now we live in the Cove area of Beverly.

161

I could write a whole book about our children, but I'll give you the condensed version. On August 13, 1988, our son Nathan Joseph was born. Nathan is currently attending Bishop Fenwick High School where he is a freshman. He enjoys school and is doing very well in his classes. His sports at Fenwick include fall soccer, winter track, and baseball. Nate is also a Red Belt in Korean Tai Kwon Do.

Our daughter Grace Alice was born on May 6, 1992. Grace is a fifth grader at St. John's School in Beverly. Grace is a fine student. She is an avid reader and is very athletic. She enjoys playing softball, basketball, and her favorite, gymnastics. Grace is a level five gymnast and recently competed in the Northeast Regional Gymnastics Competition held in Waterville, Maine.

Grace Bonaiuto

We enjoy spending time together as a family. Many of our family vacations have been camping trips. We have a small camper, so during our camping trips we are literally together! We have camped in six different states and always find something new and interesting to do or learn about. We also enjoy skiing. We all learned to ski on the same day. One Sunday about five years ago, we decided it would be fun to take a lesson. We asked that we be put together in our lesson, so the kind people at Bradford ski area accommodated us. What a site we must have been, our first time on skis! We hung out on the bunny hill that day and had so much fun! We've been skiing together ever since and thankfully not on the bunny hill any more.

Family is very important to us. We often spend time with my mom and dad and brothers and sisters. We share in the family traditions and try to respect the old ways. We try to pass on the family values that we were raised with, in the hope that our children will do the same.

Memories

Written by Nathan Bonaiuto

Nathan Bonaiuto

Every Christmas my Auntie Maria makes a walnut slice cake and every year it is a little better. I always have some. However one year, when she was frosting the cake, she took a bowl with ricotta cheese inside it rather than frosting, and she frosted the cake with ricotta cheese. My Grampy (Joseph) was the first to eat some. I still remember his face. It looked like a young kid eating a much hated vegetable. My Aunt will never live that one down.

When Easter comes around usually the weather has gotten warm and we are getting ready for the baseball season. My family always goes to my uncle's house. My Uncle Frank and Uncle Steve and I always go outside and play catch. I always treasure that kind of time with them. Sometimes they have a joke and sometimes they have a lesson, but they are always there to play catch, to give me a ride, and to love and watch over me.

When I was younger my sister and I used to sleep over my Nona and Grampy's house. When it was bedtime my Nona would bring us upstairs and tuck us in our sleeping bags and she would lie down in my Aunty Betty's bed and she would fall asleep with us. The only problem was that sometimes she used to snore and I couldn't go to sleep. I had fun anyway.

Every year on the Fourth of July my family always gets together and we have a cookout. My Aunty Betty is always the first one to jump into the pool. She always sets up a ton of games; she is so energetic. She is always the one to plan the parties. She is the first one there and the last one to leave. We love her so much.

Raviolis

Written by Grace Bonaiuto

Grace Bonaiuto

Every year most people get together for a Christmas dinner. Usually a Christmas food is ham, turkey, potatoes, etc. But I do something different. My Christmas tradition is this. Usually about a week before Christmas, we get together with my Nona and Grampy, and my Aunts and Uncles. We make delicious homemade raviolis. Here's how it works. First we make the dough. Then the guys roll the dough through the ancient roller. Yeah even my dad my brother, my Uncle Steve, Uncle Frank, and Grampy help out with this fun! It takes 5 guys to do a 2-person job! After they roll it, they give the skinny piece of dough to my mom (Elaine) and my Nona (Rose). There they put the ricotta on the strip, and fold it over. They cut them into squares or rectangles – however they come out! Next the squares are shipped to Grace (me) and my Aunty Maria. There we fork the edges so then they're sealed. When we finish that we give the raviolis to my Aunty Betty so she can put some flour on top. She also counts them (except she sometimes loses count.) Once we get going, it becomes a race for who can catch up, the stuffers, the rollers, or the forkers. We have so much FUN, that's why I love ravioli night!

My Nona has told me many stories about her childhood, when her whole family would make raviolis together. Just like we do now. I'll never forget making raviolis together; I always look forward to Christmas raviolis.

Giuseppe Serra Family Photos

Grace and Giuseppe Serra

Grace and Giuseppe Serra
Santa, Caroline, Rose and Bea Serra

Giuseppe and Grace Serra

Joseph & Rose (Serra) Bonaiuto Wedding Day

Peter, Gracia (Lazzaro) Serra, and Jane Sienkiewicz

John and Mary (Smythe) Serra

Santa (Serra) and Harold Jones

Harold, Santa and Richard Jones

Back: Betty, Frank, Steven and Joseph
Front: Grace, Marie, Joseph, Maria, Nathan and Elaine

Standing: Maria Rose Bonaiuto, Joseph F. Bonaiuto, Caroline Serra, Maria Grace Bonaiuto
Seated: Grazia (Lazzaro) Serra

Back Three: William Eggleston, Gregory Turcotte and Stephen Smith
Next Row: Quinton Smith, Sean Smith, Gerard Eggleston and Zachary Smith
Seated: Sharon Turcotte, Kim Eggleston, Margherita Eggleston and Theresa Smith
Seated Children: Daniel Eggleston and Gabriella Smith

Zackary, Steve, Sean and Quinton Smith

Theresa, Stephen
Zackary, Quinton, Sean and Gabriella Smith

Amy (Heriford) and Gregory Turcotte

Betty (Serra), Victor and Peter Sienkiewicz

Victor and Bea Sienkiewicz

William and Kim Eggleston

Caroline, John, Margherita and Maria Rose Serra

174

Giuseppe Serra Family Notes:

Happiness is having a large, loving, caring, close-knit family in another city.

--George Burns (1896-1996)

Domenico Serra and
Maria Concetta Costa Family

Life History Report

Written by Maria Charowsky with information supplied by Maria Concetta (Costa) and Domenico Serra
Photos supplied by Giovannina (Serra) Obert and Maria (Charowsky) Dombrowski

Maria Charowsky

Maria Concetta (Costa) Serra and Domenico Serra

My informants are my grandmother, Maria Concetta Costa Serra and my grandfather, Domenico Serra. I first started to do this life history report solely on my grandmother, but as I was gathering and organizing my material, I found it hard to omit my grandfather as a major character in my research. It was almost impossible to separate their lives and the effects they had on one another. To myself and to all the other grandchildren and great grandchildren, my grandmother is known as "Nonna" and my grandfather is known as "Nonno". These are the terms I would like to use throughout my report, because I feel most comfortable with them. Nonna and Nonno are my mother's parents. I chose them because ever since I was a young child I was always intrigued by their stories about their life, and how they lived in Italy. I believe they are creatures and carriers of their culture, but they also are somewhat flexible to the changing times. They live by the things they believe in, and have a very high respect for the family unit, and religion. They are truly unique people and I love, respect, and admire them very much. Doing this life history report is much more than an assignment to me, it is a special experience. It gave me a chance to find out even more about my grandparents, and to understand them all the better. I have learned so many new things throughout my life from them, things that are not in a book. The most important thing that I have learned is that your family is number one, and that you should always strive to keep it that way.

Maria Concetta Costa in Italy

Born in 1891, on December 13, in Leni, Italy. Maria Concetta Costa was born to Giovanna and Phillipo Costa. All births took place in the home with the assistance of midwives. Maria Concetta was the youngest of five children. The oldest was a boy Giuseppe, the second was a girl Angela, the third was also a girl Giovanna, the forth was yet another girl Catherina.

Giovanna (Lazzaro) and Phillipo Costa

Leni was a small town in the province of Messena, Italy. The population at that time was only about 1,000. At that time everyone from the same area of town knew one another, because they were either related or just close from living near each other for so long. Most of the families in the area owned their property, a few acres of land. Nonna's family did, they had about 3 acres of land on which they lived. The house they lived in was made out of stones and cement. It was small, having four rooms and a kitchen. The land surrounding their home was well used. They grew olive trees, lemon trees, grapevines, tomatoes, and many other vegetables. They lived off of what they grew, and stored enough to feed them throughout the winter. The mother and all the children helped with the farming. Phillipo, the father, was a sailor in the Italian Navy, and was often gone for days at a time. Phillipo took Giuseppe, who at the time was 11 years old, to Australia with him, and when it was time to return home the boy did not want to go, threatening to jump over-board if his father forced him to return to Italy. For this, reason Nonna never knew or met her only brother.

180

Back Row: Gaetano Maltese, Joseph Costa, Joseph Villanti

Seated: Giovana (Costa) Maltese, **Giovana (Lazzaro) Costa and Philip Costa**, Angela (Costa) Villanti

Children: Enzo Maltese, Joseph Costa, Angelina Maltese

Nonna's family, like all the other families in town was, very religious. Mostly all the people from Leni were Roman Catholics. The children learned their religion at very early ages, and it was a very important part of the enculturative process of the child. Catechism classes (Catholic religion classes) were started at five years of age for the children. The classes took place at the nun's quarters. The children made their Communion and Confirmation at the same time because the bishop, who preformed the ceremony, was not easily available. Nonna enjoyed studying her religion, and looked forward to the classes. She remembers that even before she ever started Catechism classes she knew most of her prayers, and said them every night before she went to bed. Her parents had taught her the prayers, and had encouraged her interest and participation in religion.

At six years of age Nonna started regular school. At that time the education of the child consisted of three years of schooling, in which they were to learn how to read, write and do basic arithmetic. The boys and girls attended separate schools, and they only attended for half the normal school day. The reason for the half day attendance was, because the children were needed to work on their families farms, and to do household chores. On days when there was no school, the children had to wake up early to help around the farm, their help was depended upon. Additional schooling was available, but not utilized by the people of Leni, because it was too costly to attend, schools were located in the larger cities and further education was not considered necessary by the people. In her spare time, Nonna and her sisters learned how to do "ricamo" (embroidery) and crocheting. Originally taught by the nuns, they learned even more by going to the houses of woman who knew the skills well, and by watching them carefully. These skills were important for the woman to learn, because this is how most of their clothes and household linens would be made. To this day Nonna has some of her finely embroidered pillowcases, because while she was young she made a lot of things to put into her hope chest to save for when she got married.

181

Maria Concetta in Young Adulthood

Nonna had told me that back then in Italy, most of the marriages were prearranged through the parents. If two families had opposite sexed children, fairly close in age, the families would persuade the children to date each other and eventually get married. If the children did not like one another, the relationship might be absolved. This decision depended on the parents, and how they viewed the situation. If for example the boy did not want to end the relationship, and was somewhat wealthy, the girl would usually have no choice but to stay in the relationship. Many times these prearranged marriages were successful, a lot having to do with the children wanting to please their parents. Something similar to this happened to Nonna. When she was eighteen, her mother's friend's son saw Nonna in church one day and was attracted to her. The boy Giuseppe Russo, told his mother, who in turn told Nonna's mother, Giovanna. After seeing a picture of Giuseppe, and hearing favorable words about him, Nonna agreed to meet him. Before they met, Giuseppe went to Australia but wrote to Nonna often and even sent her a ring. After corresponding with Giuseppe for about two years, Nonna broke the engagement, because she did not know for sure if he was returning to Italy. She was already twenty now and most girls in Italy were married by eighteen or nineteen. Soon after this she met her cousin Domenico Serra. Nonna's mother and Domenico's mother were sisters. In those days it was totally acceptable for cousins to marry. She dated Domenico for two months, and since they liked each other so much, they decided to get married. They were married in St. Giuseppe's Church, in Leni, Salina, on August 11, 1912. There was a maid of honor, and a best man. After the church ceremony, there was a celebration at the bride's home, with all the family and some close friends. They did not have a honeymoon, just a little time to relax and take a break from the daily routine. Domenico was three years older than Nonna. He was born on September 3, 1888, in Malfa, Salina, another province of Messina.

Maria Concetta (Costa) and Domenico Serra

The Transition from Italy to America

Within two months of their marriage, Nonno had decided to return to America to live with his wife, because he figured that he would have more opportunity for a better life there. He had previously been to America several times bringing his mother, three brothers, and four sisters with him. On his first trip to America he was only twelve years old and took the ship with his cousin. When the two boys arrived in the United States they went to Salem, Massachusetts to live with their uncle. So by the time Nonno was coming to America with Nonna, he had already made the migration adjustment, and he readapted easily. Where as for Nonna, the adjustment was not easy. Nonna recalls the migration as the biggest transition in her life, but being a voluntary one, she tried her hardest to adapt. The trip over by boat took about a month. During this time it was hardest for her, because of her deep sadness in leaving her family. Plus, the trip was very rough, and not being used to traveling, she got seasick often. She remembers how she cried and cried on the boat, and that the captain of the boat thought she might jump overboard. Several factors helped her to relieve some of her sadness and fears, one being that she strongly believed that a woman's place is with her husband, and a second factor being that one of her sisters, Giovanna, was living in New York. They arrived at Salem, Mass. Where they would first settle.

Nonno was now working in a grocery store, and Nonna was learning how to cook. It was the traditional marriage, where the woman's place was in the home to cook and clean. About three months later Nonno came down with typhoid fever, and he was sick for about a month. My grandmother took care of him most of the time and nursed him back to health. She prayed to the Blessed Mother everyday for him to regain his good health. She had the doctor at the house often, because with the high fever he would often act crazy, not take his medicine or spit it out. He nearly died, but with the love and patience of my grandmother, he survived the illness.

Soon after Nonno got well, in 1914, he and Nonna moved to the Bronx in New York. Here she was reunited with her two sisters Giovanna, who was already in the U.S. when Nonna came, and Catherine, who came to America soon after Nonna did. She still remembers how happy she was with her sisters. Within a few years Giovanna returned to Italy with her husband, so now it was just Nonna and Catherine in the U.S. Having at least one sister with her made her feel very secure, plus she was always especially close with Catherine.

Catherine (Costa), Dominick & son Dominick Villanti

183

While my grandparents lived in New York, Nonno worked in a fruit store. They owned property there, but never built on it, because they did not like living in the Bronx very much. At that time the "black hand," the Maffia, was controlling that area, and if you wanted to live peacefully with no trouble, you had to pay for protection. My grandparents, being very moral and religious people, wanted no part or involvement with such things. I remember Nonna saying, "I didn't want any trouble."

After living in New York for approximately three and a half years, they moved to Harrison, New Jersey. They both liked living there, and Nonno got a good job in the Hyatt Roller Bearing Company. My grandfather was a very good worker, he was well liked by his supervisors, and he received several awards for his contributions, or should I say "inventions," to help the company. My grandmother was very proud of him.

Maria Concetta and Domenico Become Parents

Soon after they were settled in Harrison, Nonna became pregnant with her first child. Being married and childless for nine years, she was very happy and welcomed the news of her pregnancy. On September 7, 1921, she gave birth to her first child, a girl, Bartolomea. They named her after Nonno's mother. Nonna breast fed all her children for about a year. Their first child was very special, as all first born are. They used to call her "princess," and Nonna used to like to display all her favorite embroidered carriage covers and crocheted blankets when she would take the baby outside.

Two years later Nonna became pregnant for the second time. During this time, Nonno's younger brother wanted him to go to Florida with him, but Nonno strongly refused because of his responsibilities to his wife, child and job. On September 20, 1923, Giovannina, another girl was born. They were both very happy to have another daughter, especially Nonno, because he loved his little girls. Nonno himself came from a large family of eight children. Nonna and Nonno both knew the real meaning of the word "family." The family was the most important thing in their lives and being able to depend on your family when you really needed them most. It was their culture which was very responsible for this belief, and I strongly have been influenced by it. Also, at this time the company Nonno was working for was planning to move to Chicago. At the same time Nonno's mother came to visit Nonna and Nonno, and she told Domenico that he should not waste his time working in a factory, and that he should move to Jersey City and go into business with his brother Salvatore who already lived there. So, not wanting to move to Chicago, and being respectful of his mother's wishes, he moved with Nonna to Jersey City. They lived on Gregory Street, and Salvatore and Nonno worked across the street in a grocery store.

Salvatore Serra

184

In 1926, Nonna delivered her third child, a son, John Battista, born on September 24. In respect and by tradition the first born female is named after the husband's mother, and the first born male is named after the husband's father. John Battista was Nonno's father's name. They were also very pleased with the birth of a son and very happy that they had him to carry on the family name.

After some saving Nonno and Salvatore bought a three family house on York Street, they shared together the apartment, while collecting rent on the other two and continuing to work at the grocery store. Salvatore was married and had three children of his own. With further savings the two brothers bought another three family house with a store below for which they should begin a business of their own, along with yet another eight family house, all on one lot on York Street. At that time property was a very good investment and all their work began to bring them much security with the happiness they had together.

Bea, Domenico, Maria Concetta and Jennie
Johnny and Mary

Two years later, on October 30, 1928, the fourth child was born, a daughter, Mary. Also, Nonna did not approve of Nonno's partnership with his brother. Nonno insisted that everything would be all right. The store was Nonno's pride and everyone helped, Nonna, Salvatore's wife Mary, who we called Commara, and the older children from both families.

Battista "John" Serra and friends in front of the Serra Store

185

The store is where Nonna learned most of her English, but it was hard for her, because she had four children, a husband, and a house to keep, plus work in the store. But though all this she was happy, because she knows that a lot of other people had it worse. She told me that during Thanksgiving and Christmas, she would make up food baskets for the poor people in the neighborhood, because she wanted other people's holidays to be happy along with hers. She devoted her life to her family's well-being and does not regret any of it.

In 1941, when WWII broke out, Nonno went to work for Air Reduction, and he was appointed as Air Raid Warden by the community. Nonna and the children took care of the store. Their only son, John Battista had enlisted in the Navy in 1944, when he was eighteen years old, because he did not want to be drafted by the Army. In 1949 Nonno sold the store to his brother and retired from business. His retirement was well deserved, because all his life he strived to have the best life he could. He believed hard work never hurts anyone, and that when you work hard for something you appreciate it more. Even after he retired, he worked part time in his friend's fresh fish market, mainly because he enjoyed it.

Their Lives Today

Today they both take interest in gardening and everyday activities. It is a joy to be with them. Recently, they sold all their property in Jersey City and are now living with my Aunt Mary, their youngest daughter, and her family in Middletown, New Jersey. Nonna is now 87 years old, and Nonna is 90. They are proud to have 20 grandchildren, and 4 great-grandchildren. They will also be celebrating their 67th wedding anniversary on August 11th. Family gatherings are still very important, for all of us; they are very happy for us, because the family is very close, and when we are all together we have such a good time. I remember at my cousin's wedding last summer in Massachusetts that Nonna and her sister Catherine walked into my uncle's house together, and my little cousin very spontaneously says, "Hey! There's two Nonnas!" I am very proud to have such "great" grandparents, and I love them very much!!!

Kathleen, Geremy, Michael, Carol Ann, Antonio
Marie and Domenico
65th Wedding Anniversary 1977

Note: This story was written in 1979 a few years before Maria and Domenico's deaths. The following story gives information on their final years.

186

Some Childhood (& Adult) Memories with Mama and Papa

Written by Maria (Serra) Goldrick
Photos supplied by Giovannina (Serra) Obert and Tony Serra

I recall many things as a youngster growing up at 267 York Street in Jersey City. Most were very happy for me. My earliest memories started probably when I was about 5 years old. Remember we lived in a 3 family house with the store on the street floor. We always spent Thanksgiving, Christmas and New Years Holidays with our cousins upstairs. There was my oldest cousin named Bea, then her brother Johnny and sisters Santa & Lena. Lena & I were the youngest in each family and spent a lot of our time with each other. Usually after we finished eating a sumptuous meal our family gathered together to play cards. It was an easy card game called seven and a half. Everyone was permitted to play but once you lost your pennies you were out of the game. It was such fun playing cards with our older sisters & brothers and all the other adults. We often had company join us. Aunt Mary's brother Tom was usually there and our friend Emily and her mom, Mrs. Vail from downstairs.

The Domenico Serra Family – circa 1938
Jennie, Mary, Mama, Johnny, Papa and Bea

One Thanksgiving Day in particular comes to my mind. It was the very first time I went to see a movie. Imagine how excited I was when Mama and Aunt Mary, "Commare", as we called her (means Godmother in Italian), decided to take all us kids to the movies. Clark Gable and Jeannette McDonald were starring in "San Francisco" at the Capitol Theater which was on Gregory Street. It was a cold afternoon and had started to snow, but we didn't care. This was a big treat for us, especially me. No one went to the movies very often in those days, too expensive for one thing. Mama bundled us up in hats, gloves, scarves and of course we all wore our galoshes (boots). We all had a good time trudging through the snow with our moms; just being with them was fun for me. Even Emily Vail and her mom went to the movies with us that day. We walked everywhere in those days, no one could afford to have a car. All I can remember about that movie of course was the earthquake and all those buildings falling down all around on top of everything and everybody. People were screaming and running helter skelter to escape the falling debris. It was VERY scary for me as a five year old. Needless to say the experience affected me badly and that night when I went to sleep I had a nightmare and woke up crying. Mama heard me and took me into bed with her and Papa. It was so warm and cozy sleeping there in between them, I felt safe and fell asleep again.

Around that same time frame, it was a Sunday afternoon and I was playing on the fence across the street from the store. As I was swinging back and forth on the gate I got my pinkie finger caught. I ran back to the store crying and screaming it hurt so badly. Papa immediately put my hand into the can of kerosene (we always had it in the store) and the pain let up, so that he was able to wrap my finger tightly to stop the bleeding. The next day Mama took me to the doctor's office. The doctor was very surprised to see that my little finger had started to heal already and he did not need to stitch it. He did have to remove the broken finger nail which hurt like blazes and I remember burying my face in Mama's fur collar. I'll never forget the pain. It took a while but the nail grew back in and my finger healed nicely. I'll never forget that day and how Papa knew just what to do for me. I also remember how strong he was and how blue his eyes were, especially if he got mad. Then they were scary!

Maria Concetta and Domenico at their 65th Wedding Anniversary party

I like to recall how well he played the mandolin and how beautiful those Italian tunes sounded to me. I love the language and was happy that I could understand and speak it with them. I miss hearing them speak it to me, even now after all these years. Papa told me he never took music lessons, but taught himself to play the mandolin. I remember him writing the music notes down on paper so my brother Johnny, playing violin and my cousin Johnny, who lived upstairs, playing the accordion could accompany him play some tunes. They made a "jolly trio" and entertained the family on Sundays and whenever the holidays rolled around. Papa loved music and wanted the records played every Sunday; it was a must for him to have a dance with us in the parlor. He taught me how to dance the Polka, the Waltz and the Tarantella and instilled the love of music and dance in me, and, I believe all us children, and later most of the grandchildren too.

I'll never forget when the war was over on "VJ Day" August 15th, 1945 and papa blocked off the street with empty garbage cans, took the old victrola downstairs in the store and we danced the Tarantella out in the middle of the street. All the neighbors came out to celebrate with us. Papa was leading the dancing and calling all the moves and everyone was laughing and having a great time. All went well until we had to "do-se-do". The Tarantella is somewhat like a square dance with partners. Of course there weren't enough boys, so Papa tied a handkerchief on some of the girls' left arms and told them that they were the "boys". This was important for the, "do-se-do", part of the dance. Well, needless to say sooner or later everyone got mixed up and it was mass confusion! We all laughed our heads off while Papa gave up in disgust. We danced well into the night doing the Polka, the Jitterbug and anything else – what a night! The people were OVERJOYED, the war was over and the boys would be coming back home again. No one wanted to go home that night. My cousin Lena and I danced until we got exhausted.

Mary's "First Holy Communion" 1936

I remember the smell of Mama's cooking, especially on Sundays and holidays. We always started with chicken soup that had the tiniest meatballs in it. Then we ate the raviolis she made in tomato sauce and lots of salad and Italian bread. By the time we finished that course of the meal, we could not eat the turkey and sweet potatoes. Mama always saved that for the next day's meal. I can still picture her rolling the dough to make the raviolis and her crooked finger on the rolling pin. Sometimes she made gigis and sphinz; I would help her deep fry them. I would also pinch the raviolis with the tines of the fork then put a tablecloth on top of the bed and place the raviolis on it to allow them to dry until we were ready to cook them. Everything was made fresh on the day we ate them. Mama never froze anything. I don't know where she got all the stamina and energy to do all that work in one day. She was amazing and so very patient. I marveled at her patience. I'm happy she taught me how to make all those things and even now my grand-daughters Grace and Julia love their favorite meal of meatballs and spaghetti and of course other Italian food I make for them. Christopher and his family also look forward to these Italian meals when they visit us.

I loved watching Mama crochet and knit. When she was knitting, the needles moved so fast all I could hear was the clicking noise they made. She made sweaters for all of us at one time or another. She tried to teach me, but I was not patient enough to learn. I'd rather go outside and play jacks, play ball or jump rope.

189

Mary and her mom, Maria Concetta Serra

In the summer time Papa would close the store early on Sunday and take the family to Coney Island for a swim. Mama packed some sandwiches for lunch. We all put our bathing suits on under our clothes and headed for the Hudson Tubes which was on Grove Street, just a few blocks from York Street. There we took the train to Brooklyn and to Coney Island. It was a long ride maybe an hour on the train but we didn't mind we looked forward to going to the beach and playing in the ocean and sand. When we got there Mama told us to go in the water for a while. Papa always went out for a good swim. He was an excellent swimmer. Mama stayed in the shallow surf with us kids and watched us play. She feared the water and never learned how to swim. After a while she would tell us it was time to eat our lunch. We had to come out of the water and let our bathing suits dry off in the sun, so they wouldn't be wet for the ride home. Papa always got a locker where he dressed and put the valise he always took with him. Then we put our clothes back on and walked up to the boardwalk. Papa always led the way and would keep us together with his whistle. He had a very distinctive way of whistling and we knew he was calling us. Everyone knew he meant business when he whistled you moved or else got left behind. He could walk faster than anyone I ever knew; even when he got older it was hard to keep up with him. On the boardwalk he bought us each an ice cream cone, put us on the "Merry-go-round" for only one ride and then it was time to walk to the train and go home. We had fun at the beach for the day; we really enjoyed the cool ocean breezes and sunshine. It was very hot on the city streets in the summertime.

We did not have television in those days, but Mama would let us listen to the radio in the evening after we finished doing our home work. The best programs were usually on Sunday evenings. We could listen to "The Green Hornet", "The Lone Ranger", "The Shadow" and others. They were called serials, much like the soap operas of today. We loved listening to the tales and used our imagination to picture and visualize what was taking place on the radio. They made good sound effects and had spooky voices sometimes. They were good wholesome stories and kept our interest. Everyone tuned in to hear what happened from week to week. We did enjoy them and missed them when they were finally taken off the air because TV was more popular later. I also remember listening to, "Your Hit Parade", sponsored by Lucky Strike Cigarettes; on Saturday evenings. They played the top ten most popular songs of the week. One song was often number one on the list for many weeks. Some of these #1 hits I remember particularly, were, "Blue Velvet", "Deep Purple" and "Smoke Gets in Your Eyes", of course there were many, many more hit tunes. These were carefree days for me as I was growing up.

As I got older, eleven, if you can call that old, I started helping Mama and Papa in our grocery store downstairs from where we lived. I helped by stocking the shelves, sweeping the floor and gradually got to wait on the customers. I was shy as a kid at that age, and had to force myself to go up to a strange adult and ask, "May I help you?" I was less afraid of the women and more afraid of the men. The years drifted by and little by little I got over my timidness and I came to know the prices better and how to read the scale to weigh potatoes, onions, sugar and the coffee which had to be ground first. I also learned how to cut the cold cuts on the machine. One time I cut my thumb pretty deep because I forgot to put the safety lever down. Again into the kerosene and got wrapped up tight no need for doctor or stitches, it healed up nicely. I can still see that scar too.

I really liked working in the grocery store. Mama taught me how to pack the groceries properly. Heavy cans on the bottom of the bag, light stuff on top & fruits like tomatoes and grapes at the top of the bag or in a separate bag if there wasn't enough room. Paper bags were expensive to buy so I had to economize and use only one bag whenever possible or I'd never hear the end of it from Mama and Papa. I learned to add, subtract and make change and not make a mistake. That helped me a lot when I had arithmetic in school. Working in the store prepared me for working diligently when I got older. (I worked for 16 years in Western Electric after graduation from Lincoln High School in 1946. I worked in the office on the first tabulating machines.)

The Domenico Serra Family in the 1940's

After the war started business in the grocery store dropped off quite a bit. The government issued coupon ration books to everyone. Rationed items included meats, butter, sugar, oils, coffee, canned goods, shoes and gasoline. As I remember our shelves were almost bare at times. No one really minded though, it was our way of helping the war effort and the boys in the service who were desperately in need of supplies. It was a long 4 years of war and all everyone ever spoke about. One day when I was in the store with Mama some ladies came in to buy something and as usual they were talking about the war. One lady said she heard that a bad typhoon hit the island of Okinawa. Mama recognized the name and almost fainted. We managed to sit her down, gave her a drink of water and she finally stopped crying and calmed down. She knew that my brother Johnny was there because before he shipped out he and I worked out a secret code where by he could tell me (us) where he was. When he wrote, the first letter he started each paragraph with, spelled out the name of the place. For example, the first paragraph started: "Oh I forgot to tell you I need so and so's address. Tell him I'll write as some as I get a chance etc, etc, etc." The next paragraph started: "Kindly remember to send me some of those great cookies Mama makes. We could sure use a package of goodies from home etc, etc, etc." The next paragraph started: "In case I forget I also can use etc, etc, etc. You get the idea. O K I N A W A. he wrote a long letter so it would not be noticeable to anyone because all letters were censored, you couldn't and didn't want to give out any military secrets. Some slogans like, "Loose Lips Sink Ships", and others I can't think of right now, appeared everywhere on billboards, in the ads on buses and trains and on the radio, in the movie theater and everywhere. It was so necessary there were spies lurking everywhere listening to conversations, we were told and probably true. When I received his letter I immediately got out the map and found the island of Okinawa in Japan that none of us ever heard of before and so far from home. Needless to say it was awfully long and unbearable especially for Mama waiting for his letter after we heard about that typhoon. Well it finally arrived and he told us he was safe and all right. What a big relief! How I wished I saved those letters now.

In the spring of 1977 Papa and Mama sold their property (two houses – a 3 family and an 8 family) on York Street in Jersey City. They came to live with Frank and me, Kathleen and Mike. We have a four bedroom home here in Middletown. We bought a big house because I knew Mama and Papa would come to live with us eventually when they got older and could no longer live alone. The first two summers Papa was here, he still had the strength to grow and take care of a garden in our back yard. There was lots of room in our yard and he grew tomatoes, green peppers, egg plants, squash, string beans, parsley, cucumbers and I forget what else. He used horse manure to fertilize the garden and everything grew fast and tasted out of this world too. He really could make anything grow and really enjoyed sitting outside and tending the garden. I helped with the watering and weeding as did Kathleen & Mike. Frank helped dig and soften the dirt and put the seeds and tomato plants in. Even Mama enjoyed the garden and weeded when she was up to it, before her knees got too bad to stand up and bend over for long.

Domenico and Maria Concetta

We took them to Mass every Sunday and of course still played the favorite records Papa liked to hear so much. He still tried to dance especially when Johnny and Bea's kids visited. It was very difficult for me to see them grow weaker and deteriorate in their old age and many times Bea came here to help and Jennie when she could and Johnny and his family came on Sundays to see Papa and Mama when ever they could. I was happy I was here and able to care for them for seven years until the end and see that they both got their wish which was to die at home and not in a hospital. We had Hospice nurses who visited and administered to Mama and Papa also during the week to help me. Papa died very suddenly of a heart attack on April 14, 1981. Bea was here. We were not aware it was a heart attack at the time so I called the ambulance and Nicky who was stationed in Red Bank at the time at the Air Force recruiting office. Nicky and I followed the ambulance to Riverview Hospital. They told us he was dead on arrival and he was taken to Pfleger's Funeral Home, here in Middletown on Tindal Road. Both Mama and Papa were waked at Pfleger's Funeral Home and interred, laid to rest, in Mt. Olivet Cemetery on Chapel Hill off Highway 35 South in Middletown, New Jersey.

We were very fortunate to have our Parish Priest from St. Mary's Church, Rev. Fr. Stanley Lukaszewski, Father Stas, as he wanted us to call him, come by every first Friday and administer Holy Communion and pray with us. He administered the last rites, "Extreme Unction", before they died. It was a Blessing and I know Mama was content up to the very end. She died peacefully in her sleep on May 21, 1984. Both Frank and I did our very best to provide a comfortable home and take good care of them both until the very end.

Serra stone at Mt. Olivet Cemetery

I also want to add that Dominick "Nicky" Charowsky was a big help to me and many times took Mama and Papa to Riverview Hospital when they got sick during those seven years. I don't know what I would have done without him. Frank worked nights at the time and was not always home when I needed a ride and I was just too nervous to drive myself.

Domenico Serra died on April 14, 1981; here is a photo of his grandchildren and great grandchildren taken at the dinner after his funeral.

Back row (left of pole): Michael Charowsky, William Dombrowski, Christopher Obert, John Serra, Edward Obert, Jacqueline Serra, Dianne Serra, and Dominick Serra

Middle row: Dominick Charowsky (in uniform), Norma Ayers, Maria Charowsky, Michael Goldrick, Patricia Obert, Robert Charowsky, Patricia Ferenc, Norma Obert, Carol Ann Serra, Donna Serra, Kathleen Goldrick

Front row: Joseph Serra, (kneeling) Geremy Ayers, Steven Lopez, Kristie Ayers, Robert Obert, Mary Obert, Heather Ayers, Michelle Obert, Anthony Serra

Happy Memories of Days Gone By

Written by Giovannina (Serra) Obert
Photos supplied by Giovannina (Serra) and Norman Obert

Giovannina (Serra) Obert

Food Shopping

When Mama went food shopping, she took Bea and me to help her carry the groceries. In the Italian section of Jersey City, called Little Italy, there was a store that sold live chickens. Mama could tell which chicken was fat enough to pick. They would kill the chicken by cutting the neck and then hang it by the feet for the blood to drain out. They had a conveyer that helped remove the feathers. You could see what was going on because they needed plenty of room for a conveyer belt that was always moving and helped to remove the feathers from the chicken. The workers did their job well, holding the chicken by the feet and turning them so all sides were clean and all feathers were removed.

This fresh chicken, when cooked, had an extra special taste. Mama taught us how to cut the chicken up in small parts just in the center of the joint, where it moved, and with a lot of smaller pieces, it cooked faster and everyone got plenty to eat. We also learned that tomato sauce tasted a lot better when cooked slow and longer on the back of the stove. We lived on chicken, macaroni, small meatballs, soup, sauce and salads.

Another store, the meat market, had a walk-in refrigeration room. When the door was open you could see in rows large pieces of beef hanging on hooks. Everything was clean and neat and there were always many customers waiting in line to be served. If we got meat, we called it chopped meat. We got one pound or two of beef, chopped in squares and it was a great change. Spare ribs were another meat change we enjoyed.

Mama always cooked and the meals were always good. Whenever she was cooking it made the kitchen smell great. One day when Mama saw a neighbor's child crying, she asked her what was the matter. She said, her mother had gone to work and her brothers ate everything she had left out for them. Mama sent her up stairs to us to give her some of what we were eating. She liked it, and ate the food. But when the girl's mother found out, she blamed her for not getting home on time and was told never to eat that food from the Serras again. The mother didn't say a thing to her mean sons who ate their sister's food.

The Ice Box

In the days when families had to keep their leftover food in the icebox, most people cooked only what would be eaten each day. The ice was sold by ice trucks that came around every three days. The ice slabs started eight times larger than the piece of ice that fit the top of our ice box. The blocks were chopped up to meet the needs of the person buying the ice. The ice box we had was not very sturdy. There was a door at the top that you had to pull up to open, to put the ice in and a door at the bottom that opened to the right to take the pan out to empty the water when the ice melted. When the ice was inside, it was top-heavy, and the water always managed to leak on the floor. At times we thought it was more trouble than it was worth. When Mama caught us sliding on the wet linoleum, she said, "That thing has got to go!", and out it went.

Michael, Ma (holding) Janice, Pa (holding) Donna, me holding Edward,
Mary, Nicky and Bea (holding) Bobby

The Serra Store

During the 1930s and up until the Second World War, Papa and his brother Salvatore were partners in the Serra Grocery Store at 267 York St. in Jersey City, New Jersey. The property they owned consisted of a large eight-family corner house and the 3 family house next to it. The store was on the first floor and three four-room apartments were above it. People that were of Irish descent lived in the first apartment over the store. Our family lived in the second apartment, and Papa's brother Uncle Sam, his wife Aunt Mary and their four children lived in the top apartment. The bad part was that the toilet facility was outside in the hall in a small room that had one toilet with a door in front and a small square opening on the side for air. The same toilet arrangement was also on the next two floors. When my brother John came home from the Navy and the war was over, the first job he did with Papa was to take a section from the large living room and provide an inside room to be the bathroom.

After the stock market crash of 1928, our country was in a long period of depression. Papa loved music, and had a mandolin that he taught himself to play. We all loved to hear him play. We would sing along with him and he would sing too. There wasn't any money for recreation, our biggest pleasure was on Sunday night when Papa had time for rest and relaxation and played his mandolin. Holidays were happy times because we got together with our relatives and friends and there was always singing and dancing and lots of good food to eat. One of Papa's good customers gave him a violin. She said now that her sons were older, they were no longer interested in taking lessons. Your son John is a young boy, maybe he would like to learn. Johnny learned to play the violin. Mama took him to New York City for music lessons. Uncle Jack's Radio Hour had a school for children to learn singing and dancing, also.

The times were very difficult for everyone in the country because there was no work available. One day Dominick said to Sam, "Two families cannot live from one small store. I'll buy your half interest or you can buy my half and that way there will be only six mouths to feed instead of twelve." Each family had three daughters and one son. Salvatore was called Sam, and the customers called Papa Mr. Dominick and Mama Mrs. Dominick.

Papa and his brother were not the least bit alike. Papa's brother Sam put up a sign in the store that said "In God We Trust, All Others Pay Cash." This was the reason for the breakup. Sam didn't want to give people credit. Papa said, "The sign must come down, the people have to eat. They will pay their bills on payday. If they don't eat, they can't work to earn the money they need." Papa told Sam "You can buy my share of the food in the store or you can sell me your share and I will pay you."

Sam took the money from Pa for his half interest and left. Now each brother had to work for his own family. Ma and Pa now were on their own and we children all had to help Mama in the store. There were a lot of small empty stores available. Sam could not get a factory job- no one was hiring. Sam opened his own store one block down on York Street. Papa said now we all have to work helping Mama in the store. Papa opened another store on Jersey Avenue because many people walked by that area to get to Newark Avenue where many clothing stores were located.

Mama and me

One afternoon while Papa was upstairs eating lunch, two policemen came into the store and asked Mama who the owner of the corner property was. Mama said, "My husband is and he is upstairs eating." Papa had finished and came down. He asked the policeman, "Is there a problem officers?" They asked him if he was the owner of the corner property. He answered, "We are half owners with my brother and his wife." The police asked, "Do you know anything about what was spotted on the roof of your property?" Papa said, "I don't know of anything being on the roof." Papa and the policemen went to the roof and Papa could not believe his eyes. A large red and black Nazi swastika was painted on the roof. Papa said, "I didn't put that there, but I recognize the paint. I can show you officers where we can see the same red paint." The window flowerboxes in front of the second floor apartment windows were painted with the same red paint. The police response was, "Not very smart, was it? Paint over the swastika with black paint and tell the parents of the boy that lives there not to do it again."

In order to purchase fresh vegetables, Papa rented a horse and wagon from the stable that was around the corner on Barrow Street. The stable was large enough only for a small number of horses and wagons-about eight or ten. The first horse Papa rented was called Barney. He was a beautiful rust-colored horse. When Barney became ill, Papa used a gray horse named Charlie.

In the 1930s, down the center of York Street, were electric trolley tracks. On Saturday morning, Papa took his horse down to the Jersey docks, and boarded the ferry boat to cross the Hudson River over to the New York City market, where the vegetables were sold. As a special treat, Papa sometimes took some of us children along. We were very happy to go on the ferry ride. To get there, buy the produce, load the wagon and then come home took about two hours all together. It was a fun trip.

197

One Saturday morning, after finishing breakfast, we heard a terrible loud crash. Papa was outside with Charlie delivering vegetables, when a trolley came by. The trolley frightened Charlie, and he ran into the road and was hit by a car. Bea was not far from the window, and looked out. She saw what happened, Charlie was bleeding very badly onto the street. Bea didn't scream, she just fainted and fell on the floor. Mama promptly picked her up and took her to the kitchen to care for her. At the same time, Papa went to get a doctor to care for the horse and stop the bleeding. We were all crying, and Papa didn't come home for a long time because it took a lot of effort to take Charlie to the stables and be treated. He never said it, but we all knew that we would never see Charlie again. Papa never took any interest in cars and he would never buy or drive one, and we all knew the reason for this was poor Charlie. Whenever he or the family traveled we always took the train.

Mama and Papa

For almost six months, Papa could not find reliable help and decided to close his second store and went back to work in a factory. He was very fortunate because he had experience working as a machinist in previous years at the Hyatt Roller Bearing Factory, in Harrison, N.J.

School and Work

We all attended Public Grammar School No. 3 around the corner from York Street, one block down on Bright Street. School No. 3 started with Grade 1 and went up to Grade 8. Lincoln High School was uptown. We got off the bus at the traffic junction, crossed a few streets, and Lincoln High was at the top of the hill. The Lincoln High School Grades 9 and 10 started from 12 o'clock noon to 5pm and Grades 11 and 12 started at 8am until 12 noon. High school was good and very interesting. Since it was not close to home, we didn't join the school clubs or other activities. Bea graduated in June 1938 and I in June 1940. Bea met Michael Charowsky in 1937 and they became good friends. After Bea graduated high school, she got a job where Mike was working in Hoboken, New Jersey at the Elram Light Company, an electric light bulb factory.

My photo and write-up in my High School Yearbook

When I graduated high school, at age 16, I was very anxious to go to work and also earn a pay so I could help at home. I never realized that I would have to work in a factory that made electric light bulbs. I applied at Elram and was hired. The large machine I worked on made the large stems. This machine would revolve around with blocks containing glass tubes. A fire heats the glass at the end to melt the glass as the machine turns. The top of the tube and the bottom of the tube were melted and pressed together as the machine turned and revolved. After this process, the block would open and the stem would fall into a tray that was ready to receive it. We learned the hard way the meaning of the term "Sweatshop". Bea worked the pronge machine that was next to the stem machine, a much smaller machine that melted the glass so that the three small prongs that hold the filament could be inserted into the stem and then put into a tray that was waiting. We learned our jobs well. I used one large handkerchief around my head and one around my neck to absorb the perspiration. If we worked six days, we received $12. At night, when I complained to Mama and Papa, Papa said, "When I worked at the factory, I earned only $1 a day. When you are eighteen you can apply for work at Western Electric, where working conditions and salary are better." On my eighteenth birthday I was very happy. I was hired at Western Electric. Hooray! I stayed employed with Western Electric in Kearny, New Jersey until I was married. I was earning $1.35 an hour, a big improvement from the $2 a day job in the sweatshop. The sad part was that I was leaving my parents home.

The Move to Amesbury, Massachusetts

I stayed employed with Western Electric in Kearny until I was married to Norman Obert and moved to Amesbury, Massachusetts in 1946. Leaving loving parents, family, friends and a good job was very difficult. The biggest shock came when I was rehired at Western Electric in Massachusetts for only 63 cents an hour, a loss of 72 cents an hour. Norman also worked for Western Electric and since Haverhill, MA was a few miles south of Amesbury, we traveled to work in Norman's car each morning. Starting time was 7:30am and work ended at 3:30pm.

Nellie, Maria Concetta and Domenico, on our wedding day

199

Right to Left: James "Sonny" McScheffy, Santa Serra, Giovanni "John" Serra, Mary Serra,
Joseph "Norman" Obert and Giovannina (Serra) Obert,
Domenico Serra, Juliette Blouin, John S. Serra, Lena Serra, Lawrence "Nugget" Greiner

Norm's mom, Nellie, worked at a shoe shop in Newburyport. We lived with her for about a year, when the upstairs apartment became available. Norm and I moved upstairs over Nellie's apartment. Four years later Norm and I finally found a large house we could afford on Elm Street in Amesbury. It was large enough for Nellie to have a kitchen, bedroom and a large living room. We enjoyed being together. We purchased the house at 177 Elm Street in 1950 and our first child Mary was born on September 13, 1951. I stayed home from work with baby Mary for about a year. After returning to work, I became pregnant again with our second child. Baby Norma Jean was born September 27, 1953. Two years later, our first son, Edward, was born on November 17, 1955. Two years after, God sent us another lovely, healthy baby daughter Patricia on September 24, 1957.

Nellie (right) with co-workers at the shoe shop

In the winter of January, 1960, my mother-in-law Nellie, Norman's dear mother, died, after her retirement from the Newburyport shoe shop, two years previous. She started getting tired and missed working and missed her friends at the shoe shop. She refused to see a doctor because she was afraid a doctor would put her in the hospital. On one cold morning she fell getting out of bed. We ran to see what had happened. We dressed her and Norman carried her to the car and drove her to the Amesbury Hospital. The X-ray showed she had progressive stomach cancer. She died a few days later at the Amesbury Hospital. We were all heart-broken. The children all cried when we told them that Memmae would not come home and play with them anymore. Jesus, Mary and Joseph took her to Heaven to be with God and the angels. We told the children we could always think of her with lots of love and remember how good she was to each one of us and she would be with us in our hearts always.

Mary, Pat, Norman, Chris, me, Ed and Norma

On July 9, 1962, Norman and I told the children Memmae asked Jesus to send them a baby brother. Now we had two boys and three girls. We were all very happy again. Christopher was a very good baby. They loved playing with him, teaching him games and reading stories to him. Christopher thrived on all the attention he got from his sisters and brother.

201

A Man Above Men

By Giovanni (John) Battista Serra

Maria Concetta and Donenico's Serra's 50th Wedding Anniversary

I got a job working for a company called "Air Reduction"; it was the same company that my father worked for. One day I was upstairs looking out the window with a couple of other fellas when I saw an elderly man far in the distance walking along the train tracks towards the company building. I knew who he was, but this other guy named Johnny Brown said "Hey look at that old guy walking down the train tracks!" I said "He might be an old man but, he's a good old man, that old man is my father Dominick Serra! He came to this country when he was about twelve years old and now he owns two apartment buildings and is in partnership with his brother and they own "Serra's Grocery Store." He has four children and, he's an Automatic Screw Machine Operator! When I told Johnny Brown all of that, I left him with his mouth hanging open. He finally said "Here I am born in this country and I pay rent, this man comes here as a kid and now he owns two houses!" My father walked every day along those tracks, he loved to walk. I can remember one time my sister Mary and myself were going to Rockaway Beach with my father and we couldn't keep up with him because he walked so fast! He told us we were gonna miss the train if we didn't hurry up and sure enough he caught the train and made it to the beach and left my sister Mary and myself in the dust! We never got there. My Father was an extraordinary man, when he set his mind on doing something he did it and no one could stop him! He worked hard all his life, in fact he was not a good man, but a great man!

Life on York Street

Written by John and Dominick Serra
Photos supplied by Tony Serra and Janice Charowsky

Maria Concetta (Costa) and Domenico Serra

One hundred and fifteen years ago my grandfather Domenico Serra was born on a small island just off the coast of Sicily. Over a century has passed since he returned to America with my grandmother to start their new lives together in America. The facts and dates of their extraordinary journey are well documented, but as I reflect, I do so, not on how, when or even why, they came to this country, but rather how they lived their lives with me and my brothers and sisters in Jersey City. The following stories are just a few of the fond memories we hold dear to our hearts, and the cherished years we spent with our grandparents (Nonno and Nonna) when they lived at 267 York Street in Jersey City.

To say the lives of my grandparents were filled with difficulties and challenges would be an understatement. Nonno lived to be ninety-two years old, and Nonna also lived to be ninety-two, which is a tremendous accomplishment in and of itself. They worked hard to survive and to raise their family, and they did it without many of the comforts that we have grown accustomed to. I can't remember them ever talking about their childhood or their hometowns. Like thousands of other immigrant families, they realized that if their lives were going to change for the better, they had to leave their home and come to America. In 1901, when he was only twelve years old, my grandfather did just that. I can just imagine the conversation he had with his mother and father, or how he was the one chosen to go. Why not his older brother? Was it his choice? Did he volunteer? What happened on the way over? What did he think when he got here? How did he survive? One thing is certain, he made it, and the rest is history, our family's history. My grandfather's bravery and courage will never be taken for granted or forgotten.

Once he arrived in America, Nonno settled in Massachusetts where he lived for a short while with his hometown companions. He worked on a farm and earned fifty cents a day, three dollars a week. He took great delight in telling me this story and in reminding me that fifty cents was a lot of money in those days. With fifty cents he said, "You could buy a loaf of bread and a gallon of milk and have change to spare." I always considered my grandmother and grandfather to be wise and thrifty people. They truly understood the value of a dollar. I can still hear Nonna's words of wisdom, "If you take care of the pennies, the dollars will take care of themselves" or "if you don't save it, you will never find it."

Their beliefs, values, and moral standards, along with their old school way of life with God, family, and prudent living at its core, was the very foundation of their lives. I will never forget Nonna's favorite saying, which she repeated to us constantly, "love each other." Nonna was always watching, always caring, always praying. She took every opportunity to tell us how important it was to do good in school, to study, and to work hard.

Nonna would always check out how we were dressed, and always remind us of how important it was to look our best when we left the house. As kids, we felt that she was always harping on something, but we listened to her none the less. Nonno and Nonna taught us a great many lessons, and helped shape our lives by their own example. I'm very grateful to them, and now that I have my own children, I can better understand that all their constant reminding was really their way of showing us how much they cared for, and loved us.

Nonno was a man of few words, but when he did speak, everyone listened, or rather, should have listened, you'd be a fool not to. To learn from him, all you had to do was watch him as he worked around the house, or in the yard in his garden, or even just sitting around the kitchen table during one of our family get togethers. It's not uncommon for Italian families to have loud, intense discussions about someone or something, and ours was no different. When the adults got together at one of our birthday parties, it didn't take much to get them started. During these heated debates, while everyone tried to get their two cents in, trying to sound like they knew what they were talking about, Nonno would just sit back and watch and listen. He would never say much, even when he was asked a question or when asked for his opinion. I remember Nonno once said, "You haven't really lived until you've seen what I have seen." How true.

Nonna was the perfect wife and homemaker. She accepted her duties as wife, mother, and grandmother with deep devotion and unwavering pride. Part of her daily ritual, was to take time out of her busy day to pray. It was not uncommon to find her sitting by the kitchen window in the afternoon or early evening, with her little black prayer book and rosary in hand, praying earnestly for her family. She would repeat and contemplate the prayers she knew so well and trusted so implicitly. Nonno and Nonna never had the luxury or the opportunity of a formal education, but they learned more from life than they could from any book.

John and Donna (Gennace) Serra

Nonno worked very hard, and had many different jobs. When they lived in Harrison New Jersey. Nonno took a job as a machinist and worked as a screw machine and lathe operator for the Hyatt Roller Bearing Company. I was amazed to find out that when the Hyatt Roller Bearing Company went out of business, the very same factory building where Nonno worked for many years was taken over by the Hartz Mountain Corporation where I worked for six years. Imagine my surprise was when I found out that I was working in the very same building where my grandfather worked nearly seventy years earlier!

Nonno and Nonna moved from Harrison and purchased a piece of property on the corner of York and Mercer Streets diagonally across from Van Vorst Park in Jersey City. The property consisted of two brownstone multi-dwelling apartment houses 267 and 271 York Street. On the second floor of 267 in a very small apartment was where Nonno and Nonna lived. There was a storefront in 267 where Nonno and his brother Salvatore operated a grocery store where they sold household goods, candy, fresh fruits, and vegetables. We lived just down the block at 245 York Street for only a few years and then moved to 271 York Street. We were very young at the time, and there were just three of us, my brother Dominick who was three, my sister Donna who was only two, and I was just an infant. We lived on the second floor just across from Nonno and Nonna's apartment. My mother told us once that whenever her or Nonna wanted to talk to each other, they would pull on the squeaky clothesline in order to get each others attention.

Despite the fact that Nonno never had a driver's license, and never owned, or drove a car for that matter, he knew how to go anywhere. He walked everywhere, and if he couldn't walk to his destination, he would take the train or the bus. Nothing stopped him. He knew the trains and buses better than anyone. When we were boys, my brother Dominick and I were Nonno's travel companions and took turns accompanying him to Massachusetts for weddings or funerals. If no one was available to drive him, that didn't stop him, it was too important to him. He would pack up a small suitcase, while Nonna made us lunch. We would take the number nine bus, or walk, to the Journal Square bus station where he would buy two round trip tickets for Boston. We boarded the Greyhound bus and were on our way.

The day finally came when my brother and I got our first cars, my brother Dominick bought an old 66 Chevy Bel Air, and a few years later I bought a 1971 Dodge Dart. We were glad to be able to drive Nonno wherever he wanted to go. Dom used to pick him up and drive him to church on Sundays. Nonno's the one who taught me how to get to Massachusetts, he never needed a map, he knew the route to Aunt Jenny's house so well, he could get there with his eyes closed. He knew the towns and streets in Massachusetts as well as the ones in New Jersey, including every major highway in between.

Dominick and Diane (McGuirl) Serra

One day when I was driving Nonno home from our house, I stopped for a red light on the corner of Grand and Henderson Streets. Nonno turned to me, and pointing to a gas station on the corner and said to me "do you know what was on this corner before that gas station?" No! I replied. He said "a stable where I kept my horse and wagon". He said his horse's name was Charlie (Charlie Horse). He went on to tell me how he would hook up Charlie to the wagon and drive him down to the Hudson River Ferry where he would cross over into New York. A few times he even let my father, who was about fifteen at the time, drive the cart. They took the ferry to the farmers market where he loaded up the wagon with fresh produce that he sold in the grocery store on 267 York Street.

Countless times we walked with him all over Jersey City, as he ran his errands to the hardware store or the A&P on Jersey Ave., or to the live poultry store on Brunswick Street. On the weekends, Nonno would go food shopping at the Shop-Rite on Grove Street. He showed me how to pick the freshest fruit, and told me to always look at the loaves of Italian bread to make sure they weren't burnt on the bottom. A bag of groceries in each hand, and something for me to carry, we headed home. I can remember as we walked, Nonno's stride was long and fast, I had to double step just to keep up with him. He slowed down over the years, but he never stopped walking. He walked to our house on Morris Street nearly everyday. When we were little playing in front of our house, I remember we would get so excited when we saw Nonno turn the corner. As he walked towards us with his cane in hand and his cotton cap on his head, we dropped everything and raced to see who could get to him first.

Whenever we went to Nonno and Nonna's house on York Street, we would speed up as we got closer to their house because we knew if the store was opened, there was a good chance we were going to get a treat, a piece of candy from Nonno's store. That is of course if Nonno's brother Salvatore wasn't there. He never liked us taking candy without paying for it.

Nonno and Nonna's house was a very special place for us. They always made us feel special and welcome. I can still remember the details of the apartment on the second floor of 267 York Street. It was a small, simple apartment with only two very small connecting bedrooms, a living room, kitchen, and bathroom that was converted from a half bath that at one time you could only access from the hallway outside the apartment. I can't believe that Nonno, Nonna, my father, John, Aunt Bea, Aunt Jennie, and Aunt Mary all lived in that little apartment.

If I close my eyes I can see the apartment just as I remember it; the pressed tin decorative ceiling, the wallpaper in the kitchen with the little cuckoo clocks, the trunk in the kitchen by the window; with the old fashioned radio that also played 45 records, the metal top kitchen table with simulated wood grain finish, the old black and white TV, real cedar closets in the bedroom and parlor, and the peddle operated Singer sewing machine that Nonna operated like a pro. My brother Dominick even remembers the little blue parakeet they had as a pet.

I always looked forward to going to Nonno and Nonna's house, Nonna seemed to always know when I was coming. I didn't know how she knew, I think my mother would call her and tell her. As I entered the hallway of 267 York Street, I would push the middle button marked "Serra", and wait a moment until Nonna buzzed me in.

They say you never really get to know someone until you live with them, my brother Dominick and I were fortunate to have had the opportunity to live with Nonno and Nonna, for several years. We experienced first hand the daily routine of their simple happy life at 267 York Street in Jersey City. It started out as weekend sleepovers with me and my brother Dominick taking turns, then as we got older and started working in the fish store, we would walk home with Nonno, stay for supper and stay the night. This was great, and it was easier for Nonno, since he didn't have to walk us home every night.

We would leave for school, and Nonno would leave for the fish store. When we got home, we would always find Nonna anxiously awaiting our arrival as she had dinner well under way. Nonna once told me that when Nonno asked her to marry him, her response to him was, "But I don't know how to cook." He replied "Don't worry, you'll learn." The rest is history because not only did she learn, she was the best.

Nonna wasn't a fancy cook, like everything else she kept it simple. With a few plain ingredients, she made some of the best meals we ever had. You could gain weight just by inhaling the aromas that came from her kitchen. Breaking pasta, thin spaghetti, always Ronzoni, into little pieces in a bowl to prepare a dish of "Pasta-and-Peas" was a daily routine. I loved to watch her while she worked, grating a piece of fresh Italian bread into a bowl, then adding a pound of ground beef then sticking her hands in the bowl to mix it up thoroughly. She would then begin to form her delicious, tender little meatballs that were out of this world.

When we were little, we used to eat there every Sunday. Whenever she made her homemade ravioli, she would always let us help. We had so much fun. After she combined all the ingredients to make the dough, we would help her knead it until it was just right, Nonna would then roll it out on the table at just the right thickness and texture. She would then cut the dough into equal size squares. Then she would get the Ricotta cheese filling out of the icebox, and would carefully measure the right amount of filling and place it in the center of each square then we would cover each with another dough square. The last step was the fun part. Nonna showed us how to seal all four sides of each Ravioli using a fork. Then we would very carefully carry them to the bedroom, yes the bedroom, which was right next to the kitchen, and place them on the bed, yes the bed, on a clean white sheet that she covered with flour in order to let them dry.

After dinner each night, Nonna would clean up, we would do our homework, (Dom was still doing his homework there all through college) draw, or read one of our comic books that we hid under the cushion of the parlor chairs. Nonno would go into the parlor, lay down on the couch, and put his feet up to relax and watch the Six O'clock Evening News with Walter Cronkite. Nonno never missed the news. He was up on all the current events. I remember during the Viet Nam War, Nonno couldn't wait to turn on the news to see what was going on.

When the News was finished, we would all sit in the parlor and watch one of their favorite TV shows, Lawrence Welk, Ed Sullivan, The Red Skelton Show, or Wrestling on their black and white television. Nonno and Nonna loved to watch Wrestling, it seemed more real then, not like today. There was not a lot of show boating, just wrestling but it was good, and it was funny. Nonno's favorite wrestlers were Bruno Samartino, Gorilla Monsoon, and Haystack Calhoun, and they both liked the midgets, I never saw them laugh so hard. When their program was finished, off went the TV and we got ready for bed. Nonno was in bed by nine o'clock every night.

Nonno loved music, and always wanted us to learn how to play a musical instrument. He would always find time at the end of the day to sit on the couch and play a few tunes for us on his mandolin. I loved watching him play, he only knew a few songs, but he enjoyed playing them for us. His repertoire consisted of only a few Italian favorites and two American songs "Red River Valley" and "In the Shade of the Old Apple Tree". Whenever the families got together, Nonno always took the opportunity to gather up the kids to teach us how to dance the Italian jig, otherwise known as "The Tarantella". This old Italian favorite could be danced to any Italian tune especially Cella Luna.

Besides watching their favorite TV shows, they also enjoyed playing cards or playing checkers. Checkers was Nonno's favorite. He was the best checker player I ever saw. Once the game started, it wouldn't take him long to reach your side of the board, get a few kings, and proceed to wipe you out. Occasionally he would let us win. He loved setting you up for some of his special moves like a triple zig-zag jump, or getting you caught in what he referred to as a "pair of pants". This was a move where he would strategically place one of his checkers between two of yours. You knew that no matter which one of your checkers you moved to safety, you still lost the other one. He was so good when he pulled off one of these moves, you never saw it coming. Playing cards was another favorite, you didn't have to ask them twice, they were always up for a challenging game of "Scoppa" or "Brishcola"

Every night, Nonno would lay out his clothes for the next day, and shine his black leather ankle high oxfords. On cold winter nights, Nonno would take two house bricks and put them on the stove in the kitchen to heat up, while he got ready for bed. He would wrap up the hot bricks in a towel and place them under the covers at the foot of his bed to keep his feet warm during the night. He said that "Your feet should always be warm, and your head should always be cool, if it was the other way around, you're in trouble."

Nonno and Nonna were very faithful and devout Catholics, Nonno never missed Sunday Mass, and made every effort to insure that we didn't either. He was also very dedicated to his job, which he held for many years as Secretary of the Congregation of the Blessed Mother Maria S.S. Del Terzito. Once again this was another part of his life that he felt was important enough to pass down to his grandchildren. Every summer in the month of July, Nonno would fulfill his duties as secretary and make the necessary arrangements for the upcoming celebration. He started weeks in advance, and of course involved my brother Dominick and me in the activities. First we would make a visit to a local florist in Jersey City, where Nonno would order 10 floral bouquets made up mostly of carnations, they were his favorite and he could get more of them because they were the least expensive. He was very meticulous and shrewd when placing his order with the florist. Nonno always stood firm when the florist would try to increase the cost of the flowers. He always refused to pay the increase, and would threaten to take his business elsewhere. The florist, as usual would always be the first to give in. The next thing on his checklist was to update the pamphlets that were mailed out to all the members each year.

Maria Concetta and Domenico Serra

Nonno would take us by train into New York City. Once there we walked for several blocks to a small print shop where Nonno would review the revisions with the printer and order the new pamphlets. The last thing on the list and the most important, was to visit the Church. In September, about a week or so before the actual date of the celebration, we went to the church in order to remove the statue of the Blessed Mother from her designated alcove high above the sanctuary floor. The statue, which felt like it weighed several hundred pounds, had to be taken down, and placed on the altar in preparation of the celebratory Mass. But taking the statue down was no easy task. Nonno was too old, so he supervised the job as my brother Dominick and I carefully, and very nervously removed the statue using two old rickety ladders and a few wooden planks. It was hard, and dangerous, but we did it for him. We knew that he took his duties very seriously, and he was very proud to be in charge of such an important responsibility.

Our grandparents were simple people. The only real wealth they accumulated over the years was their family, three daughters, one son, 20 grandchildren, and 27 great grandchildren. They didn't leave much behind in the way of earthly possessions, but what they did leave us, is priceless.

There's an old Bible proverb that says, "A good name is rather to be chosen than great riches, and loving favor than silver or gold." Whenever I read this verse, I think of my grandparents. Nonno and Nonna left us not only these precious memories, but also the legacy of their life long dedication and love for their family, and their good name which I am proud to have as my own. Thank you Nonno and Nonna for everything.

Serra Memories of their Grandparents

Written by the Serra Family
Photos supplied by Mary (Serra) Goldrick and Giovannina (Serra) Obert

Domenico Serra, Maria Concetta Serra
Donna Serra, Dominick Serra and Mary Lynn Serra

L to R: Mary Lynn Serra, Donna Serra, Carol Ann Serra, Domenico Serra, Maria Concetta Serra,
Kathleen Goldrick, Maria Goldrick (holding) Michael Goldrick, John Serra, Jackie Serra,
Johnny Serra and Dominick Serra

Part One
Written by Dominick Serra

I can't really say much about the last couple of years of Nonno & Nonna's lives since I only got to see them occasionally on the weekends after they moved in with Aunt Mary & Uncle Frank. I used to walk around their back yard with Nonno and we would talk about what he had seen on the news. The last time I spent with him was a day or two before he passed away. I spent a couple of hours with him, just holding his hand as he lay in his bed that Sunday afternoon.

Dominick Serra

However, I used to spend almost every evening with them before they moved. I would stop by after working at the fish market to do my college homework. Nonno would help me with my Italian homework. Sometimes we would play cards or just watch some TV before I went home.

"Nonno always impressed upon me the value of getting the best education that I could, in order to have a good career and make a good living for myself and my family"

"Nonna taught me how important it is that we love one another, long before John Lennon made it fashionable and newsworthy"

Part Two
Written by Donna (Serra) Lorusso

My fondest memories of my Nonna and Nonno are of the times we spent with them at their home on York Street. I am so thankful that we had them with us for as long as we did, and that we were able to see them so often. Like going to church with them on Sunday and the family gatherings at their house, with the homemade raviolis on the bed. The dollar bills my grandfather would slip into our hands after church. I guess it was his way of showing us that he was also grateful for us spending time with him.

I remember the gardens he used to plant in our back yard with the cucumbers and tomatoes. He could make anything grow! He would walk eight to ten blocks from his house to ours just to tend to it. I remember stopping at their house on my way home from school because you knew Nonna was always cooking something good and you were going to eat. I remember all those haircuts that I didn't want as a kid, but was too afraid to say anything. Besides, my bangs always grew back! I remember the trips to Massachusetts in the station wagon eating those cheese on whole wheat sandwiches, and getting yelled at for throwing the crust out the back window.

Donna Serra

My memories of my grandparents are long and precious to me. They were the glue that kept the family together. They were always there when you needed them, and they gave you guidance and unconditional love. I'll never forget the day I went to the Hospital to have Steven and Nonna came to see me. I was very sick and almost died, and when I was allowed to have visitors, she was one of the first ones there to see me. She brought me some pears. I'll never forget that!

I think we were very lucky to have them for as long as we did. I only wish I could have learned to speak Italian or play the Mandolin. I wish that I had paid more attention to Nonna when she was cooking. I would give anything to have some of her recipes today. I remember her sewing with her crooked finger on that old black Singer sewing machine, and the way she ate the heads of the fishes that Nonno brought home from his hard day at Raymond's fish market. I miss going to their house in Jersey City, I miss their broken English. But most of all I just miss them!

211

Nonno was always up on what was happening in the world, He watched Walter Cronkite religiously every night. I think about Nonno and Nonna all the time, and enjoy very much telling my sons about them. I think your idea of putting together a

Johnny Serra

family tree/biography is good for everyone because it helps us to reflect on all the good times we had with our grandparents. What Nonno started over a hundred years ago has reached and touched all of our lives. The way I remember Nonno and Nonna, was that they were all about family, they loved and cared for everyone, no exceptions. Nonna's favorite saying was "Love Each Other" That was what was most important to them, that is the very reason why Nonno came to America.

Part Four
Written by Jackie Serra

I remember the time when I was about 8 years old. Aunt Mary gave me a pair of Hush Puppies shoes and I stepped on a nail and it went through the sole of the shoe and into my foot. Nonno came over every day and bathed my foot for me and put some Black drawing salve on it to heal it. It never got infected and went away with no problems. I never had to go to the doctor.

I remember when I was sewing something and Nonno told me a story about the Devil and the angel that had a sewing race. He said the Devil threaded his needle with a long thread so he wouldn't have to thread it over again he thought he would win by saving time and cheating the Angel. The angel's with a short thread. While sewing the Devil was sitting next to a rose bush and his thread became tangled up in the bush because it was so long but the angel who had the short thread just kept on sewing won the race.

I also remember Nonna cooking in the kitchen and the smells of what she was cooking were so good. I sat by the window with the peach pits and watched all the cats in the yard while Nonno made us fresh lemonade then played the Mandolin and showed us how to dance in the living room. When we went to their house I remember playing checkers with Nonno no one could beat him but he would let me win sometimes.

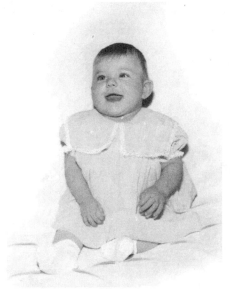

Jackie Serra

There was one time when Nonno came to get us to go to church on a Sunday morning and we were all sleeping because we were up late making a jigsaw puzzle. Nonno tapped me on my feet with his cane to wake me up. When I went into the kitchen Daddy was sitting at the table with the puzzle and Nonno started yelling at him and with his hand swiped the puzzle off the table and all the pieces went flying all over the kitchen. We were still finding puzzle pieces 2 years later. It was very funny later but not at the time.

I remember the times I worked with Nonno in the Garden and he showed me how to plant tomatoes. I thought to my self that my grandparents were so special! Especially Nonno for coming here to America by himself and making a life here for his family .He was only a boy and didn't know anything about America he didn't even speak English but he managed to bring over Nonna and his Brothers and sisters, buy land and raise a family all this during a time of depression he truly had wisdom and courage.

I wish they were still here with us all the good times and how loved they made me feel. I thought to myself when I was a little girl how proud I was to be part of our Family.

213

Part Five
Written by Tony Serra

The one thought that comes to my mind about my grandfather, Domenico Serra is that he always made me feel accepted and loved, 100%. He never judged me or made comments about my appearance, he simply saw me as his family - a grandson which he loved with all his heart! I believe he had a special insight that not many people have, he had a strong spirit, and I am very fortunate to have known him, and to have had him as my Nonno.

When I was young, I remember my grandmother always telling me to get my hair out of my eyes! I had very thick hair when I was little and lots of it, so when ever I used to go over to my grandparents house, Nonna would get a soup bowl out of the closet and put it on my head and cut all around the edge of the bowl, and would you believe after she was done I looked like the little Dutch boy on the paint can! It wasn't bad at all, I have seen pictures of myself as a little kid and I was pretty darn cute- sloppy but cute.

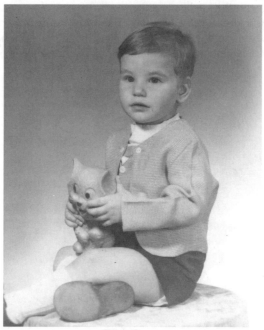

Tony Serra

Did you know that Nonno put my hand in a jar of kerosene one time when I was little - I accidentally slammed it in the car door of my dad's station wagon getting out going up to their apt at 267 York Street? I almost forgot about that - Its amazing how much comes back to you. I also remember that my brother John used to weed the front of the apt bldg 271 York Street and one time he told me and Carol that if we helped him, he would take us to the movies! We did and he took us to see "Jaws". He told us not to tell Nonno and Nonna! They didn't go for that sort of thing -movies you know, not to mention a killer shark movie- its still today one of my favorite all time films and a great memory of being with my brother and sister.

If any one was to ask me if I ever had a hero in my life, without hesitation I would say my Grandfather Domenico Serra, he was a strong intelligent man who gave of himself with out question, as a young man he was brave and determined on making a better life for his family, I remember him always working very hard, and always teaching us how to make the right choices, and even if we had to struggle through something, never to give up! There are not many men around like my grandfather these days; he was one of a kind! A true hero to me, I will see you and Nonna again someday, until then, you're always in my heart, mind, and soul. I love you both!

214

Recollections...

Written by Christopher Obert

I have been asking everyone to send in memories, so I figured I better write down a few of my own memories. When I think of the past here is a few of the images that pop into my head...

I can picture Nonno and my dad sitting in the living room at York Street discussing President Nixon and the Vietnam War. I just sat there listening to them go back and forth debating the issues. It is the only discussion I can remember between the two of them.

I can recall one time in the kitchen on York Street, my grandfather, Nonno was telling a joke in Italian. I cannot remember who he was telling the joke to, but I can picture him standing next to the washing machine with the roller on top. The joke was something about a group of guys that, for some reason, could not blow their noses. Each one had to somehow hide the fact that they were wiping their nose. I can only remember how one guy did it. As he pointed out a flock of birds flying overhead he wipes his nose on his shoulder sleeve. It is the only time I remember Nonno telling a joke.

Once, back in the 1970's, when the movie the Godfather was making news, I asked Nonno if we had any family members in the Mafia. He looked at me with a look I never saw him use before. It was a very stern and serious look. He said, "Yes, we are never to talk of this again!" I never did...

I vividly remember the summer my mom and I spent a few weeks on vacation on the Jersey shore. We stayed at the Charowsky's bungalow. I had a great time and spent most of the time with Michael Charowsky, Bobby Charowsky and his girlfriend Patty Ferenc. I spent most of my time with Patty's sister Alicia. I will never forget that summer!

I can recall all the times we visited the Goldrick's. Mike, Kathleen and I would play all the time. Mike and I would watch wrestling on TV and then roll around on the floor. Every now and then Kathleen would join in. One of the things I can remember best is when Mike and I would whine until we got our parents to buy us "cheese cake", which is our favorite.

Another one of my recollections is when we would visit with the Serras. I remember one year Dominick gave me a bunch of his US Navy models. I felt like I had just won the lottery. I played with those ships for years. I can also remember looking through comic books with Dominick, Johnny and Tony. We would always have long discussions about our favorite heroes.

I can remember playing dozens and dozens of games of "Stratego" with my brother Ed and never winning one game... even after turning the board around and swapping sides. Ed used to play hide and go seek with me and would always hide so well that I could not find him. Just as I was about to complain that I could not find him he would show up sitting on the couch next to me. I never could figure out how he did that. I can also remember when we were younger and we would divide up our collection of religious icons that we slept with. I could never get both the black Crucifix and the blue, glow in the dark Blessed Mother icons, which were our two favorite pieces.

I also remember that one of the legs on my parent's bed had the tendency to slip out and the bed would fall to the ground. One day while I was playing in my room, my brother and sisters were running around in our parent's room and they bumped the bed and it collapsed. They ran in my room picked me up and put me on the bed, then quickly disappeared. When my parents came upstairs to see what the noise was, they found me on the broken bed... Thanks guys!

My Grandpa the Immigrant

Written by Kathleen Goldrick in 1977
Photos supplied by Giovannina (Serra) Obert

Kathleen Goldrick

Dominick Serra came to America in 1901 on a ship called the Liguria.
This is how he described it…

I came from Naples Italy when I was 12 years old. The boat trip was hard and long and we hit a lot of rough water. I came here with some friends. When I got to America it was a whole different place. We landed in New York and stayed over night. The next day we took the electric trolley car because that was the only transportation there was on land. We took it to get the boat to go to Boston, Massachusetts. I got a job on a farm. It was a good job because a lot of people were out of work. I worked 10 hours a day and my job paid 50 cents a day ($3.00 a week). In 1912 I went back to get my girlfriend to marry me and we got married in Leni, Italy.

Kathleen Goldrick and Mr. and Mrs. Dominick Serra

216

The Story of Domenico Serra and the Comic Strip "Ching Chow"

Written by Christopher Obert as told to him by Mary (Serra) Goldrick
Photo and images supplied by Mary (Serra) Goldrick

Marie Concetta and Domenico Serra

One year when I was visiting with my Aunt Mary, I asked her to tell me a story about my grandfather. She told me something I never knew, Domenico Serra liked to play the numbers! It was not this fact that surprised me but how he picked his numbers. He got his numbers from "Ching Chow". Ching Chow was a comic that ran in the newspaper. The comic had a Chinese saying and a cartoon that went with the quote. He would cut the comic out of the paper and glue it into old magazines. Aunt Mary gave me 3 magazines full of these clippings.

Magazine 1) Marian Helpers Bulletin Oct. - Dec. 1965

Magazine 2) New Jersey Bell Telephone Company, Telephone Almanac for 1962

Magazine 3) Airco Tank Talks September, 1963

On each comic is a three digit number hand written in pencil. Aunt Mary told me these numbers were the numbers he would play. He somehow got the number from the cartoon. I tried to determine how, but could not figure it out. Then I found the answer. In one of the magazines was a torn page from a book. "Magical Spiritual Dream Book" by Mme. Fu Futtam. The book seems to give you clues as to what your dreams mean. Each entry has a three digit number associated with it. My grandfather would pick the principal image or idea in the cartoon, look it up in the book, and get the corresponding number.

I copied the torn page and a page of the Ching Chow clippings. Enjoy…

SWING—To see children swing denotes honor and wealth in the
near future. 481
SWITCHBOARD—Operator denotes vexation and change of occupa-
tion, residence and special friend. 656—234
SWORD—To dream of a sword shows a life of distress, danger and
suffering, happily ending in honor. 833
SYRUP—To dream of syrup denotes that you will be deceived. 881
TABASCO SAUCE—To dream of it denotes a new position in up-
to-date quarters. 927
TABERNACLE—To enter one denotes good luck in everything you
undertake. 325
To see worshippers shows your relatives from whom you are far
apart are spending sleepless nights over you. 713
TABLE—To see one nicely set with flowers shows death in you
neighborhood. 444
EMPTY TABLE—Denotes money in a handful. 248
TABLE CLOTH—Clean, denotes an unexpected visitor. 490
If dirty denotes sickness or disappointment. 833—4
TABLE SPOONS—Denotes the arrival of a loving
life partner. 601
TABLETS—Shows that you are being misled by t
your best friends. 400
ACKS—To dream of tacks denotes everlas
forts among two of the opposite sex.
AG—To see a tag hanging denotes yo
off your post. 808
AIL—To see animals' tails denot
TAILOR—To dream of a tail
his suit to you. 160
TALE BEARER—Denot
ALISMAN—To ho

TASK MASTER—Denotes your home will be broken up by the
influence of one you've taken in confidence. 012
TASSELS—To dream of tassels you will be sure to get money. 258
TASTE—To dream of tasting anything shows you will have many
admirers. 641
TAXES—To dream of paying taxes denotes you will occupy a good
position socially and in business. 111
TAXICAB—See cab.
TEA—To dream of tea in any form denotes gain by long travel in
foreign country. 854
To serve tea shows a present and future slate of happiness and success. 169
EACHING—To dream of teaching denotes that your industry and
wise judgment in handling your affairs will be the source of
your comforts in later years. 510
POT—To dream of a tea pot shows an enlightened mind towards
ing an honest living smartly. 805
DROPS—To see tear drops shows love and consolation from
of the opposite sex. 539
—Denotes a visitor with a very pleasing personality
sk to return. 428
—Death news. 415, 90 back
you will be hampered by difficulties. 481
k. 208 Dirty teeth—hardships. 376
ing one is sure to bring at some time
ions. 998
te of your mind. 332
tender denotes
ve it or not
disturb

Torn page from the book. "Magical Spiritual Dream Book" by Mme. Fu Futtam

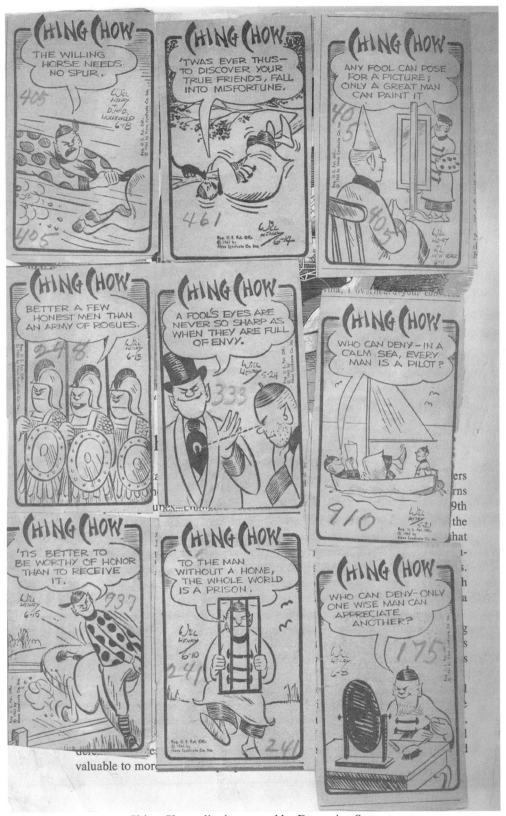

Ching Chow clippings saved by Domenico Serra

The Dish Girls and Dish Night at the Palace

Written by Mary (Serra) Goldrick
Photos supplied by Giovannina Obert and The Dan McNulty Collection

Bea, Bea, Santa, Jennie and Lena

When my sisters and I were growing up in Jersey City, there were no shopping malls anywhere. Our shopping district was located within walking distance on Newark Avenue, about five blocks from York Street. There were many stores lined up one after the other. Some were clothing shops for men, and others sold dresses for women. There were also stores such as *Miles*, *A. S. Beck*, and *National* that sold shoes for men, women and children. And of course every district had a *Woolworth 5 & 10 Cent Store*. It was great! Everything was reasonable priced very affordable. You could buy almost anything you needed at the *5 & 10*. Many of the neighborhood girls worked at the counters there. Those stores were in every town across American and only recently went out of business. Someone even wrote a song about the store. The title was "I Met a Million Dollar Baby at the 5 & 10 Cent Store." It was a cute little ditty, and went something like this.

"I met a million dollar baby at the 5 & 10 cent store,
She was selling china and when she rolled those eyes,
I kept buying china until the crowd got wise,
Incidentally, if you should run into a shower,
Just step inside my cottage door,
And meet the million dollar baby,
From the 5 & 10 cent store!"

220

Mary, Lena and Santa Serra

Monarch's Studio was also on Newark Avenue. All our Communion, graduation and wedding photos were taken by Mr. Monarch. He was a nice man and everyone went there to be photographed for special occasions. Next door to him was the *Palace Theater*. When the war was over in 1945, the *Palace* started having "Ladies Night" every Thursday. The price of a ticket was a dime, (Years later it went up to 20 cents). Remember, hardly anyone had a TV to watch at home, so we went to the local theater for our entertainment. By this time we were all working and could afford to go out. Every girl who bought a ticket got a dish on "Ladies Night." My sisters and I liked to go with our cousins and friends every week so we could get our 'free' dishes. A different dish was given each week, until one place setting was completed, then over again until you could complete a service for four, eight or twelve. The dishes were very nice and I think every girl in our neighborhood managed to collect a set.

During the show, someone would get up and you'd hear a loud crash. The audience roared with laughter. It was funny so long as it wasn't your plate that got broken. For a dime you could see a double feature movie, a couple of cartoons, a newsreel, a chapter and always next week's 'Coming Attractions' AND get a free dish. Those were carefree, happy times and we all had so much fun! They were lovingly known as "The Good Old Days!"

Palace Theatre, Jersey City

221

Pioneer Village
Circa 1940s

Written by Christopher Obert and Giovannina Obert
Photos supplied by Giovannina Obert

Photos of Emma Clemenzi, Jenny Villanti, Jennie Serra, Santa Serra and Bea Serra

Sometime during the 1940's the Serra cousins, Emma Clemenzi, Jennie Villanti, Jennie Serra, Santa Serra and Bea Serra, went on a day trip to Pioneer Village. My mother told me "I think that's what it was called." She said "I remember having a lot of fun. We took a bunch of photos!" One day, as was going through her photo albums for pictures for the Serra book, I came across a bunch of photos of that day, and I put them together here for a short photo story. I hope you enjoy it.

The Serra Cousins being silly

Bea Serra's Wedding Day

Monday November 19, 1945

Reprint of the letter Marie Serra wrote to her brother Giovanni "John"
while he was over-seas during WWII.
Photos supplied by Giovannina (Serra) Obert

Michael Charowsky and Bartolomea Serra

Dear Johnny,

Well, here it is the day after Bea's Wedding. Everyone is feeling fine, although we are all pretty tired from yesterday's festivities. I'll start from the beginning.

Everyone got up about 7 o'clock on Sunday morning. Mike's brother slept overnight and Lena Villanti slept over too. Betty Serra slept upstairs as did Margie and Aunt Grace who also came from Beverly for the wedding. All went to mass and received Holy Communion. Then we came back and had coffee and cake. Mike and his brother Johnny went home to Carteret to get dressed. About 12:00, I started to set the table for dinner. Everyone who was upstairs came down to eat with us. Mama cooked chicken soup and roasted chickens in the oven and pasta. Oh boy, it was a good meal! When Uncle Tom and Edna and son Tommy arrived from NYC, they joined us at the table and ate too. We then cleared the dishes and started to iron the gowns. Bea and her brides-maids got dressed. Gee Papa sure look cute with his tuxedo on. At about a quarter to three the flowers arrived and Mama and I wore corsages of red roses, so did Mike's Mother and sisters

Helen and Mary. All the men had white carnations in their lapels. The photographer arrived at about 3 o'clock. He took some pictures of Bea in front of the mirror. She looked so beautiful! Then the cars (3 big black limousines) pulled up in front of the house. Johnny and Eleanor Zulinski decorated the cars with white streamers, the bride's car had a sign in the back window said "Just Married". We put the sign up after they came out of church. Helen Charowsky dressed up three little dolls one in white like a bride with veil and all. One in pink for the maid of honor's car and one in blue for the bride maids' car. They were then attached to the radiator cap on each car. The cars looked really great! All the neighbors were outside watching everything.

Then we all proceeded to walk downstairs. The maids went first in front of Bea and Papa. As they came out of the doorway they were showered with rice and confetti. The photographer snapped a picture of each in turn and then Papa and Bea together. Everyone got into the cars and we drove down to St. Peters church. The wedding was to start at 4 o'clock.

The alter was beautifully decorated with baskets of flowers and a long white rug was laid down the isle of the church just before the brides maids started down to the alter. The priest, Mike and the ushers were waiting at the alter. While the organist played "Here Comes the Bride" they marched in, Lana V. first then Betty, then Bea "Commare" followed by Jennie as the Maid of Honor. Then came Bea and Papa. Bea looking positively beautiful and I couldn't help crying a little as I looked at her. She looked like she was floating on a white cloud. When they reached the first pew Papa lifted Bea's veil and kissed her and then shook Mike's hand. Bea took hold of Mike's arm and walked up the alter steps to the priest. Father Rowland performed the wedding ceremony.

The church was very quiet; you could almost hear a pin drop as the priest said. "Do you B.S. take M.C. for your husband and she said "I do". Then "Do you M.C. take B.S. for your etc." and he said "I do." As the priest blessed them the choir girl sang Ave Maria. It was so beautiful I couldn't help crying. Then they exchanged rings and kissed. The music sounded again and they marched down the isle again… as "Man and Wife". On the steps of the church more pictures were taken then they got into the cars and boy did they blow those car horns and off they went to Monarch's studio to have pictures taken. Pete Chiola and I didn't stay there though. Pete took me back home and all the relatives came up to the house from church.

Nancy and Tom Stewart came from Beverly. Katie and Kenny Stone came from Bloomfield and Aunt Caroline DeLorenzo and daughter Bea came from Beverly also.

Right to Left: Steven Scampsky, Bartolomea Serra, John Charowsky, Giovannina Serra, Michael Charowsky, Bartolomea (Serra) Charowsky, Tony Chiola, Bartolomea Serra, Henry Syzpanski, Lina Villanti

Summers Down the Jersey Shore

Written by Lorraine Charowsky

This is dedicated to Bartolomea (Serra) Charowsky and Michael Charowsky and all their children and grandchildren. May the smell of a warm, summer breeze spark as many fond memories for you as they have for me.

Michael and Bartolomea (Serra) Charowsky

Isn't it strange that one whiff of a particular scent can sometimes recall a lifetime of memories? We all have a few favorite smells like freshly baked cookies, a campfire, newly mowed grass that remind us of good times long past. There are smells that mark tradition like Christmas trees in winter. They are smells you can always count on to remind you of home, holidays, your loved ones, and all the memories related to those special times. And then, there are other more elusive smells like a faint wisp of perfume as a woman walks by that reminds you of someone used to know, and suddenly all these memories coming flooding back to you with an eerie clarity, as if they only happened yesterday.

Sometimes when the wind is just right and it's a balmy day in late spring, I can smell summer coming. I can't really describe what I mean. Maybe it's the smell of the ocean wafting in on a warm breeze, but whatever that smell is, it makes me smile. Summer is my favorite time of year, and the smells of summer time always bring me memories of my grandparents. For at least the first decade of my life, I spent several weeks every summer down the Jersey shore at my father's parents' bungalow in Ortley Beach. I loved it – the beach, the boardwalk, the fun, the food. I loved it all! But, I especially loved spending time with my family.

There's just something special about grandparents. Maybe it's because they love to spoil their grandchildren. Maybe it's because they are like our parents, but minus the disciplining part. Either way, I just know I got very excited whenever they came over or we visited them. Visiting at the shore was very special because it was usually a long visit, so I didn't have to rush to fit everything I wanted to do with them into a short time. It felt like I had forever on my side. We were on vacation. Life was slow and leisurely. I couldn't have wanted more. All those summers seem so long past. It's funny because now, so many years later, all I remember are the little things, just all the mundane details that add up to life down at the shore.

If I think hard enough, I can smell the old wood, the salty, musty odor of that bungalow. I smell peaches ripening on the kitchen counter, and I remember going to the farmer's market to get fresh produce. My grandma and I loved fresh peaches. At the sink, I can smell Palmolive dish liquid. We used to make homemade soap bubbles and blow bubbles on the front porch. There's a pitcher of lemonade on the kitchen table. My grandma taught me how to make lemonade. I still make it the way she showed me. The secret is to add one lime with all those lemons. I spent many mornings sitting in that little kitchen talking with my grandma about everything and nothing. In the hall, there's a chest of drawers where my grandmother kept the linens. The linens smelled like lavender. I liked the smell, and I remember asking Grandma why the towels smelled that way. She explained to me what a sachet is and that it makes your linens smell good and helps keep bugs away. I think I was the only kid in third grade who knew what a sachet was. My grandmother loved all pretty smelling things. The hall closet was always full of scented soaps, lotions, perfumes, and talcum powders. And, of course, I tried every one of them! I learned everything I know about being "girly" from my grandmother. Sometimes she would take me with her to the salon down there, and she'd even let me pick out what color nail polish she should get done on her fingernails. No matter how bright the shade of pink I chose would inevitably be, she always liked it and told me I had made a beautiful choice.

Bartolomea (Serra) Charowsky

Some days, we would all go to play miniature golf, go for ice cream or to the Italian bakery for bread, pastries, and cookies, but most days we'd be at the beach. My grandmother was the consummate sun worshipper. She always had several different kinds of tropical coconut scented suntan lotions and oils. I can still picture her lying out, her Sicilian complexion deeply bronzed, wearing those oversized dark sunglasses of hers, waving to me as I played in the surf. My aunts, uncles, and cousins would all come down in the summer, too. There would be plenty of people around all the time, and lots of other kids to play with. We spent so many hours on that beach. Late in the afternoon, the adults would begin rounding up their respective children, and we kids always wanted to stay just a little bit longer. Then it would be pointed out to us that the sooner we all went back to shower, change, and have dinner, the sooner we would get to the boardwalk. If everyone was visiting, we'd have to go back in shifts, so there wasn't as long of a wait for the shower.

Then, the adults would make dinner arrangements. Fish dinners were a special treat down the shore. Someone would go for the flounder or haddock at the market, either pre-made with French fries and Cole slaw, or someone would bread it and fry it up at the bungalow. We'd take dinner out to the front porch and all eat together. Somehow, we'd still have room for dessert at the boardwalk. We might get cotton candy, orange/vanilla swirled ice cream cones, funnel cake, waffle ice cream sandwiches, oversized lollipops, red rope licorice, and of course we would pick out a mix of salt-water taffy to take home. All the grandchildren would ride the "kiddie" rides, and some of the adults would ride the "big" rides. We would try to win prizes playing the games and play skeeball. Some nights we'd stay for the fireworks display. We'd get all tuckered out and head back to the bungalow.

My grandfather was a night person, like myself. Sometimes, I would sleep in "the little room," and I remember my grandpa checking on me every now and then. I had trouble falling asleep when I was young, and I was afraid of the dark. I would remind him to keep a light on for me. Some nights he would cook himself a little late night snack, and if I was awake, it always smelled so yummy. One thing I remember him making was this mix of cut up hot dogs with onions and baked beans. Sometimes I would come out if I couldn't sleep, and he'd give me a little plate and share with me. I still don't know exactly what he did or added to make it taste so good, but to this day, I've never had better "beanie-weenie."

Michael Charowsky

Being that my grandfather was a late riser, my grandmother would often ask me to wake him in the morning. I think it took me nearly a whole summer to master the art of waking my grandpa up without the little dog Ebony nipping my heels as I left the room. Ebony was very protective and attached to my grandfather. Whenever he would leave to go to the store, Ebony would sit on the porch looking out the window whimpering and whining until his return. Grandpa would come back with the newspaper, and sometimes he might bring me something special like Cracker Jack, Tootsie Rolls, or Dum-Dum Pops. I remember sitting on the porch playing while he read the paper or clipped coupons. He would always offer me the funnies to read.

Lorraine and Eileen Charowsky

Sometimes, if it was rainy and we had to stay in, we might do something crafty with the old newspapers. We folded paper hats. He taught me all sorts of little tricks, most of which I've long forgotten, but one I do remember is how to turn a newspaper back into a tree. He would roll a few pages together and snip the top of it a few times and pull it a particular way until it started to look like a palm tree. I just loved that kind of stuff. Another favorite rainy day past time was playing cards. I remember "helping" my grandparents play solitaire, or playing war, go fish, or gin rummy with one or both of them. My grandmother tried to teach me how to play poker, but I could never (still can't, in fact) remember what all the hands are and which ones beat which. Maybe someday I'll master the game of poker, although by then, I'll probably have grandchildren of my own…

I never knew it until much later, but I was very fortunate. I was so lucky to have had all those fun times with my family down the shore and shared all those moments with my grandparents. I was the first of seven grandchildren, and there are at least five years between the ages of myself and the rest of my cousins, so I had a great amount of attention from my grandparents all to myself for a long while. I had the chance to get to know them, and I have so many fond memories that I will never forget. My grandparents both passed in the mid-1990s, but I hope we'll all hold onto whatever wonderful memories we have of them. For me, whenever I catch the smell of summer floating in on the breeze, I will think of all those days down the shore with a smile on my face and love in my heart.

Peir-Lian Charowsky, Kathleen and Grace Wilson, Eileen and Lorraine Charowsky

My "Big" Sister Bartolomea
Written by Maria (Serra) Goldrick
Photo supplied by Janice Charowsky

Bartolomea (Serra) Charowsky

I would like to write something about my oldest sister, who was named Bartolomea, after my father's mother. A very unusual name to be sure. I have never heard the name outside our own Serra family. As we were growing up, my mother lovingly called her "Bartoleda," "Beda," or "Bea" for short. She was always my "big" sister to me, but was teased a lot because of her strange name. My parents were married for nine years before Beta was born and she was a very welcome little baby indeed!

My cousin Dominick Villanti once told me my parents were so happy they treated her like she was a little princess for a long time, I guess until the rest of us were born. Bea and I were seven years apart in age and her circle of friends were different than mine as youngsters.

As time went on, Bea met and married Michael Charowsky and they eventually raised five children. Bea and I grew closer as adults, I often baby-sat for her children after I came home from work, and spent many happy years with my nieces and nephews while they were growing up on Duncan Ave. in Jersey City.

Bea always loved perfumes, make-up and beautiful jewelry and had a great flare for selling Avon products, which she did for over forty years. She was known as the "Avon Lady" by friends and neighbors in Jersey City. I was among her steady list of customers and I often joked with her, saying she could sell *anything* to *anyone*, even ice to as Eskimo. She would just laugh, she was quite happy selling Avon products from her home, which provided her with a little income and a little diversion as well- two things necessary when raising five small children.

After I got married Bea often baby-sat for my children Kathleen and Michael too.

Bea taught me many things: how to polish my nails and apply make-up, but especially to love each other and to cherish family. My sister loved her children, grandchildren and all her nieces and nephews very much.

I have many fond memories of us all at Ortley Beach down at the Jersey Shore where Bea and Mike had their summer bungalow and invited us down for vacations year after year. I will never forget her cheerfulness and love for life. I love her very much and still miss her terribly. May God Bless you, Bea, my "big" sister Bartolomea.

A Personal note from your God-Mother
Written by Mary (Serra) Goldrick
Photo supplied by Giovannina (Serra) Obert

    I would like to say how particularly proud I have always been of my nephew Michael Jude Charowsky and his dear wife Elena. With a specially equipped car Michael has been able to drive himself and Elena to their jobs each day and any place else they need to get to for the tasks of daily living. Their love, determination and dedication to each other have enabled them to maintain a loving marriage and home for the past twenty-two years. Although Michael was born with a physical handicap and is short in stature, he has always stood head and shoulders ABOVE the rest of us. Mike and Elena will *always* have my *love, respect* and *admiration*. I congratulate their courage and wish them my heartfelt happiness in their lives together. They are truly "beautiful!" May God Bless and protect them each day.

Elena (Mercante) and Michael Charowsky
Wedding Day - October 18, 1981

My Sister Jennie

Written by Mary (Serra) Goldrick
Photos supplied by Giovannina (Serra) Obert

Giovannina (Serra) Obert

Jennie always helped me do my homework. She was a great inspiration for me. We wrote, (I should say she wrote) this poem that was one of my homework assignments in grammar school. I memorized it and never forgot it.

Abe Lincoln

Lincoln was poor when he was a babe,
But we all remember him as "Honest Abe"
Lincoln was loyal, honest and true
But greatest of all, he was President too
Lincoln loved people no matter what faith
In a crowded movie house, he met his fate!

I still have the little book with the original written by her. I guess I must have been in the 5th grade at the time. I know she will probably remember writing this for me. I also have a story she wrote for me about the first "Thanksgiving" in the "New Land".

Our Christmas's were not extravagant. We were lucky to get one toy, a ball or something small. We were quite poor growing up. The first doll I ever got was from my sister, Giovannina after she got her first job in ElRam and it was a "Dytee Doll" (one that drinks and wets) and I was 11 years old. I remember my sister took me to the '5 and 10 Cent Store' and asked the lady for the doll. She looked at me and said, "Aren't you a little too old for a doll?" Of course, I started to cry; little did she realize it was my very *first* doll. Oh well, some thing just stick in our memories. But I'll always love and cherish my sister for being so good to her little sister. She always was and still is a wonderful sister, always thinking of others and very generous to everyone!

Because of my sister Jennie's advice to take the commercial course in Lincoln High School, I learned business courses, typing, shorthand, and how to use the business machines of those days, such as the Dictaphone. I was able to graduate and get an "office" job in Western Electric in stead of having to work in the factory where she and Bea and Mike and Cousin Bea and my brother Johnny worked. Also the starting salary was more for the office workers. Office hours were from 8:30 AM to 5:15 PM. One hour for lunch. It was quite a luxury not to start work at 7 AM and work to 3:30, with only a ½ hour lunch. In the factory working on the noisy punch press machines or whatever. Jennie always wanted me to go to college, but my father refused to let me go to school for any longer than the law demanded.

Giovannina (Serra) Obert and Marie (Serra) Goldrick

Que Sera, Sera – Whatever Will Be, Will Be

Written by Christopher Obert
Photos supplied by Nancy (Blanchette) Obert and Giovannina (Serra) Obert

If I think back, the oldest memory I have is of my mother. She has always been there for me. I did not always know this at the time, but I know it now. I suppose that most children think that they have the best mom in the world, and I am sure that from their point of view they are right. I am no different. I think my mom is the greatest. Anything she has ever done, she always had the best interests for me and my brother and sisters in mind. Now don't get me wrong, my mom is not perfect. She, like all of us, has made lots of mistakes and stumbled from time to time but it is the fact that she just keeps getting back up and trying again that I am the most proud of. It is this lesson, "Never Give Up" which she has taught me that was the driving force behind this book being printed.

My mom, Giovannina Serra Obert

Christopher Obert

My oldest memory is from when I was very young and my mother would hold me in her arms and sing, "Que Sera, Sera". I never felt so happy and safe as I did when she would hold me and sing. As I sit here and type this, I hold back the tears and smile. For a long time now, I have been a little too big and she has been a little too small to hold me in her arms, but I have not forgotten the feeling. I never thought I would ever feel that way again, but I was wrong. Years later, when I held my children in my arms, I had a similar feeling. I felt so happy and now it was my job to make my children feel safe. I do not remember singing to them, but I do remember so many other things. I hope that my children can remember something special from that time that they will treasure and carry into the future.

Four generations: Maria Concetta, Chris, Giovannina and Shari.

Another memory of my mom is from 1975 when I was in the 7th grade. I had to write two poems for English class. I hated reading poems, never mind writing them. My mother sat down with me and we wrote this poem together…

The Chores of Mother Nature
By Giovannina Obert and Christopher Obert

The Chores of Mother Nature
Are Wondrous to Behold.
Each season tells a story,
That always is retold.

Skies of Blue, Rainbow Bright
Sea of Color, Majestic White
Winter, Spring, Summer and Fall
Mother Nature did it all!

I can still remember sitting there. It was a kind of heaven and hell at the same time that all children go through when doing homework with their parent. I did not want to be there but I appreciated the help. When we were done with the two poems, I was very happy. The poems were very good and I was very proud of them. The second poem has been lost through the years but I still have "The Chores of Mother Nature". This one event changed me. After that day, I started to write poems, and now, 28 years later, I am thinking that my next book may be a collection of my poetry; all of this because my mom took the time to help me with a homework assignment.

Some of My Memories...

By Mary Fortin

Mary (Obert) Fortin

Growing up, the summers seemed so long, but some of the best times were when Nonna & Nonno would visit us. Nonno and my Dad would play pinochle till all hours of the night. They loved playing and boy, could it get LOUD!! It seemed so exciting! One summer, they taught me how to play. I was thrilled. The thrill didn't last long though. I discovered that they both had amazing memories. If I put a certain card down and it was wrong they'd say "Why didn't you play that two hands ago, when he put that down and I put this down." It quickly got to the point where I didn't want to play anymore. I was content just to watch them, safely out of the line of fire!

The worst night of my life was when my brother Ed turned 17. We had had a little party for him, just the family, that night. Then he went over to his girlfriend Heather's house. Later that evening, I answered the phone. It was Officer Michaud from the Amesbury Police. He wanted to talk to my Dad. He asked him to come to the hospital and identify his son. Didn't say if he was alive or dead, just come down and identify him. After he left, my Mother gathered us all around her. We knelt down on the floor & started saying the rosary. It seemed like years before we heard from Dad. Ed was alive but in very critical condition. We later learned that when he left Heather's, he started to fall asleep at the wheel. He awoke with a start, saw a mailbox, and swerved to avoid hitting it. By doing that, he hit the only tree in the area. He later remembers hearing someone say "Why are you rushing to get him out. He's already dead!" Thank God that they did. Ed was in the hospital for some time, but he survived!!!

My Granddaughter Laura was just 2 at the time. She was supposed to be eating her grilled cheese sandwich, but just wasn't hungry. I asked her if she wanted any more. She looked at me with big brown eyes and said, "No, but I don't suppose you have any Lollipops around!" Lollypops are her favorite, even to this day. She knew that her limit was 1 a day. Grandpa kept them hidden in his tool chest. We caught her one day with her hand in the chest. "Laura" we told her "You already had one." She answered back, "I know, I'm just browsing!!!"

Sun Rise, Sun Set

Written by Christopher Obert

As I sit here and compile this book, I wonder why this book project has become so important to me. What is the reason? As I write this section, I believe I have found my answer. My family! To know and understand our past is very important. To know and understand our relatives is equally important. But we do not live in the past nor do we reside with our relatives. We live in the present with our immediate families. All of creation revolves around family and it is our highest duty to love, nurture and honor them. It is them, our family, yours and mine, that is the reason for this book. So while I collect stories about other people and families I have to make sure to include the story of me and my family.

Nancy Blanchette, the girl I fell in love with!

Many years ago, someone came into my life that changed me completely. I did not know it instantly but it did not take long to figure out that my life had been altered. This person was Nancy Blanchette. A friend of mine had set us up on a bind date. She was the only blind date I had ever been on and I can truly say that I was blind before I met her. She has opened my eyes to so many things and emotions. I am extremely indebted to her. I can still remember our second date. We went to a Chinese restaurant and the little yellow slip of paper in my fortune cookie said "Stop searching forever, happiness is just next to you!" I kidded "Does this mean that I'm going to marry you?" We laughed and smiled and continued on our date. Nancy did not see me save that fortune.

STOP SEARCHING FOREVER
HAPPINESS IS JUST NEXT TO YOU.

I still have and carry my fortune

We dated for a year, and what a year. We fought like cats and dogs but we loved like Romeo and Juliet. She helped me to find myself and she helped me find something I treasure even more. Together we found our children. Everyone thought we were too young to be starting a family, but God knew best. Shari Lyn Obert was born in 1982. Shari is our sweet angel and made our life even better. Jason Edward Obert was born in 1985. He was our quiet boy that made life wonderful just by smiling at you.

237

Nancy and Chris at Nancy's Prom 1981

Jason and Chris

Nancy and Shari

Jason and Shari not wanting to go to bed!

Jason and Shari playing nicely, for a change!

Nancy Sue (Blanchette) Obert

Nancy is the daughter of Hervè and Agnes Blanchette. She grew up in Methuen and graduated from St. Mary's in Lawrence. She has worked in the banking world on and off since her senior year of high school, only leaving the field for eight years to operate an in home day care center in order to be home with our children, and to work for one year at Microfab Inc in Amesbury. She has been an active member of the Haverhill Greenleaf PTA and was instrumental in the playground project. She loves reading, gardening and traveling, but spends most of her time taking care of me and the kids… of which she does an excellent job!

Shari Lyn Obert

She was one of the most intelligent and talkative children I have ever seen. She loves to read and has read more books than anyone I have ever known. I can still remember the day she told me she was "just about done" reading all of the books in the children section of the Haverhill Library. Shari was also a very active child, participating in dance, gymnastics and "T-Ball". She has a Silver Award from The Girls Scouts. She has been to Italy twice, once during her sophomore year and once during her senior year of high school. She plans a return visit during the summer of 2004. She was on the Math Team and a member of the Key Club in high school. In addition, she volunteered at the Haverhill Public Library and was a visiting volunteer in Virginia. Today, Shari is a senior, attending Boston College with a double major in English and History.

Jason Edward Obert

Jason was a very quiet child that expressed himself with his eyes. Jason was an active child engaging in floor hockey, soccer and indoor wall climbing. He enjoyed going on bike rides and going fishing. He could also sit for hours playing with his Hot Wheels and Matchbox cars or building things with his Legos. Jason has just graduated from Whittier Vocational Technical High School studying carpentry. While in school, he worked on many projects big and small, such as tables, shelves and sheds. He worked off the school grounds doing on-site construction. Today he, like most other 18 year olds, loves automobiles. He has worked full time in house construction and is now woring full time at Circuit City. He also attends classes at Northern Essex Community College.

Christopher Paul Obert

I am a student of science and a fan of science fiction. I love to read and collect books and comic books. I like to write poetry and songs. I enjoy many styles of music. Some of my favorite performers are: Black Sabbath, Dean Martin, The Monkees, Joan Jett, Bobby Sherman and my ultimate favorite… KISS.

I am to some extent, a career student. I have been going to college since 1983. I love to learn new things and plan on taking courses forever. I have attended classes at Northern Essex Community College (NECC), University of Lowell, and Boston's Museum of Science. I have completed courses and certificates online and through the mail at NECC, California State University, Sacramento and North American Correspondence Schools. I have attended lectures at the Museum of Science and Harvard. I have a Bachelor of Science in Manufacturing Technology from Trinity College and University. I have two certificates from NECC, one in Wastewater Technology and one in Web Page Design and Development. I have an Associate in Arts, General Studies from NECC and will complete another Associate in Arts, Computer & Information Sciences, in the fall.

I volunteered at the Boston Museum of Science, and I worked as a technician at Nucletronix Inc. for two years. My career has been working for Western Electric / AT&T / Lucent for the past 18 years. In August of 2001, I took a package to leave the company to go back to school in order to update my computer skills. In addition, I started to do serious work on my mother's family tree and the book that you now hold in your hands.

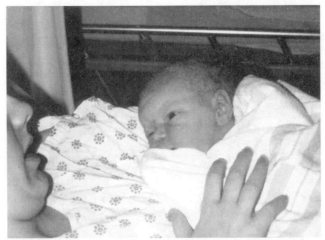

The day our life changed, April 29, 1982, the day Shari was born.

Lightning strikes again, May 31, 1985, the day Jason is born.

My Family (1985) Shari, Nancy, Jason and Precious

241

Shari Lyn Obert

Shari Obert

Jason Edward Obert
with Tiger and Bo-Bo Jason's teddy bears
and Tiger and Charlie, Chris' teddy bears.

Jason Obert

Anyone that knows me well understands that I could not write a story about my family without mentioning Cook. Precious was the name of my best friend, his nick-name was "Cook". If you asked me, I could tell you hundreds of stories about our adventures together. If you are wondering why I would include a few words about a cat, I will leave you with this question: "How complete would a biography of Charlie Brown be without mentioning Snoopy?" He was, and still is, the best friend I could every have. I love you buddy!

Precious "Cook", he was not my pet, he was my friend

I cannot find the words to tell you just how much my family means to me, except that they are a part of my soul. They are all that I live for and have made me believe much more strongly in God and myself. As I said in the beginning of this book, "I am nothing without them."

My Family (2001) Jason, Nancy, Shari & me

Look out Mr. Roberts

Written by Christopher Obert

Most Serra family members have seen the old movie "Mr. Roberts". The light hearted comedy starred Henry Fonda, Jack Lemmon and James Cagney. But few family members know the Geremy Ayers/Mr. Roberts story.

Back in November of 1991, while Geremy was still attending Haverhill High School, he worked as a part-time actor at the local theatre. Geremy played a Navy midshipman in the Amesbury Playhouse version of "Mr. Roberts". One night backstage during the evenings performance, a prop gun, used as a sound effect, accidentally went off and shot Geremy in the stomach. He received painful 2nd degree powder burns to his midsection. He was rushed to the local hospital still wearing his Navy bellbottoms and button-down shirt. Geremy was treated and released. Unfortunately, he did not make it back for the second act, but he did perform the next day and finished out the show's run. The cast and crew wanted to show their support and thanks for Geremy. One evening after a show, Pat Rosano, the actor who played the captain, presented Geremy with an authentic Purple Heart medal. Mr. Rosano pinned it on Geremy stating, "for being wounded in the line of duty" as the cast looked on.

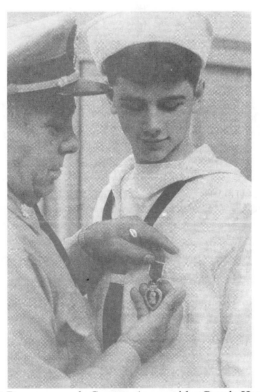

Pat Rosano awards Geremy Ayers with a Purple Heart.

Star Trek and the Family

Written by Christopher Obert

James "Scotty" Doohan and Jason Obert

What is it about Star Trek that has kept it one of the greatest American mythologies? It has endured for more than 30 years, exploring the human condition. It is a story that has been told through five TV series, one animated series, numerous motion pictures, dozens of comic book series, hundreds of paperback books and scores of technical manuals and blueprints. Whatever it is, it has infected the Serra family. Many of the Serras consider themselves Star Trek fans. Many looked forward to each week's episode. The Obert family (also Star Trek fans) would talk for hours among themselves and with their Serra cousins about the future.

Mary Obert wrote to Walter Koenig (Pavel Chekov) back in the 1960's and got sent a photo of Walter (that I stole from her... I mean, "borrowed" from her!). Like my sister, I also love Star Trek. I follow all the TV shows, movies and books. I remember back in the 1970's looking at books and blueprints with my cousins and then running to the local library to make copies for everyone. I also wrote letters to some of the stars of the show, in which many sent photos back. My favorite is from Whoopi Goldberg (Guinan).

I wrote to apologize to Whoopi! I was not happy when I first heard that she was joining Star Trek – The Next Generation. It is not that I did not like her, I did. It was just that I felt that she was not right for Star Trek. But after I watched her performance on the show, I thought she was excellent. I especially liked the episode "Yesterday's Enterprise". So I wrote her telling her that I was originally against her joining the Star Trek team, but that she has done an excellent job. She sent me a photo thanking me. That was so cool! In the 1990's my wife Nancy and I took our son Jason to the local mall so he could meet James Doohan (Montgomery "Scotty" Scott). We had a great time; we got autographs and a quick photo. I have no doubt that Star Trek will still be popular for my grandkids...

One last Serra / Star Trek note: one of the last scenes in the 2002 Star Trek movie "Nemesis", shows the USS Enterprise in space dock above Italy, Sicily and the Aeolian Islands!

A Trip to the USS Nautilus and Submarine Museum

Written by Christopher Obert
Photos by Christopher & Nancy Obert

In July 2002 I turned 40. To celebrate, my wife, Nancy, took me to Foxwoods Casino in Connecticut. The next day on the way home, we were going to stop at a local winery. My wife was looking at a tourist map and said that we could stop at a nearby museum about submarines. Nancy knew that I liked submarines and thought I would like that. She said that they had some sub there named Nautilus. I said "What, THE Nautilus?" The USS Nautilus was the world's first nuclear submarine and one of my favorite things growing up. I could not believe it, The USS Nautilus. The reason I have included this story is not the historic adventures of the USS Nautilus and her crew. Those stories are important but it is because of a relatively small submarine that is sitting in front of the museum. It is a Japanese Submarine, the kind used during WWII. When we went to the museum, I instantly recognized this type of submarine. When I was younger, I used to look through a scrapbook of postcards that my mother (Giovannina Serra) had collected. The postcards were from WWII and I thought that they were awesome. There was one that I really liked. It showed a Japanese Suicide Submarine. That postcard is one of the images that I have included in the World War II section of this book. This was not the same sub, but I just had to include this story to show people that you never know when you may someday come face to face with a piece of history that ties you to other family members!

Nancy (Blanchette) Obert in front of the Japanese Submarine

Christopher Obert in front of the USS Nautilus

Christmas through Children's Eyes
Written by Charlotte (Simms) Serra

Carlotte on her wedding day

       One of my warmest memories of Christmas is from a time long ago. It was our first Christmas at the Wartberg Orphan Farm School. You see my sister Margie and I were placed in an orphanage when our parents William and Anna passed away within a month apart. My sister Mary would join us later, she was taken to my aunt and uncle's but being sad and unhappy, she missed us and wanted to be with her two younger sisters & nothing can replace a home with loving parents and a big family however, what we were about to experience for the first time was magical to three little girls from Brooklyn. Christmas at the orphanage was warm and beautiful, early Christmas eve we the lighting of the tree. The tree was a big pine tree that stood in the center of the front lawn, it had hand made ornaments the orphan children made out of tin can tops, toy blocks, beads and almost anything the children found that could be crafted into sparkling tree decorations. The pastor said a Christmas prayer and when he said - LET THERE BE LIGHT, - the tree lit up to all the children's wonder and amazement. We sung traditional Christmas carols around the tree and then, it was time for the Christmas pageant. We were all gathered together and brought to the pastor's house there, the pastor's wife and her sister dressed us in white silk robes, angels' wings and, gold garland for halos on our head & we were all given small candles to hold and then it was off to St. John's Lutheran church. When we arrived at the church all the lights were out as we walked down the isles of the church with our lit candles, we sang very softly Christmas carols such as "Silent Night" and "Away in a Manger". When we reached the alter we formed the cross, it was breath taking to behold. People came from all over to see our Christmas Pageant. It was a tradition for many of the visitors. After our position of the cross we all went to our seats and with out delay the show began with the Nativity.

       The Children of the orphanage played all the roles of the nativity, the Baby Jesus was a large flashlight wrapped in a small blanket, so it looked like rays of Heaven's light shining from our Lord's tiny face. The wise man said their verses and the other characters spoke. Then we were up again and placed around the piano. We sang more carols such as "Hark the Herald Angels Sing" and "Joy to the World". The church was packed. Everyone wanted to witness our beautiful pageant. It was truly a magical night. After the pageant ended we went back to our cottages, hung our long light brown cotton stockings on the foot of the bed post, washed our faces, brushed our teeth and went to bed. As we lay in our beds dozing off to sleep you couldn't hear a thing. The silence was so peaceful. Then in the far distance we heard sleigh bells. We all jumped up out of our beds and ran to the window. It was snowing and the ground looked like it was covered with millions of tiny diamonds glimmering in the moonlight just like the cover of a Christmas card. What we saw next was the most exciting for three little city girls, it was Santa Clause coming down from outside the gates, he was pulled in a big sleigh by two white horses and the straps had jingle bells on them. Santa drove all around the cottages so that all the children could see him, what excitement it was to see Santa Clause right in front of our very eyes. When Santa had gone we all jumped back into our beds and quickly went back to sleep. Christmas morning was filled with goodies and surprises, the stockings were filled to overflowing with candy, peppermint canes, marzipan, nuts, tangerines and apples. We all dressed and went down stairs for breakfast. After breakfast we were off to church again for morning services, then it was back to the cottages to open presents under the tree some of the gifts I received were a pair of white ice skates, a skirt, a sweater, new socks, a small bottle of perfume, gloves, and ear muffs. After opening our gifts we would enjoy a wonderful Christmas holiday, sleigh riding and ice skating, God was certainly with us, watching over all the orphan children, making sure we all had a joyous Christmas.

Charlotte Serra and her children Christmas 1963
Donna, Jackie, Mary Lynn, Dominick and Johnny

Charlotte (Simms) Serra

Written by Antonio "Tony" Serra

Tony Serra

Charlotte Simms Serra is the most beautiful woman that I have ever known. Her love for children has no limits and her strength of spirit is unsurpassed. Charlotte has had to face many obstacles in her life, as a small child she lost her parents within a month apart. She was placed in an orphanage soon after and although she was cared for and nurtured; it can never take the place of the loving parents she adored. Charlotte remained in the orphanage till the age of eighteen. About a year later she met and married Giovani Battista Serra. She would have eight children with him: Dominick, Donna, John, Mary, Jacqueline, Carol, Anthony and Joseph. I have often heard her say "raising my babies was the happiest times of my life", and I believe this to be true. When ever she is around babies or children her face lights up and you can't help feel the overflow of joy and love that comes from her heart. Charlotte is a very special woman; she is kind, gentle, and very giving. If she knows that you are in need she will make sure you are taken care of without any questions asked! I believe when God created her he took extra time to make her so beautiful and special. I am very blessed to have her and thank God every day for letting me be a part of her life. How do I know so much about Charlotte Simms Serra, you ask? Well, she's my mom and I have experienced all of her love first hand. That is why I asked her to put as many of her memories in this book. I used to sit on the floor in our living room and she would tell us these heart warming stories about a time when peace and love was given more freely, and people cherished the simple things in life. My mom just went through an awful time in her life, she developed breast cancer and underwent surgery to have it removed, she is fighting to stay healthy, and I pray everyday that God will bless her, and give her many more years of happiness!

Charlotte dancing with her son Tony

Note: Sadly during the time Tony and I were working on this book, Charlotte, Tony's mom passed away. She was a very kind and giving person, and I wish the Serra family well.

Mom & Dad
Written by Donna (Serra) Lorusso

Today is a day to celebrate
The moment in your life
When two hearts came together
And rejoiced as man and wife

Remember on your wedding day
The promises you have made
The years have quickly come and gone
But memories never fade

Our wish for you is simple
To live your whole life through
To count your many blessings
That God has given you

Start each day with a kiss
End it with a prayer
Remember when you first met
And the joy that you two shared

Treat each other with respect
In happiness and strife
Be thoughtful and considerate
All the days of your life

You mean so much to all of us
How could we ever say
All that is wished for you
Today and every day

"We Love You"

A Dedication
John & Charlotte Serra
"50th" Wedding Anniversary
October 12, 2002

John Serra Comic Book Art Work

Written by Christopher Obert

Johnny Serra

One of my favorite memories from the 1970's is that every year we would take a trip to New Jersey to visit our grandparents, aunts and uncles and cousins. One of the things I remember most from those trips was visiting with John and Charlotte Serra and their children. We had so much in common that we always had a great time. One of the things we had in common was that we grew up loving comic books. We would sit on the bed and go through stacks of comic books. Although we liked all comics, our favorite was Marvel Comics. We would hang around for hours asking questions like, "Who was stronger, Thor or Hulk?", "Who do you like better, The Fantastic Four or the X-Men?" or "Who is your favorite superhero?" We had a great time.

One of the other things I remember was that my cousin Johnny not only liked reading comics, but liked to draw them. I would sit there just watching him sketch hero after hero. He was great! I wished that I could draw like that. I used to think how cool it would be to work with Stan Lee over at Marvel Comics. I knew that some day Johnny would work making his own comics and be famous. Well, over the years he stopped drawing and never became a famous comic book artist but he made me feel like I grew up knowing one. This story is my way of saying thanks.❧.

Here are a few examples of some of Johnny Serra's great work…

There's a Hole in My Skyline

Written by Danielle Serra
Photo by the Goldrick Family

There's a hole in my skyline. I suppose to the outside world unaccustomed to gazing at them, the absence of the Twin Towers of the World Trade Center, would be overlooked or worse yet---shrugged off. I myself found it hard to believe that I found nothing in the very spot where they stood like a beacon of success, power…maybe invincibility. Watching the events of September 11th unfold before my eyes on nearly every station was to me such a surreal experience. It wasn't happening. It couldn't have happened. The planes plummeting into the 110-story buildings. The buildings billowing smoke and fire and then crumbling to the ground. It was like something out of a Jerry Bruckheimer film. I was half expecting to see Bruce Willis or Ben Affleck coming to save the day.

But despite every clip, every replay I saw on the news or read in the paper it was still too much for me to comprehend. No one hell-bent or evil enough to do what those men did. We were safe here in the US. We're invincible. No one can touch us. That's what I wanted and needed to believe because THAT was MY skyline. My backyard. That was near home. Someone had attacked New York as well as the Pentagon and a small town in Pennsylvania using planes full of innocent civilians as bombs. Places a few hours or even minutes from my home. It must have been a movie. It just wasn't real.

I'm from Bergen County. More specifically a small suburb of New York in Jersey called Cliffside Park. I'm literally a few minutes from THE city by the George Washington Bridge or the ferry in Weehawken. From my town on the Palisades you can see right across the Hudson to the majestic skyline of NYC. At night it's got this magical glow about it. It radiates energy. But after going home this past weekend, I finally came to realize that the glow, all though not diminished, has weakened at bit. The hole in my skyline took away some of that light. What's sad is I almost couldn't tell where the Towers had been. I had to use other buildings to guide me to the spot. The smoke is still rising. You have to search a while for it but its still there. The smoke and the rubble are all that's left. It did in fact happen and this was reality. It occurred to me maybe even for the first time, when I saw the hole and the smoke snaking into the sky from it. This is our reality.

I needed to go home to see for myself that all the horror I had seen every time I put on the news was real. And now that I know this isn't fiction I have to admit I'm scared and even more saddened and heartbroken for all those innocent people that have lost their lives and all the people mourning for them. It's still too much to comprehend but it happened.

Faced with the depressing truth, I now try to focus on anything positive. Positive things such as the heroes that have gone to Ground Zero day in and day out to search the rubble with heavy hearts in the hopes of finding maybe one more person. At least I hope they do even if that flies in the face of reality at this point. But I pray and hope just the same. I think most Americans hope against hope together for something like that.
It's amazing to see Americans unite in order to revive some of that strength we've lost. Flags in windows, patriotic songs on the radio, charities and fundraising and vigils showing that although we might not be invincible and impervious to the violence of the world, our spirits are invincible. I am trying to hold on to this patriotic feeling. It's sad that it took tragedy to test our love for this country and each other. It's sad that it took a horrific act of violence to provoke this feeling of unity and pride for our country. It is this unity that is helping many of us heal.

I did not lose anyone close to me in the terrorist attack. But if this had happened a little over ten years ago I might be fatherless right now. My father worked in the North Tower for the Port Authority when I was younger. I remember going to work with him on occasion and being in awe of the massive structure he worked in. I can remember standing on one of the windowsills, resting my forehead against the glass, peering down at the street below and feeling like a giant. In fact the last time I was close to the Towers was in January when my friends and I were driving back from some club. That night I peered up instead of down at the towers and was still in complete awe.

World Trade Center, New York City

I assumed they'd always be there, part of my skyline, part of that light. Now that they're gone, it'll take some getting used to. Their absence will be an inescapable reminder of all those lives lost as well as our shaken sense of security. But I, and other Americans can learn from harsh reality created on the 11th of September. Instead of responding in hate and anger, many of us have pulled together to help those afflicted by the attack. This is the America people need to see. This is another aspect of my reality, something to fill the hole in my heart caused by the hole in my skyline.

When I looked out over the Hudson for the first time since IT happened and saw that hole in the skyline I felt fear, anger and deep-rooted sadness, but I also felt an overwhelming gratitude. It would be wrong of me to shed a few tears and go back to the way things were. Because now things are different. Now I'm grateful for a lot of things I took for granted. Grateful to be a part of this re-united America, grateful for the life I have and the freedom I have to live it as I see fit and grateful for the opportunity to watch something other than smoke rise from the hole in my skyline. A new, stronger, more united America was born from those ashes and I've never been more proud to be part of this country having witnessed what incredibly resilient men and women call this place home.

My Grandmother

Written by Gina Lorusso

Gina Bina… That's what my grandmother calls me. I love her with all my heart. She is a truly beautiful person and that is why I chose her for this character sketch.

My grandmother's name is Charlotte. She is very special to me. She is giving, loving, trusting and forgiving. I am beginning to wonder how she came to attain all of these great qualities, considering the life that she had. My grandmother did not have an easy life; in fact she had it very hard. My grandmother was born on October 18, 1931, the tenth child of eleven children to her parents Anna Lillian and William Frederick Simms. She grew up during the depression and there was not much to go around. Life was poor for her and her family. They didn't have much. I guess that is why my grandmother really appreciates everything she has in life. When my grandmother was eight years old; both of her parents died. Her and her younger sister was immediately put into an orphanage. She had many chores to do. But, I think her favorite, and it really wasn't a chore at all, was caring for the babies in the nursery. She had to feed them, wash them, clean their cribs and just make sure they were happy. This was easy for her because she loved children so much.

When my grandmother turned 18, she left the orphanage to go to work. Her life as a career woman was very short-lived, because at the age of 20 she met and married my grandfather (John). More than anything else, she wanted to have children. So, I guess when she became pregnant right away, it was a blessing. My grandmother did not plan to have eight children, but she felt that each one was a blessing from God. My mother tells me a story that when my grandmother was pregnant with her eight child, my Uncle Joe, she wanted to have a little girl. She even had the name already chosen for her. I think deep down inside she knew this would be her last baby, because she was not getting any younger. After all, she was 41 years old! The day she delivered the baby, she knew she couldn't use the name she had chosen. My grandmother tells me that my Uncle Joe was a beautiful baby and that she was never disappointed that he was not a girl. She loved him very much!

My mother made a promise to her on that day. She told her that when she got married and had her first daughter, she would give her that name that she had chosen. She would name her Gina Marie, and she did! I think that is why my grandmother and I have this special bond. Whenever we are together, we have a lot of fun, playing cards, watching old movies or just talking. My mother and I try to visit her as often as we can and when I do not see her for a long time, I really miss her. I think of her often and I know she is always thinking of me, because she is my grandma and I am her Gina Bina!

John and Charlotte Serra

Goldrick Memories

Written by Mary (Serra) Goldrick
Photos supplied by Mary Goldrick

Frank and Mary Goldrick

Frank & Mary's "Early Married Years"

When we were first married Frank and I lived in Newark, NJ on Hawkins Street right next door to his Mom, Dad and brothers, Johnny and Billy. Frank's grandmother, Elizabeth McElroy lived just around the corner with her daughter, Florence. His aunts and uncles lived at the end of the same street as we did and had cousins on the next block as well. Frank was born in Newark as was his Mom, Dad and brother and many of his relatives as well. They were of Irish descent and were always a very close knit family, just as our family was. Frank's Dad was born in the house on Hawkins St. All his family loved Italian food, so I cooked many dinners for them and we enjoyed many family get-togethers.

On St. Patrick's Day (March 17th) Frank always rented a top hat and tails and marched in the parade in Newark. He and his friends, all of whom were Irish, marched with him. The section where we lived was known as "Down Neck" in Newark. The parade started uptown at Broad and Market Streets. The shopping district was located there, with department stores such as Bamberger's, Kline's, Orbachs, etc. It was a huge parade and I often took some of my nieces and nephews to watch Frank march. They *loved* parades. That evening Frank's Mom cooked a big meal of corned beef, cabbage and potatoes. I learned to cook many of Frank's favorite meals from his Mom. She was a great baker of pies and cakes as well. I taught her how to make meatballs, tomato sauce and lasagna. We got along very well.

We lived in Newark for five years. In 1965 Frank was promoted to Supervisor and was transferred to a new Western Electric Data Center that was opening up in Maryland. Our parents were quite upset that we were moving so far away. But, it was just a 3 hour distance away and we promised to visit often, which we did every other weekend. Maryland was a lovely state and we bought a 3 bedroom ranch house in Timonium, a small town outside of Baltimore. It was a little lonesome for us being alone all of a sudden, so we decided to buy a puppy. We bought a Boston Terrier and named him Murphy. He was a frisky pup and we always took him in the car when we went back to NJ for our visits. He had a great time running around after my in-law's Boston Terrier Skippy in their back yard.

While we were living in MD, our daughter Kathleen was born in 1966. You can imagine our happiness! We had waited a long time to become parents and Kathleen was such a beautiful little baby and our pride and joy. As she grew to be a toddler she'd chase Murphy around taking his toys and playing with him. It was fun to watch her dressing him up in doll clothes. They got along so well, Murphy was patient to a point, but when he had his fill, he would run away and hide, so he could rest and take a nap. Frank was then transferred again this time back to NJ. Our parents were delighted! As were we! We settled in a beautiful town in the mountains of NJ named Livingston. We again bought a new house. It was a 3 bedroom ranch with a little brook along the back part of the yard. It was a beautiful residential town and we lived there on Deal Lane for the next ten years. In the meantime, our son Michael was born in 1967. He was such a cute blue eyed baby boy and such a joy to us. Kathleen had a baby brother to play with, our little family was now complete. Our happiness knew no bounds. He was such a happy baby and our pride and joy! Now we were closer to our families again and were able to have company for holidays and birthdays. We had many happy times visiting with my sisters Bea, Jennie and my brother Johnny and their children. Kathleen and Mike were elated to be with their cousins again. We had many, many birthday parties and spent all the holidays together, going to Newark to see Frank's family then to Jersey City to see my family. At Easter time we generally drove my Mom and Dad up to Massachusetts to visit with my sister Jennie and her children and sometimes at Thanksgiving time if there wasn't too much snow.

Kathleen took dancing lessons for many years and Mike joined the baseball team. He loved sports as much as Kathleen loved dancing and later joined Little League. We went to all his ball games and enjoyed watching him play with his friends. They won the championship and each boy received a trophy. Mike was so proud! Everyone in the family came to see Kathleen perform on stage in her annual recitals. It was a wonderful, carefree time for all of us. Frank and I really enjoyed seeing our children growing up and maturing to wonderful adults who both also went on to receive their college degrees.

Mary and Frank Goldrick

Honeymoon & Oranges

Frank and I met as co-workers in Western Electric Co. in Kearny, NJ. We were immediately attracted to each other and when the Korean War broke out and Frank enlisted in the Army, we kept up a correspondence with each other while he was away from home. In 1955 he was released from the service and returned to work in W. E. We continued to date each other more seriously now and soon became engaged. We wee then married in 1960. We had a beautiful wedding and many of our aunts and uncles and cousins from Massachusetts attended the wedding and reception in Jersey City. While I was dancing with cousin Battista Clemenzi he asked me where we were going for our honeymoon. When I told him we were driving to Miami Beach, Florida, he told me tat his uncle Alexander Clemenzi lived there. He had an orange grove along the Sunshine Highway and we would be passing right by his place so why not stop in and visit him. We did find him and was he and his wife surprised to see these 'strangers' approach. I immediately explained that my father was Domenico Serra from Italy. With that his face broke out in a big smile of recognition. He then knew who I was related to and welcomed us warmly. We had a very pleasant visit and spoke of Battista and all the relatives in Massachusetts and New Jersey. As we were getting back into our car to leave, he took a long handled pole with a small basket at the end of it and picked us some oranges and grapefruit off the trees in his front yard. His driveway was lined with beautiful tall palm trees on either side which Alexander said he planted himself. I'll *never* forget the taste of those delicious oranges and grapefruits as we continued on our trip. I can remember it so clearly as if it was yesterday even after all these years. They were definitely the best we ever ate! Nothing bcats fresh picked fruit!

Mary and Frank Goldrick

Vacations at the Jersey Shore

Janice Charowsky, Bea Charowsky, Maria Charowsky, Mary Goldrick (holding Mike Goldrick)
Front: Kathleen Goldrick

      When our children Kathleen and Mike were youngsters we spent many vacations at the Jersey Shore. Every year in July, the Western Electric Co. in Kearny, NJ closed the plant down for two weeks. In those days everyone in our family worked for the W. E. Co. so we all took vacation at the same time. My sister Bea and her husband Mike had two bungalows in Ortley Beach, which was right next to Seaside Heights where the boardwalk and rides were located. Bea and Mike and their five children stayed in the front bungalow all summer and rented the back bungalow. It was a good arrangement for us. Everyone went up on the beach in the daytime and then we would go for dinner and stroll the boardwalk in Seaside Heights in the evenings with my nieces and nephews. They were all older than Kath and Mike and loved their company and attention, they went on lots of rides together and had lots of fun with their cousins. Frank often played the wheels and won stuffed animals, toys or candy for the children. They were all delighted to win something on the boardwalk. It made their day complete. At times we won so much 'stuff' it was difficult to reload the car when it was time to go home. Nevertheless, we had loads of fun and especially when Jennie came down with the children or Johnny and Charlotte came down with their family.

Kathleen and Mike Goldrick

260

An Ode to Domenico

Written by Michael Goldrick

Michael Goldrick posing with a photo of Giovani Serra at the 2002 Serra Reunion

As the deadline nears for submission to the Serra Family History, I feel I would be remiss if I ignored Chris Obert's endless request for family stories, as I have repeatedly done over the past several months. I'm told that I was introduced into the Serra family in 1968, as an adopted baby boy. My mother has further told me that I was originally named Vinny, so I clearly possess an inherent biological appreciation for the Sicilian flavors of scungilli, antipasti and the like. Although I haven't had the opportunity to learn my true biological identity, I have had the unique opportunity to have been welcomed into a close knit unit and loving family that I have never thought of as anything but my own. Although the adoption market for such a perfect match has dwindled, my sister has been also been lucky enough to add a few more members to the Serra clan through adoption. Bottom line is that it has been a wonderful experience that I wouldn't trade for the world.

Mike Goldrick helped Chris Obert with the important job of
taking down the Serra Reunion signs after the party

Western Electric Softball

Written by Mary (Serra) Goldrick

When I was 17 I joined a Western Electric softball team. We played ball on our lunch hour for several years. I was the team captain when we won the W.E. Championship. I loved sports especially playing ball.

GIRLS' SOFTBALL CHAMPS are these Building 170 ball-tossers who defeated the Merchandise girls 11-0 in the title play-off. . . Winning team members include Elaine Paraskeuas, Anne Montamaro, Lucy Cioffi, Helen Zazula, Angela Beveridge, Marie Serra, Nancy Viggiano, Agnes Piechota, Irene Jizwick, Lorraine Nordstrom, Madeleine Dunbar, Florence Wurgel, Dorothy Bruen, and Doris Steele; while men in the photo are Coaches Herb Leadenham and Stan Gniazdowski.

Softball Oct. 1947

GIRLS' SOFTBALL CHAMPIONS RECEIVE AWARDS for their league victory, at the end of the Wekearny Club season. Left to right are Club President Kenneth D. Snyder, 8250; Marie Howard, 695; Helen Zazula, 5280-5; Rennie Kozian, 915-5; Dorothy Brienza, 5282-1; Katharine Cass, 1141; Team Captain Marie Serra, 1116-3; Wekearny Club Director Marge Lawson, 5490-3; Stephie Sielick, 1232; Elaine Paraskevas, 1129-2; Anna Nordstrom, 1141-2; Dot DeCicco, 1265, and Marion Sprake, 1141-2. . . . On the team but absent when the photograph was made were Helen Pizaravich, Beatrice Giacobbe, and Mickey Wehrle. *1948* . . . .

Mary receiving the softball award, 1948

262

My Maternal Grandparents

Written by Mary (Serra) Goldrick
Photo supplied by Mary Goldrick

Giovanna (Lazzaro) and Phillipo Costa
With their son Joseph, and grandson Joseph

My maternal grandfather, Phillipo Costa, was born in 1845 on the Island of Salina, Province of Messina, in Italy. He was a sailor in the Italian Navy and was in the War of Lissa. After his release, he went to South America where he spent four years working as a merchant seaman. On his return to Italy, he married my grandmother Giovanna Lazzaro. (She was a sister of Bartolomea Lazzaro, my father's mother. It was permissible in those days for first cousins to marry.)

Philip and Giovanna had seven children, of which only five survived. The oldest was Angela, then came Giovanna, Catherine, brother Joseph and the youngest was my mother Maria Concetta. Two other brothers died when they were small boys. In 1891 when my grandmother Giovanna was pregnant with my mother her husband decided to leave for Australia. He took his twelve year old son Joseph with him. They stayed and worked there for seven years. Grandfather Philip returned to Italy alone in 1898.

His son Joseph remained in Australia where he was working in the Savoy Restaurant. Eventually he worked his way to become the manager of a large and successful business concern in Sydney. He later married an English woman and they had a son named Joseph. Sometime after 1912 Joseph took his son who was about six years old to Italy to meet his grandparents. It was the only trip he made back to Italy as far as we know.

My mother Maria Concetta never met or saw her brother Joseph, because she was born in December of 1891, after he left for Australia, and she was gone to America when he went back to visit his parents with his son. I can't imagine how hard that was for her, never to know or see her own brother. She often talked about this with sadness.

Grandfather Philip took up his usual farm duties of growing grapes from which he made wine to be sold. His olive trees were producing now and they made olive oil which was also sold. They grew onions, potatoes and other vegetables as well.

By now all his children were married and away on their own. It was difficult work for my grandparents, but they managed the best they could until my grandmother became sick. She was sick for some time and died of heart trouble in 1928, (the year I was born).

Two years later my mother sent the passport for her father to come to America. However, due to a sudden illness, he became very sick. The operation they performed was not successful and he died in 1931. My mother never saw her parents after she got married and went to America in 1912.

Maria (Costa) & Domenico Serra 50th Wedding Anniversary
August 11, 1962

Back Row: Giovanni "John" Serra and Marie (Serra) Goldrick
Front Row: Bartolomea (Serra) Charowsky and Giovannina (Serra) Obert
Serra Family Reunion Summer 1986

Left to right: Mr. & Mrs. John Serra, Mr. & Mrs. Norman Obert, Mrs. & Mr. Domenico Serra,
Mrs. & Mr. Michael Charowsky and Mrs. & Mr. Frank Goldrick

Back: Mary, Maria w/Chris, Domenico, Michael
Dominic, Johnny, Mary Lynn, Norma, Donna, Ed, Pat, Maria, Janice, Nicky, Bobby

Back Row: Maria Concetta (Costa) Serra & Domenico Serra
Middle Row: Janice, Robert & Michael Charowsky
Front Row: Dominick & Maria Charowsky

Michael, Robert, Bea, Peir-Lian, Dominick, Mike, Janice and Maria Charowsky

Chris and Edward
Norma, Pat and Mary Obert

Nellie, Norman, Edward, Mary, Norma, Jenny, Patricia Obert

Joe, Tony, John, Dom, Donna
Carol Ann, Jackie, Charlotte, John, Mary Serra

Back: Steven, Danielle, Dominick, Gina, Daniel
Front: David, Matthew, Noelle, Rebecca and Daniel

269

Robert and Kathleen (holding Julia) Wilson
and Frank (holding Grace) & Mary Goldrick

Back: Frank & Mary Goldrick, Ed Ryan
Mike and Pam (Ryan) Goldrick, Betty Ryan

Robert and Patricia (Ferenc) Charowsky

Bobby, Heather, Patty and Robert Charowsky

271

Jennifer, Kimberly, Maria (holding Grace Wilson), Christina and Billy Dombrowski

Christina, Kimberly and Jennifer Dombrowski

Mary and Roger Fortin and Michelle Obert

Back: Michael Sova and Larry Ayers
Sitting: Kristine Sova, Zackary Sova, Heather Ayers, Geremy Ayers, Norma Ayers
Front: Amy Ayers and Kelly

Robert, Norma (Grandmont) and Ed Obert

Pat, Shirley, Bob, Angela and Ryan Ponticelli

Shari, Nancy (Blanchette), Chris and Jason Obert

Back: Edward, Norma and Mary
Murphy (dog), Patricia and Christopher

Back: Ed, Norma and Norman
Front: Cheryl (Laliberty), Rob (holding Katherine) and Giovannina (Serra) Obert

Matthew and Katherine Obert

276

Dominick, Tony, Dominick and Daniel Serra

Dominick, Danielle and Diane (McGuirl) Serra

Harry, Donna (Serra) Steven and Gina Lorusso

Harry and Donna (Serra) Lorusso

278

Roberto and Mary Lynn (Serra) Gonzalez

Carol Ann (Serra) and Daniel Downing

Mary Lynn, Carol Ann, Jacqueline and Donna

Matthew and David Serra

Robert Lewitt, Christine Flynn, Mike Goldrick, Evelyn Cranwell, Robert Wilson and Kathleen (Goldrick) Wilson, Janice Charowsky, John Wilson, Kelley Wilhelmsen, Maureen McDowall and Anthony Forgione

Frank, Mildred, Mary, Maureen and Bill Goldrick
Pam (Ryan) and Mike Goldrick, and Tony Hannan

Norma, Johnny, Janice, Bobby, Donna, Ed, Mary, Dom
Mike, Maria, Mary Lynn, Pat, Jackie, Chris
Kathleen, Mike, Joe, Maria Concetta and Domenico, Carol Ann, Tony

Shari, Chris Jason, Pam (Friend), Mike, Robert, Kathleen
In front of the Ellis Island Wall of Remembrance

282

Standing: Jason Obert
Front: Jennifer Dombrowski, Heather and Robert Charowsky, Shari Obert and Christina Dombrowski

Lorraine, Shari, Michelle, Geremy
Eileen, Ryan, Amy, Christina
Heather, Robert, Jason, Jennifer, Angela

283

Roger and Mary Fortin with Michelle Obert and daughter Emma

Cathy, Dominick and Lorraine Charowsky

Robert, Heather, Patty and Bobby Charowsky

Frank and Mary Goldrick (holding) Julia Wilson with Michael Goldrick (holding Grace Wilson)
Robert Wilson and Kathleen Wilson

William, Jennifer, Kimberly, Christina and Maria Dombrowski

1st cousins
Back: Chris, Dominick, Mary, Patricia and Maria
Front: Kathleen, Norma, Michael and Robert

2nd cousins with one 2nd cousin once removed (baby Emma)
Left to Right: Jason, Geremy, Angela, Shari, Michelle (holding Emma), Amy, Grace, Lorraine
Robert, Kimberly, Jennifer, Christina (holding Julia) and Heather

286

Domenico Serra Family Notes:

History is the ship carrying living memories into the future.

--Stephen Spender (1909-1995)

Maria Concetta Serra and Giovanni Clemenzi Family

The Great Salem Fire - 25 June 1914

Written by Ann Clemenzi.

What I remember from my father's (Angelo Clemenzi) telling of the story, my grandparents John and Concetta (Serra) Clemenzi were living in Salem. They were expecting one child at that time - Sophie (Clemenzi) Villanti. My grandfather loaded up the truck with as much as he could from their home including wife and child. As they were leaving Salem, they passed an orphanage. The orphanage had no way of getting the children out of Salem. John Clemenzi dumped their belongings and loaded as many kids in his truck as possible. They made it to Beverly and lost all their belongings.

Written by Sophie (Clemenzi) Villanti

My parents could only save a fan (with streamers attached) from the fruit store. When they were crossing the bridge my father said "What good is just a fan?" and then threw it over into the river. "We're starting over from scratch!"

Salem Fire Poem

When I was three, I watched the Salem fire.
It burned all night (or then I thought it did)
and I stood in my crib & watched it burn.
The sky was bright red; everything was red
out on the lawn, my mother's white dress looked
rose-red; my white enameled crib was red
and my hands holding to its rods—
the brass knobs holding specks of fire—

Elizabeth Bishop

Note: The Great Salem Fire devastated 252 acres, destroyed 1,800 buildings, and rendered 15,000 people homeless.

Post cards of the Great Salem Fire

Homeless endeavoring to save their household goods at the big Salem fire.

Bird's eye view of ruins of Great Salem Fire.

Post cards of the Great Salem Fire

Feeding homeless children at the Great Salem Fire.

The Great Salem Fire

Memories from Sophia (Clemenzi) Villanti.

Written by Catherine (Villanti) Constantelo and Angela Villanti
as told to them by Sophia (Clemenzi) Villanti

Sophia Villanti

Sophia was the oldest of John and Maria Concetta's seven children. As the oldest, she was told to always take care of her siblings and to set the "right example" for the younger ones. Concetta did not like to cook so Sophia watched what others did in the kitchen and went home and tried to make the dish herself.

She recalls at age 12 joining the 4-H club because her mother heard that they would teach her how to sew, tat and can. At that time the club met at the Washington School in Beverly and Miss Parker was the instructor. Students were to bring the fruits or vegetables or what ever they wanted to can and that is where she started her cooking. Her father taught her at an early age how to pick blueberries and edible mushrooms.

At age 13 Sophia heard classmates talking about having turkey for Thanksgiving dinner. She asked her father if they could have turkey. He wanted to know who would cook it and of course she said, "I will". He went out and bought the family's first turkey. Sophia had a Fannie Farmer cookbook and followed the directions in it.

Word got out to extended family that she had prepared a turkey and now they all started to cook turkey. At that point it was decided that Sophia knew enough about cooking to keep on preparing meals for the family.

John Clemenzi always had a garden at his home on Elliott St. where he grew lots of tomatoes. Labor Day was always dreaded because the tomatoes had to be canned and made into puree. On the average the garden yielded 300 jars a year! Sophia also made cordials with "bootleg" alcohol (100 proof) such as anisette, strega, rasolio and rum for rum cakes.

Always a well-behaved youngster, Sophia brags that she never once was kept after school. Shortly before she turned 16 years old, Sophia told her father that she wanted to learn how to drive. He gave her permission and taught her on a seven passenger Buick. She got her driver's license the day she turned sixteen. The day she got her license her mother asked her to take her to Boston, which, of course she did. At that point she was elected to drive any older Italian woman to doctor appointments. In those days there were very few cars and also a few horses on the road.

Sophia has many fond memories of picnics with her extended family. They would prepare a picnic basket and all gather at Salem Willows, Stage Fort Park in Gloucester, Centennial Grove in Essex and once in a while Salisbury beach. She remembers seeing gypsies on the road in Salisbury selling their wares and telling fortunes. Her mother warned Sophia and the other children to stay away from them for fear that they would try to kidnap them. Once a year the Clemenzis, the Costas and the DeLorenzos would drive to New Jersey to visit with Uncle Dom's and Uncle Sal's families in Jersey City.

Sophia (seated) and friends

Sophia finished high school in 1932 in the midst of the depression. After high school she worked at Corte's Italian grocery store in Beverly, MA. In 1934 she went to nursing school in Boston. Then she started her nursing career at Trumble Hospital in Brookline Village where she stayed until 1938. At that time she began doing private duty nursing until her marriage in 1940.

Sophia met Dominick A. Villanti in 1936 when he and his brother Philip came to visit her family in Beverly and it was love at first sight. He had just returned from Italy where he had been in college. Because Dominick's parents were born in Italy, the Italian government considered him an Italian citizen even though he was born in New York. In those days Mussolini was in power and was striving to reestablish the Roman Empire. Due to his dual citizenship, Dominick was in danger of being drafted by the Italians. He had very strong feelings against Mussolini so he returned to America without completing his college education.

Dominick Villanti (left) trip to Italy

Sophia was immediately impressed by the way he spoke Italian so perfectly and by his intelligence. After his weekend visit, he returned to his home in New York and the two corresponded by mail. They were married on August 25, 1940 at St. Mary Star of the Sea Church in Beverly, MA. As newly weds they lived in the Williamsburg section of the Bronx. In 1942 Dominick received a very important letter. It said "Greetings, you have been selected to serve your country." He was in the Army from 1942 to 1946, in both Germany and France. The government sent Sophia $50 a month and Dominick's pay was a whopping $21 a month! When Dominick was drafted, Sophia returned to her parents' home in Beverly. When Dominick returned to the U.S. after the war, Sophia was so anxious to see him that she took her first airplane flight from Boston to New York to meet him. Sophia really did not want to live in New York and Dominick said he had been thinking of living on a farm so they started their new life in Ipswich, Massachusetts.

Sophie and Dominick Villanti

Dominick worked for Joseph Marini at his farm on Linebrook Road in Ipswich for many years. They always wanted to have children and on September 8, 1947 they were blessed with the birth of Catherine. As the first child, she was named after her paternal grandmother in the Italian tradition. Catherine loved the country, having pets and seeing deer in the back yard. She has fond memories of picking strawberries, blueberries, asparagus and running in open space. Catherine is still very close to many of her childhood friends from Ipswich.

On May 12, 1951 Dominick and Sophia's second daughter, Maria Concetta, was born. Maria was named after her maternal grandmother. She was a very quiet child who liked to color and do puzzles. She remembers the elaborate New Years Eve parties at the Marini home with many people, lots of food, party hats and noisemakers. Maria loved living on the farm, picking apples, blueberries, peaches and cherries. In strawberry season, she picked the delicious fruit and was paid 5 cents per quart. After earning 35 cents, she would ride her bicycle three miles to Quint's drug store in downtown Ipswich to buy an ice cream sundae. In winter, she enjoyed ice-skating on the ponds behind her home.

Sophia surprised many of her friends and relatives with her "change of life baby" Angela who was born on March 29, 1957. Living on the farm, there were no other children her age in the area, so Angela invented an imaginary playmate, Cousin Carol, whom she said lived in a green house with purple shutters.

The family moved to Beverly in March of 1963 and the girls attended school there, Catherine at Beverly High School, Maria at St. Mary's just across the street from the family home. Angela had been in kindergarten at the time at St. Stanislaus School in Ipswich, but since there was no kindergarten class at St. Mary's she became a kindergarten dropout! Maybe that is what inspired her to stay in school and become a teacher. Angela went to Fitchburg State College, where she earned both her B.S. and Master's of Education degrees. She has taught special education in the Beverly public schools since her graduation in 1979. Angela loves to travel to places all over the globe. She has visited Europe several times as well as Mexico and many Caribbean islands. In the summer of 2002, she went to Sri Lanka.

Catherine, Maria and Angela Villanti

To this day Sophia still enjoys cooking and entertaining friends and family at her home in Beverly. It is not unusual for her to prepare a Sunday dinner for anywhere from four or five to up to twenty five people, even today at the age of eighty-eight. Some of her specialties are homemade pasta, lasagna, and gnocchi. She also loves to bake pies, cookies and creampuffs and makes pizzelle on a regular basis to send to various friends and relatives who like them.

Catherine is now married to George Constantelo and they live in Beverly. They have two daughters, Kristen and Alana. Catherine has worked at The Gap at the Northshore Mall since 1996. George is originally from Lynn, MA and he has worked for General Electric ever since 1971. Kristen now lives in Amesbury, MA. She has two children, Anthony and Kaitlyn, and gave birth to her third child, a son, named Jared Michael on June 22, 2003. (He was six weeks premature, but still weighed in at 5 pounds 2 ounces and mother and baby are doing well.) Alana lives with her parents in Beverly. She works at Curious Creatures in Peabody during the week and for Creative Catering of Beverly on weekends.

Maria married Dennis Parent in 1984. They live upstairs from Sophia at her home in Beverly. Maria has worked for the Massachusetts Department of Revenue since she graduated from high school in 1969. Dennis also worked for the state for many years, first at Danvers State Hospital until it closed, then at Tewksbury State Hospital until his retirement in 2002.

Aunt Sophie A Great Woman
Written by Christine di Grandi Jones

We all respect Aunt Sophie for her love of family, her boundless generosity, piety, sensitivity, directness, cheesecakes, and banquets on Chapman Street! She never misses a family function. At age 89, she still makes the 225mile trip to celebrate with our family in Hyde Park.

Priests at Saint Mary's are all the happier and well fed because of Sophie's church devotion. (Not forgetting her & Dominick's faithful Friday night Beno) She is often the subject of the priests loving humor and appreciation of her.

From the time Sophie was a child, she cared for her younger brothers and sisters… Angelo & Emma even called her mama. She took Angelo everywhere even to Washington DC when she went with her girlfriends.

Sophie converted her living room to a bedroom for her mother where she cared for Concetta until her last days. Sophie has raised Catherine, Maria, and Angela with the same love of family and caring hearts.

Catherine's hands are creative, have a green thumb, and are always there to help! Her heart is giving and extends to those in need. She is a prophet in her own way bringing the word of God to little ones in CCD, serving on her Parish Counsel, bringing the devotion of Saint Dymphna to Beverly and beyond those who need emotional and psychological healing. She and George love children - especially the grandchildren! I remember what a popular teenager she was-she knew everyone especially those in convertibles! She even wore a headband like Olivia Newton John!

Maria is fondly referred to as Sophie's mother. Maria, who lives above her mother, with her husband Dennis and bird "Frankie" looks after her with care and concern-scolding her for doing too much! Maria is known for her expert shopping skills.

Angela has hosted many family functions. She has also hosted me in her warm, comfortable, and inviting home during several of my visits to Beverly. She carries the family history in her head. She was on the Serra family reunion committee. If you want to know a fact, ask Angela! Invite her to a party and ask her to bring stuffed mushrooms…mmmmm

Thank you dear Matriarch for being the glue of the family… I am proud to be called your gemella!

Dominick Villanti and his Turkeys

Written by Christopher and Nancy Obert with information supplied by Sophia Villanti
Photos supplied by Sophia Villanti

Dominick and Sophie Villanti

The same day we were visiting Sophie Villanti, and she told us the story about Emma Villanti and her cakes, she told us another story about her husband Dominick. We were looking through photos albums and we came across a photo of Dominick and a tray of chicks. Chris asked, "What is the story behind this?" Sophie told us that they used to raise turkeys. We did not know this.

Dominick and the chicks

We then came across a second photo of Dominick with the adult turkeys. She told us that Dominick called it Willowdale Turkey Farm and that at their peak they had about 2,000 turkeys.

Dominick being watched by the turkeys

Sophie said it was hard work and that they did all that work themselves. She also told us that it was very busy around Thanksgiving and Christmas, the two biggest turkey eating days of the year. She said that their hands would get so tired and sore because of all the work, that at times she would not look forward to the holiday season.

Regardless of all the hard work, we could tell that Dominick and Sophie would still make the holiday season special for their family. Every time we meet with them, we can see the close family bonds that can only be made through years of loving and caring.

The di Grandis of New York

Written by the di Grandi Family

The history of our family was compiled by the five children of Marietta Stephanie Clemenzi and George Joseph di Grandi. We are second generation Americans and are 5 of 32 grandchildren of Concetta (b. April 13, 1890 in Malfa-Island of Salina-Provincia di Messina daughter of Battista Serra & Bartola Lazzaro) and Giovanni (John) Clemenzi (b. February 11, 1885 in Turania, Provincia di Reiti, son of Dominico Clemenzi & Sofia Marapodi), more lovingly known as Nonna and Nonno. We believe that Concetta arrived on Ellis Island, New York in 1910 with her brothers, Domenico and Salvatore, her sister Caroline, her mother Bartolomeo Lazzaro of Salina, Messina, Sicily, and her mother's sister Catherine.

Concetta Serra and Giovanni Clemenzi met at the store Concetta's uncle owned in Salem. Giovanni was building the church (Many Italian immigrants worked as masons when they came to the United States) across the street from the store and used to frequent there many times just to see Concetta. Giovanni asked Concetta's uncle for her hand in marriage. Since her uncle knew little of Giovanni, he told Giovanni to get a letter of recommendation from the Mayor. Giovanni went to the Mayor and received a glowing letter. Little did Concetta's uncle know that the Mayor was a relative of Giovanni. Concetta Serra and Giovannni Clemenzi were married at Sacred Heart Church in Boston's North End, on February 25, 1912. Their second child, our mother, Marie Mary Stephanie Clemenzi, was born June 8, 1916 in Beverly, MA. Mary was a pretty, curly-haired little girl who, as a young woman, attracted many suitors. At the age of 7, she learned to play the piano by ear. Her closest friends were her sisters, Sophie and Emma, and her first cousins, Katie, Teresa, and Rosie. The family lived in Salem until the great Salem fire, when they moved to Beverly.

After leaving school, Mary worked as a supervisor at CBS Hytron, a local factory, where several of her suggestions for more efficient operations were implemented by management. She conceived the Time and Motion inventions, won awards during WWII, and suggested and implemented the "coffee break." She also worked in her father's construction business doing income tax and bookkeeping. Later in life, as a single parent, Mary worked at several jobs including receptionist at the historical Nelson House and the world famous Culinary Institute of America. Mom also attended many college courses at Marist College and Dutchess Community College in Accounting, Typing, General Business, and Art.

To this day, at the age of 87, she still maintains an interest in business. She is active in the stock market, tripled her own mother's assets, and manages her son Ronald's real estate rentals and investments. Mom is devoted to her children and grandchildren. She has spent endless hours filling their stomachs with pasta and their hearts and minds with stories, beautiful thoughts and memories.

On a bus trip to Beverly from the Bronx, having visited her sister Sophie Villanti, Mary met our father, George di Grandi, the eldest son of Italian immigrants, Rosa Lusco from Cefalu Sicily, and Pasquale "Patrick" di Grandi from Ragusa in Sicily. Dad was in the Army stationed at Fort Edwards, MA. He fought at Monte Casino and Anzio in World War II and was awarded a Purple Heart and two Silver Stars. Their wartime romance led to marriage on October 29, 1944 in Beverly, MA. We have spent many hours reading their love letters stored in a trunk in the basement.

Our parents moved from the "family house" on Elliot Street, where most of the young married Clemenzi children lived at some point, to a four-family home they purchased for $6,000 at 14 Chapman Street, Beverly, MA. The house was across the street from St. Mary's Star of the Sea School and the convent which Mom's father built. Mom worked hard at renovating the first floor so that the seven of us lived comfortably in a beautiful home. Their five children, Diana, Ronald, Christine, Patricia and Francine, were raised here. Our home had a clear view of the school and asphalt playground where the Sisters of Notre Dame walked and prayed. We always had to be on our best behavior or we'd hear about it from the nuns in school the next day. We also watched the Saint Mary Cardinals and Crusaders Drum and Bugle Corps practice there (Ronny was a member). We are pleased to say that we can still visit this house today since Aunt Sophia owns it.

Visiting Nonna and Nonno at 24 Neptune Street was a Sunday afternoon ritual. Our aunts, uncles, and cousins convened for family dinners on the basement level of this two-story brick house (which our Nonno built) with its summer kitchen and long tables of plywood and wood horses. In an adjacent, small, cool room, Nonno made wine from his homegrown grapes. We all shared the last bottle of his wine on Mom's 75th birthday in 1991. Nonno stood 5'4" and reared sons all over 6 feet tall. He had bright blue eyes, all his own teeth and a full head of hair. He would chatter his teeth to show us they were all his. A self-educated man, Nonno had a keen knowledge and interest in art and opera, which he tried to impart to his grandchildren. He knew and was loved by everyone. At his funeral mass at Saint Mary's Church, the main street was closed to accommodate the 7 limousines for the family and the innumerable cars filled with friends and acquaintances that came to pay their last respects.

Nonna was a quiet and stoic woman. But every now and then she would regale us with old Sicilian stories, poems and songs. Some of us remember her in the kitchen plucking pigeons, chickens or skinning a rabbit Nonno had caught for supper. The adolescent girls also remember her checking our progress by pinching our budding bosoms as she would a ripening peach. Most of us still have one of the beautiful afghans she crocheted for our wedding or baby showers (a tradition continued by her daughter Sophie). Every grandchild has at least one if not a dozen knitted slippers and vests. She lived through the deaths of her husband, two children and a grandchild. We were blessed to have Nonna in our lives until she was 96 years old. May her great Serra longevity genes continue to be passed down to all our future generations. So far, so good!

In 1962, our family moved to the Hudson River Valley in New York because Dad was made general manager of an American Motors' Rambler Dealership in Poughkeepsie, NY. He soon opened his own dealership, Riverview Rambler, in Newburgh, NY, as well as a used car lot. Dad was generous, personable, and loved to live on the high side. He earned many awards (Best Salesman Nationwide), prizes (our bunk bed set we still have) and trips for car sales. Mom and Dad traveled to places like Europe and Mexico, and we couldn't wait until they got home to see the many gifts they bought for us. When they were away, we had loving people like, Nonno diGrandi or Kenny and Georgina D'Eon come stay with us. With five children, it must have been a tremendous task for them. We have vivid memories of Nonno cooking a delicious spaghetti sauce for dinner, and treating us to 'ring dings' everyday after school.

Our parents built a home, which mom designed, in the village of Historic Hyde Park, New York. It is a bit less modest than the Vanderbilt and Roosevelt Mansions it is situated between. Installing an in-ground swimming pool made us popular in the neighborhood. It also made our home more of a vacation spot for our families from Massachusetts.

Our cousins were our early childhood friends, many of whom have grown to be our dearest and best friends. The 225 mile distance has not kept us from sharing special family events and spending time together. Many of us communicate daily via the Internet. We also keep in touch with our cousins in Italy with whom we have had the good fortune to visit many times.

Christine, Fran, Ron, Patricia and Diana

We Five Children

Written by the di Grandi Family

Diana Rose graduated from Mount St. Mary's College, SUNY at New Paltz and New York University with a BA, MS, MA, CAS in Educational Administration and English. She was editor and writer for a regional education quarterly and has had many of her works published in literary and poetry periodicals. Diana has retired from teaching Special Education and is now an English and Theater Arts Teacher. She also produces, directs and acts at the Center for Performing Arts in Rhinebeck, NY where she is a member of the Board of Directors. She also heads her own production company, Up in One Productions. She has produced and directed both locally and off-off-Broadway. She studies acting in New York City at the Phillips Actors Studio and is the director of the Children's Theater at the Center of Performing Arts. Married three times, Diana has no children of her own, but positively dotes on her nieces and nephew.

Ron, our only brother, was born on March 3, 1947. He graduated with a BS in Electronic Engineering from the University of Detroit, an MBA from Marist College and a J.D. from Columbia Pacific University. While in high school and college Ron worked many part-time jobs to help support his mother and sisters. After graduation Ron worked for many years at IBM and is still employed in the semiconductor industry. Ron excels at interacting with people and has been successful at semiconductor sales. For a short time he pursued his dreams of becoming a college professor by teaching both at Marist College and at Rochester Institute of Technology. He continued his love for the drum corps and played a soprano in the 20th Century Senior Drum and Bugle corps. He has been studying martial arts for over 10 years and has recently earned his second black belt. Ron met his wife, Pao-Lien, while working in Taiwan. They were married on 4/10/1983. Their daughter, Patricia-Chen DiGrandi was born on May 25,1986 in Rhinebeck, New York. Patty is soft spoken, both in Chinese and English, and is a good student. Patty has been training with her father in the martial arts for the last two years and has already earned three belt promotions. She is now an orange belt. Ron and Pao-Lien are actively involved in the Roman Catholic Chinese Church. Ron teaches CCD and Pao-Lien sings in the choir and also teaches Chinese in the church's Chinese School. She has received the coveted "Confucius Teachers Merit Award" for her teaching efforts. She also sang with her group, the Mid-Hudson Community Chorus, in tribute to the victims of the Tiananmen Square tragedy at Lincoln Center in NYC in 1989. Ron, Pao-Lien and Patty-Chen temporarily live in Northern California.

Christine Constance. "The middle child." Dad always teased that I was inoculated with a phonograph needle because I talked non-stop. (As I write this in such a techno age, I realize what an ancient implement that is) I am sure this ease with people is why I have a real estate career. As a teen, there was never time to be bored. I was a drum majorette of the Vagabond Drum and Bugle Corps. When I graduated from Roosevelt High School, I was distinguished with a varsity letter for being the most active student. I belonged to many school clubs and as an adult continued with organization involvement. My sisters and I worked as waitresses while attending school. I was an adult when I returned to complete my under graduate work. I was the first graduate of Marist College with an Integrated Major. I did Masters studies in Political Science at Marist College as well as Religious Studies at St. Joseph's Catechetical Institute and received a Masters Degree in Marriage and Family from Iona College and have had a small counseling practice. I have taught at Marist College, Dutchess Community College, and for the Realtors association where I served as Chairwoman of Education. I have also obtained professional designations. I have served as President of the Hyde Park Chamber of Commerce, Eucharistic Minister and Lector for Regina Coeli Church, devoted a heap of time to the kids at DAYTOP. Exchange students and challenged teens have found a home with my family. When I was a child, I would beg my parents to take in orphans for the holidays. Today I honor graduates with awards in the name of Eleanor Roosevelt, my beloved son, and Mother Theresa.

Traveling is one of my favorite things to do. I have had the good fortune to visit dozens of countries and have even been paid for escorting groups of passengers on cruises and Canada. My favorite place to go is Italy! Last year, I spent a few weeks visiting the birthplaces or my four grandparents! It is a wonderful visiting our cousins in Italy! I was the first of my siblings to be married on June 8, 1968 to my high school boyfriend, Mace Earl Jones, son of Mace Navy Jones, Cambridge Maryland and Janet Hodge Jones of Poughkeepsie, NY, daughter of Mildred Meyer and Earl Hodge. We were married for 23 years divorcing in October 1993.

God had blessed me with three children: Trisha Marie Jones, 12/20/1970; Mace di Grandi Jones 3/22/78; and Deanna di Grandi Jones 9/9/1979. I have had a real estate practice for 33years "Christine Jones Realty", am a real estate investor, and soon to be a developer. As each day comes to an end, I try my best to get home to witness spectacular sunsets over the Hudson River and Catskill Mountains. Come join me! Trisha Marie is the first-born child to this next generation. December 20, 1970. She was a great older sister who often looked after Mace and Deanna. She attended Regina Coeli Catholic Grammar School before she was 5. While a student at Franklin Delano Roosevelt High School, Trisha was a peer leader and traveled to other school districts to speak to superintendents and principals and conducted team-building exercises. Before graduating, she had earned a semester of college credit. Trisha as well as her siblings, learned to down hill ski shortly after becoming proficient at walking! She loved the family outings of tubing the Esopus River, climbing Mohawk Mountain, vacations in Mexico and Italy! Early on, Trisha acquired a taste to travel, which she and Jon enjoy today. Trisha married her high school sweetheart, Jonathan Freiermuth of Hyde Park, NY on November 23, 1989. Trisha graduated with a Bachelor Degree in Biology from the University of North Carolina at Wilmington while Jonathan was an enlisted Marine at Camp LeJune. I was shocked to learn that they sold their blood so that Jon could take flying lessons! Jonathan's outstanding scholastic achievements made him a shoe-in at Rochester Institute of Technology until a computer groundbreaking company scooped him up. Jonathan remarked that he couldn't believe that he got paid for doing something he enjoyed so much! Trisha has worked for hospitals in the Rochester area in the computer field. Trisha and Jon have recently sold their Dutch Colonial in Honeoye Falls, NY to move where the sun shines in Tampa, Florida. Trisha enjoys Eastern dance and her group has performed publicly.

Mace di Grandi Jones born on March 22, 1978 was a curly head platinum blonde. Often times, when we would call him, he'd respond: "Shhh, I am thinking!" At age 2 or 3 he would quote: "To be or not to be, that is the question!" Before attending school, Mace decided that he wanted to be called "Ryan Ready". I clearly remember how proud he was at his nursery school graduation that he finished a group recitation before anyone else! Mace was an out going young man who was always looking out for the younger and weaker kids. When he was little, he played soccer, won a medal in Judo and became an altar boy. He loved to shock people with bold statements, not unlike his mother, and he loved to make people laugh. Mace was a talented violinist chosen to play at Carnegie hall. His teacher said he excelled faster than any student she ever taught. (He practiced for hours each day). He loved to entertain us at restaurants, and even brought his violin to Mexico to play! Mace played at a concert the day he began his eternal life on March 27, 1993. He was 15 years of age for one week at the time of a tragic car accident. He was a passenger in a friend's car. Mace played football for F.D. Roosevelt High School. He loved long hot showers until the smoke alarm went off! We were sure he fell asleep in the shower! Mace was adventurous: climbing trees (that terrified his mother), was a fearless skier who no one could keep up with and was told he even played Tarzan on a balcony in Hawaii! Mace climbed down the smallest volcano in the world and played on the top of the Alps! On his own volition, he made his way to shake the hand of President of the United States, Bill Clinton, twice! Mace served Regina and St. Paul's Church as an altar server into his teens. He was open in conversations and loved to shock people with bold statements, not unlike his mother, and he loved to make people laugh. He had great values and was concerned about the environment. Mace, as well as his sister Trisha, excelled in Math scoring 100% in state regions exams. The only Christmas gift he wanted was a video, which would teach him to do higher math calculations in his head. A two+ hour waiting line in the freezing winter did not deter family, friends, and acquaintances from paying respect at his wake. 13 violinists, 33 altar servers, 7 priests and a Bishop participated in his Rite of Christian burial. Each year, a graduate of Regina Coeli School and Roosevelt High School is selected by their peers to be the recipient of the Mace di Grandi Jones Award for Joyful and Selfless Giving.

Deanna di Grandi Jones was born on September 6, 1979 at Northern Dutchess Hospital in Rhinebeck. Referred to by her dad as "Bugsy," Deanna was born 17 months after her brother, Mace. What a beautiful baby! When they were young, Deanna and Mace helped out at the nursing home-They loved wheeling the patients around and the elderly were delighted to see the kids. Deanna loved skiing, horseback riding, traveling, gymnastics, tubing the Esopus River and anything fun! A Social creature for sure! Spending time with friends was a big part of her teens. She has shown artistic talents that are yet to be tapped. Mace and Danna had Italian tutoring. In their playful way, they loved trying to shock the teacher by asking her to teach them certain words! Mother would pay them for each Italian word they learned (nice words, that is!) Deanna was involved in peer leadership in high school and graduated while living in Rochester with Trisha. The principal, who was fond of Deanna, awarded her with the "WOW" Award -"Watch Out World!" Deanna is eager to earn a bachelor's degree in Math. Bettina, "a bundle of joy", was born to Deanna on September 14,

303

1999. Deanna was a sport doing this naturally and putting up with the women of our family all being present with Movies, photos, advice, and food! What a sweet, delightful, polite, beautiful, and bright child! (Spoken like a true Nonna who cannot wait for her to get her passport!). We are all looking forward to Deanna and Bettina living in Hyde Park. She may write her own book!

Patricia Joan is starting her 30th year at the Dutchess County Legislature. She heads the administrative office for the Legislature, is Parliamentarian and Advisor, as well as fundraiser for the Majority Party (Republican) of the Legislature. She had taken a year off in 1977 to work for the State Assembly. She married John in 1988 and has three lovely children: Stefanie, age 12; Sarah, age 11 and Robert, age 6. John is an engineer and managing director of National Bandwidth, a telecommunications consulting company. He is intelligent, creative and a good husband and father. John teaches by example, and has taught his children the fundamentals of life, love of God, and love of self. John's constant hospitalization for chronic ulcerative colitis, which leads to the removal of his large intestine, caused him to lose his job at IBM. This was his opportunity to utilize his God-given talents. He started his own business, which had led him in many different paths. He is always coming up with different ideas, which lead him to many opportunities. He once wrote and published his own book, "If Life's a Game, What's Your Score?" For fun, he acts and directs at the Rhinebeck Performing Arts Center (a comedian known to all). He loves working with young actors. Stefanie and Sarah follow in his footsteps and have been acting for about four years now. Sarah is in her second opera with principles from the Metropolitan Opera Company (a true performer). In addition to Stefanie's performances, she is a strong swimmer in our local swim team. She is entering a 4H program and will be breeding and showing rabbits. Stefanie is a lovely young lady, with a wonderful sense of humor and a particular sensitivity to her Nonni. She is an altar server at Regina Coeli School and had attended St. Peter's Catholic School in the 6th and 7th grades. She had taken ballet since she was four years old, gymnastics since she was six, and plays the violin, flute and has taken piano lessons. Sarah is a beautiful young lady, with a free spirit. She loves to laugh and play, and often times displays her dramatic talents. Sarah has played the cello since 4th grade, had taken piano lessons, ballet lessons since four years old, gymnastics since she was six, and has been a girl scout for five years. She intends to be a cadet in another year. Sarah loves to help people and is saving up for her own personal laptop computer. She is versed in the computer and Internet, and loves to explore all the functions of the computer. Her Aunt Franny calls her a "computer nerd." Both Sarah and Stefanie love to cook and experiment. In fact, Sarah made a special pancake cake for Gina's graduation – her own idea and concoction – everyone loved it. Robert is a wonderful, precocious, intelligent young boy who has mastered Playstation videos. He has just completed kindergarten with strong academic grades. He attended St. Peter's Catholic School pre-K, and attended Dutchess Community College Lab Nursery School. He loves hot wheels cars and Yugioh cards. He can match his cousin in any card game – his cousin is five years older. Patty's family had lived in the home Patty built 21 years ago where chickens grazed, rabbits basked in the sun in the driveway welcoming them home, cats scurrying around, and dogs bringing them gifts they stole from their neighbors. She had tiled her own bathrooms, stained all the wood in her chalet loft, and took cabinet making courses to learn how to build her bedroom cabinet doors. She had traded her tiling expertise for electrical work in her house. Since her family of five had grown out of their 2-bedroom chalet, they sold their home immediately after 9-11-01 for a newer, bigger home. They first lived with her sister, Franny, for 5 months, and have been living with Nonni for the past year in the same house that Patty was brought up in. Patty and John have entered that never-ending project of building a home. Her e-mail address is wishahome24@aol.com.

Francine Concetta was entering second grade when we moved to New York. She vividly remembers the culture shock the first time she met a new friend's grandmother who spoke to her in perfect English. She stared at her in awe; she had never heard an elderly person who didn't speak Italian or have a thick Italian accent. Her greatest accomplishment has been raising her beautiful teenage daughter, Gina, entirely on her own. Gina was born on June 24, 1985, the happiest year of Francine's life. Gina is intelligent and ambitiously pursuing a college education in hopes of one day becoming an attorney. One of Gina's many interests is softball, which she has played for 10 years. At age 7, she inherited her cousin Mace's baseball bat after his untimely death. It was twice her size but she insisted on using it no matter how hard her coaches tried to persuade her to give it up. Gina had admired her cousin immensely. She even took violin lessons to be like him and absolutely beamed the few times she got to play with him in concert. Gina was very active growing up, which kept her mother running. She took piano lessons, violin lessons, and baton lessons, belonged to girl scouts, and played basketball as well as softball. Prior to becoming a mother at age 30, Francine had designed and general contracted the building of 3 homes, and remodeled a 4th. Doing house plans for others became a "not for profit" sideline. With the coming of the computer age she found a new passion in computer technology and a new "not for profit" sideline. At age 44, she decided that there must be a more fulfilling way to be giving and decided to become a certified foster parent. Francine is a civil engineer for the local county government. She attended school nights to obtain an associate's degree in civil engineering and computer science. While going to school, she spent many afternoons doing her homework on her lap in the bleachers while watching her daughter play softball. After working at her career for 18 years, Francine found herself obtaining the services of the Federal government to pursue a sexual discrimination suit against the county, which after almost two years was found in her favor. Now she looks forward to an early retirement so that she may pursue a new career (not yet determined).

Grand Children

Deanna DiGrandi Jones, Daughter of Christine DiGrandi Jones. I was born on September 6, 1979 in Rhinebeck, NY. I grew up in Hyde Park and Staatsburg, NY attending Regina Coeli Parochial School from ages 3 - 13 years old. As a child I had the benefit of learning and experiencing wonderful things in life such as being involved in dance, soccer, gymnastics, piano, Judo, Girl Scouts, 4-H and a world traveler by 8yrs old. With strong family roots I fondly remember my Aunts Patty and Franny attending every recital, school play, and concert I was in as well as extended family from MA visiting in the summer and being there for rights of passage like my First Communion. My brother Mace and I, only a year and a half apart in age, grew up doing everything together. We were usually at each other's throats, but we used to have a lot of fun too. I fondly remember ice-skating with him on our pond in the winter and in the summer we used to make a ramp up to it and ride bikes off the ramp and land in the pond. He was a friend to everyone, and I always followed him around wanting to be just like him, which made his tragic death in 1993 exceptionally painful. At this time, my sister Trisha moved back home while her husband Jonathan served his 6th and final year of the Marines overseas. A year after Jon came back (when I was 16) Trish, Jon, and I moved to Rochester, NY where I completed high school and entered Monroe Community College. As a "free spirit", I spent the next few years moving around and trying to find my niche. This also included covering myself with body piercings and some tattoos. In April of 1998, I met and fell in love with Justin Paige Quarcini-Thomas of Niagara Falls, NY born in October of 1977. Justin and I became the proud parents of Bettina Quarcini-Thomas Jones on September 14, 1999 born in Rhinebeck, NY. Bettina is the 1st grandchild of Christine and Mace Jones, and the 1st great grandchild of Mary di Grandi. I found my niche doing Computer IT support in Rochester, NY but miss being around family so I am currently in the process of relocating, with Bettina, back to Hyde Park, NY.

Francine, Patricia, Christine, Diana and Ron

Marrieta Di Grandi's Memoirs

Written by Marrieta "Mary" (Clemenzi) di Grandi

Mary di Grandi

First and foremost I wish to thank Chris Obert, for devoting so much time and effort in writing the Serra book, and inviting me to add my memoirs. I am so proud of my Serra, Clemenzi heritage, especially of my Nonna Bartolomea, my mom and dad, and my Uncles Zio Domenico and Zio Salvatore. My nonna Bartolomea worked with her uncle, in Salina Sicily, who was a doctor, and had hand written a book "REMEDIES TRIED AND TRUE " Lucia Clemenzi has the original in her possession, she found it in the house where my grandparents lived, in Salina, Sicily. My Nonna Bartolomea, knew how to set broken bones, use massages, and herbs. People, who lived on the Island, would come to her, seeking her cures, most of them would bring her eggs and chickens, in payment for her services. My Grandfather, whom I never knew, was a "LITTLE OLE WINE MAKER "he made the best wine on the Island, because he grew the best grapes.

My left arm was dislocated when I was born, and I couldn't move it, my grandmother massaged it every day till I was able to move it. I spent a lot of time with my nonna Bartolmea, who lived with my aunt Caroline Serra DeLorenzo, until she died, at the age of 96 or 106, no one really knows. My Uncle Guy DeLorenzo, said she was hiding 10 years, so she could get into this country. When my daughter Christina went to Sicily, she could not find her birth records. Did you know, that Nonna did not have a gray on her head? We also had a Zio Antonio, who lived with the DeLorenzos, one day he left home and never returned. My parents and all my relatives, searched everywhere, but could never find him.

After Zio Domenico, who was the "Brains", of the family, brought them all to America they lived in Salem, Ma., until the Salem fire. They owned a large Grocery Store, My father was a Hero, during the fire, he went around with his truck and saved all the Nuns and Orphans. My aunts, Uncles, my mom and dad lost everything they owned, except a Provaloni cheese, which they grabbed, when they ran for their lives to the Salem Common.

After the Salem fire, my parents, Aunts and Uncles, and Nonna Bartolomea, moved to Beverly, all except Zio Domenico and Zio Salvatore, they moved to Jersey City, N.J. Our trips to New Jersey were one of the biggest events of the year. It was an all day trip to go from Ma. To N.J. there was no Mass Highway at that time, we would travel on Rt.1A all the way. We had a caravan of 3 large Packard cars, with over 21 people. The DeLorenzos, the Costa and Clemenzi families. When it was time for bed, we children slept on the floor. Zio Domenico and Zio Salvatore would come in to check on us, and we would giggle, when we saw the white Nitecaps they wore on their heads. On one trip, when I was about 15, it was Lena Scibetta's Christening day and I was her Godmother. She was such a cute little girl.

Johnnie Serra, Uncle Domenico's son (there are so many John Serras) came to stay with us in Beverly, Ma., one summer, when he was a little boy, Johnnie had such a beautiful voice, he sounded like Bobby Breen, who at that time was a very famous child star and singer. We would go to the playground, and the kids would all gather around him to hear him sing. I was so proud to say he was my cousin. Johnnie always called me Marietta. One day, when I was seven, my mom took us shopping to buy a piano, when she found the one she liked, she told us to remember the serial number to make sure we were getting the same piano she liked; so when the salesman said "Let's see that was serial number…", and I blurted out the sixteen digit number I had memorized. He was amazed. I have a very good memory for numbers. I memorized my husband's army serial number from over 50 years ago. I have all my children's and grandchildren's social security numbers in my head, also account numbers, telephone etc, but I'm not so good on remembering names. Anyway, my mom hired a piano teacher to give me lessons. She thought playing piano would help my left arm that was dislocated. Every time I would sit at the piano, to practice, my sister Sophie would come and pull my hair, so I didn't want to take any more lessons, and learned to play the piano by ear. Mom had a good sense of humor, she would cook the meals and pass the food around the table, but my siblings, who were all finicky, would not take any, so when she got to me she would say "Here Marietta, you eat it, no one else wants it!"
As a teenager I took care of my father's books, payroll, billing and Income Tax When I saw what he had to pay for Income Taxes, I said to him "Papa you have seven kids, you should not have to pay so much Income Taxes." So I did them for him, until my brothers came back from World War II and went into business with him, then they hired a CPA. I am very proud of my father. He came from Italy as a very poor young man, and worked very hard and became one of the most prominent Building Contractors in Massachusetts; constructing such buildings, as The Prudential Center and King's Grant, and for companies such as AT&T.

Mary di Grandi and grandkids

Memories

Written by Patty DiGrandi Hohmann, Francine Di Grandi and the di Grandi children

Giovanni Clemenzi:

I remember sitting on Nonno's lap, as he bounced his leg up and down, making me laugh. I remember sitting at the dinner table with a glass of homemade wine, and he telling me to drink it, that it was good for me. (I was only 7 or 8). I remember him spraying his peach trees in the backyard with some big contraption on his back. He would always pick up a peach and eat it, give me one to eat too. He always had lots of peaches. I remembered being very loved! - Patty DiGrandi Hohmann

I have all the same memories as my sister Patty as vividly as if it were yesterday. I also remember the time when he was building the convent across the street from our home in Beverly. He would come over for lunch, and he always had room on his lap for a grandchild or two. Sitting on Nonno's lap was the best. I can also remember when he was sick in the hospital near the end of his life. I was around 9. Everyone wanted to see him and there was not enough visiting hours in the day to accommodate us all. We would all sneak in to his room and pack into the bathroom when the nurse came around. His funeral procession was the longest the town had ever seen with seven limousines to accommodate his seven children's families. - Francine di Grandi

Concetta Serra Clemenzi:

Nonna didn't drive, so Aunti Sophie would bring Nonna and mom shopping. Oh, how mom and Nonna loved to shop, and shop, and shop. I would sit in the back seat, and Nonna turned around to look at me, and in broken English asked me to put out my hands. She always had Nestlé's chocolate bits in a little plastic bag that she would give to us. It was my treat for waiting so patiently while her and mom shopped, and shopped, and shopped. Don't think that I don't open a bag of Nestlé's chocolate bits now, without thinking back to those days! When she was in her nineties, Nonna would come and visit in Hyde Park. I remember strolling her up and down the street in her wheel chair. We used to have heartwarming talks. I felt great that I could finally do something good for my Nonna, even if it was driving her around, too! - Patty DiGrandi Hohmann

Nonna was already in her 70's when I was born. I remember her as a quiet, loving elderly woman. I also remember those delicious chocolate bits that she carried in her big black bag. But mostly I remember her sitting in her recliner chair knitting or crocheting even as she napped. Her hands were always going. I also remember the multitudes of paper bags that she had stored in all her closets. Most of them filled with yarn. This was a trait passed down through the generations. My mother kept everything in bags. Whenever we packed the car to travel, out would come the bags of who knows what to be strategically placed around the car for different purposes. You can imagine my horror the first time I went to get a piece of wrapping paper from one of my closets, and I had to first remove about 5 other bags to get to it! - Francine di Grandi

Emma (Clemenzi) Villanti:

I remember watching Aunti Emma make her huge, wonderful cakes in her special kitchen in the cellar of 24 Neptune Place. We helped her make (and eat) the frosting, lots and lots of it. To this day, I can remember the taste of her delicious frosting, with that touch of lemon. Aunti Emma loved keeping us busy. As soon as we entered her apartment upstairs from Nonna, she would put a dust rag in our hands, and teach us the proper way of dusting. She had a beautiful cascade water fountain made of stone that Nonno built for her in the corner of her living room. I loved watching her cook. I sat on the wooden, built in bench in her kitchen situated under a window, next to her counter. She had such patience explaining how she was making the gnocchi which was my favorite. - Patty DiGrandi Hohmann

Aunt Emma, lived above Nonna and Nonno. We loved visiting her. She was a talented woman who fashioned cakes into impressive works of art. Sugar cube churches with music, chocolate paths, sugar swans, even fish bowls were imbedded in her cakes. Moving vans had to transport these one hundred pound cakes to the

Cardinal or for a family function. Nonno used to say that had Emma been a boy, she would have been the best builder among them. We children were allowed to help make icing and patrol her confectionery sculptures to keep the younger ones from touching them. Many of us received her famous doll cakes. She loved kids and made us feel important. Auntie Emma left this world too young. - The DiGrandi Children

Ah, yes, the cakes and the frosting! I remember all the bowls lined up of different colored frosting that I would stick my fingers in to taste. I guess the dusting was a small price to pay to be able to test all the frosting. But what was up with the cinnamon ingredient in the homemade gnocchi! Sorry Aunt Emma, but it was not my cup of tea. - Francine di Grandi

Sophie (Clemenzi) Villanti:

I have few memories of visiting Aunti Sophie and Uncle Dominick at their farmhouse in Ipswich, though I do remember lots of Turkeys. All my memories are of 14 Chapman Street. Aunti Sophie bought our 200 year old home from mom and dad right before we moved to New York. I loved going there, it was still "home" for me. Aunti Sophie must have had the biggest table on earth. So many families sat around her table AT THE SAME TIME! I struggled to understand what everyone was saying – they all spoke in Italian. So I reverted to being chased by my cousins, Peter James, Mark, Johnny, etc. around the house. The boys were always chasing the girls. Kids running around, the grownups carrying on several conversations at once, and Aunti Sophie busily cooking her absolutely delicious 12 course dinners for 30 or more, were the most loving and lasting memories of all. Aunti Sophie never stops loving, sharing and cooking. - Patty DiGrandi Hohmann

When I think Aunt Sophie, I think cheesecake, cream puffs, ravioli and Pecorino Romano cheese. When we travel back home to visit I can always plan on gaining an easy 5 pounds just eating at Aunt Sophie. She is the matriarch, the center of the family, the glue that holds us all together. - Francine di Grandi

John Battista Clemenzi: (son of Concetta and Giovanni Clemenzi)

In my eyes, Uncle Battista was such a big man. He stood tall, strong, had a deep and powerful voice; but yet he was such a sensitive, loving and caring uncle. He demanded respect, and you gave it reverently. Showing respect was important, not to just your elders, but respect for family. Uncle Battista was the epitome of family, and taught us the importance of the family unit. Everyone loved being around him, he was a magnet. I loved hearing his stories, he made everyone laugh. He had the greatest memory of all, and he was always right! Because I was close to my cousin, Marie, I spent many summers with Uncle Battista and Aunti Olga. Aunti Olga would wait on everyone hand and foot. She was amazing. She was in the kitchen when we went to bed, and was cooking or running errands hours before we even got up. You could always count on hot muffins, buns, bacon, and precut grapefruits for breakfast. We all put in our individual egg requests after Uncle Battista received his perfect 3 minute eggs. I thank Uncle Battista for so many things, things which have made lasting effects in my life. - Patty DiGrandi Hohmann

I can't say enough about my Uncle John. I learned so much from him. He was my male identity in life. He was always giving and always thinking of the children. Like Nonno, Uncle John was most comfortable with a child or two on his lap. My daughter also found her place on Uncle John's knee. He gave so much of himself to me through every stage of my life. I miss him so much that I can't ever think of him without tears in my eyes as I have now. Uncle John's home was my second home. The door was truly always open for me and everyone who dropped by. I'm not certain whether or not I called ahead or just showed up at the doorstep whenever my car would steer its way in that direction. His home was the center of family gatherings for many years as the patriarch of the family. Aunt Olga was always by his side caring for him in sickness and in health. On my many visits there, she would wake me early in the morning with the loud aroma of homemade blueberry muffins baking in the oven and bacon sizzling on the stove. I could write a book of my own on my warm memories of Uncle John and Aunt Olga. - Francine di Grandi

Dominick Clemenzi: (son of Concetta and Giovanni Clemenzi)

Every summer memory consists of Uncle Dominick and Aunti Helen. Memories that include my sister Franny, cousin Cheryle and myself getting lost: enjoying beautiful Wingaersheek Beach at Uncle Dominick's house, we three drifted off in the ocean on a blowup lounger. We lost our bearings, and walked back to the beach at an unknown place in the neighborhood. We cried terribly, we were so lost and scared. We finally went to a stranger's house to call Uncle Dominick, only to find that we were at a house right behind his. Embarrassed and ashamed, we walked back to Uncle Dominick's house with cousin Dickie who came to get us. We never lived that one down. Uncle Dominick taught us all how to clam. We had to get up at 5am to do it, but we did, and it was an experience. Aunti Helen had to cut all those clams that we brought back, and she made the best crab cakes in the world! I spent many summers at Aunti Helen's, playing with my cousin, Mary Catherine. In fact, Aunti Helen taught me how to sew a pattern. I sewed my very first dress with her. There is not one pattern I sew without those fond memories of Aunti Helen. Uncle Dominick is such a strong, talented man. He has made the most beautiful stone/cement flower pots. They are bigger and much heavier than a pot, and are such a creative work of art. I am proud to own one of these treasures, as well as the artistic trivets he has made, hanging in my kitchen. Uncle Dominick is such a hard-working man. I love hearing his stories of the war, of the family, his business, etc., -they are life experiences my children also appreciate. - Patty DiGrandi Hohmann

Uncle Peter:

If it wasn't for Uncle Peter and his love of adventure, I would never have been to the places in New York that I have visited. Uncle Peter, Aunti Rose and the 5 boys would spend their summer vacations with us in New York. Uncle Peter always wanted to travel to someplace he had never been in New York. I was so happy to be their guide and companion. One place Aunti Rose loved especially was the Baseball Hall of Fame in Cooperstown. She loved baseball! Uncle Peter loved anywhere he went. He and the family were so much fun to be with. We used to sit around and talked while he did Aunti Rose's hair in Mom's sun porch (Uncle Peter was a hairdresser). To this day, I thank him for the information and grooming tips I kept with me, and teach my children in turn. Uncle Peter loved the pool, and loved to sun bathe. At the end of his 2 week stay, he would be so very tanned. He cleaned mom's pool everyday, and trimmed her bushes and trees. Uncle Peter is so pleasant, and a thoughtful, loving person. - Patty DiGrandi Hohmann

Uncle Angelo:

I loved going to Uncle Angelo's beautiful house. My cousins always gathered there for parties. I remember that family was very important to Uncle Angelo. I remember that he was so concerned when dad left us, that he privately talked with me and counseled me with love and understanding. He was a quiet, cerebral man, who I respected and found very interesting. I loved hearing about his trip to China, and admired the beautiful things he brought from there. He passed away much too young, and I wish I had known him better. - Patty DiGrandi Hohmann

Vacation Memories:

I have vivid memories of going to the White Mountains with the family, and hiking to the Flume, seeing the "Man in the Mountains" and watching Dad trying to fit through the "Lemon Squeeze". It is because of these fond memories, that in my adult life, I have been visiting the White Mountains every year, and now bring my children to the same places. I also remember going to Lake George with Mom and Dad's dear friends, Kenny and Georgina (who still remain dear friends to us all) and visiting "Gaslight Village". We rode around the town all night long, until Mom found a place to her liking to stay. Dad and Mom would go in, we'd wait then they would come back out arguing why Mom didn't like that place either. Once we found a place, a couple of us would go in with Mom and Dad, then the rest of us would sneak in the back. (It must have been hard to find a place that would fit the 7 of us in one room). - Patty DiGrandi Hohmann

Family Memories

Written by Diana di Grandi

Diana di Grandi

Bartolomea Serra (Great Grandma)

When I was 2 years old, my mother took me by the hand into a bedroom saying "Come, see great grandma die." She was lying in a hospital bed that was the highest bed I'd ever seen. The bed was surrounded by relatives. I think this was my earliest memory.

Dominic Serra (Nonna's brother)

I remember visiting him and his family in New Jersey. He would always give us ice cream and candy from his store.

Angelina (Nonna's sister)

I remember her as an elderly woman with black hair in a net. She was a widow who had to support her family. She dyed her hair in order to appear younger to get work.

Concetta Serra Clemenzi (Nonna)

Nonna was a very quiet woman. Because of this, I found it difficult to really know her.

Her favorite pastime was crocheting afghans and vests for the family.

I remember her plucking chickens and skinning rabbits (that Nonno had shot).

She had an herbal tea for anything that ailed you.

I remember her being very frugal. Yet she loved to shop.

I think she was a bit hypochondrical. She complained often of aches and stomach problems.

During my second divorce, she telephoned me saying "Deanna, listen to your husband. Do what he says. He's the man; he knows best." She didn't know from Gloria Steinam

She seemed very stoic at the deaths of her children and grandchild (Aunt Emma, Uncle Angelo, Bobby). While I'm sure she mourned, she seemed to accept it as part of life's cycle.

When I was about 9 years old, I ran away from home to Nonna's. She sympathized with my plight that no one at home understood me. Then went into the other room and telephoned my mother to let her know I was there. In many ways, my mother is very much like Nonna.

311

John Clemenzi (Nonno)

I remember Nonno as a very vital man, interested in everything and everyone. He loved Italian art, architecture and opera. He listened to Italian radio and read Italian newspapers everyday.

He loved children. He would play with us often.

It seemed like he knew everyone. He would stop to talk to people on the street every time I was with him. He even took me to several wakes of people I never met.

He went to church every Sunday, then would stop at our house to visit. Often he brought fresh vegetables from his garden.

He let us help him make wine from his home grown grapes in his cellar at Neptune Street. He would always let us sample a little. I remember hating the taste of it.

When I was a toddler, I memorized all my books and nursery rhymes. Once Nonno saw me "reading" from a book and marveled that I read all the words correctly.

When he learned that he was to die, he completely closed off from everyone. He would scribble nonsensical lines on paper in an effort to communicate. He died when I was a teenager. His death left a deep void in the family.

Uncle Johnny reminded me most of Nonno.

Sophia Clemenzi Villanti (Aunt Sophie)

(Married Dominic Villanti – Children: Catharine, Maria, Angela)

Aunt Sophie is the head and heart of the family.

As a child I loved visiting her and her family at their turkey farm in Ipswich. Turkeys ran all over the yard. We children would pick blueberries and strawberries. Aunt Sophie used to bake pies and short cakes with them in a great old oven in her country kitchen.

Of the three sisters, Aunt Sophie was the serious, pragmatic one. She wouldn't abide nonsense or foolishness. She always, to this day, loved company. She prepares feasts for all who visit her.

Emma Clemenzi Villanti (Aunt Emma)

(Married Phillip Villanti – Children: Roberta, Phillip (Alvin))

She was a handsome woman, who took pride in her appearance. She would never leave the house without make-up or a girdle. At home, she wore colorful housedresses.

She was always fun to be with. She loved children and had a special way with them.

I remember staying with her on Elliot Street. Sometimes I would sleep in Roberta's room. There were stars on the ceiling that glowed in the dark. I would wake up to the sound of their pet bird chirping; a sound I always associate with their home. Today, when I stay with Roberta, I wake up to that same sound.

She was always yelling for and at "Alvin," who was usually involved in some sort of mischief. When the Chipmunk song was released we were sure they modeled it after our cousin, Alvin.

She created cakes that were works of art. Some of them were featured in the newspapers. I remember the cakes she made for Cardinal Cushing and Nonno and Nonna's anniversary. They featured sugar cube buildings, chocolate roads, swans, lamp posts, candy stone walls, and ponds. We loved watching her decorate the cakes. Nonno used to say that had she been a boy, she would have been the best builder in his construction company.

I thought she was a great cook. I particularly remember her gnocchi and her blue cheese dip.

My sister, Chris looks very much like Aunt Emma.

Dominic Clemenzi (Uncle Dom)

(Married Helen – Children: Robert, Richard, Dorothy, David, Mary Cathrine)

I stayed overnight at their home in Danvers often. Dorothy and I were very close as children. Uncle Dom always had something amusing to say. To this day, he is known for his stories and novelty items. He used to tease that Aunt Helen was from an American Indian family (she is not).

Visiting his Winkersheek Beach home in Gloucester where he makes his famous clam cakes.

His garden and art work with paint and stone.

John Battista Clemenzi (Uncle Johnny)
(Married: Olga Vandi – Children: Marie, John, Cheryl Ann, Alex)
Uncle Battista was big in size and heart. He was always generous, sometimes to a fault, to friends and family. Like Nonno, he was very sociable and knew everyone in town (though, at times, he would confuse people's names to a comical end). Family gatherings often took place at his home in Wenham. He loved us children and took the time to play games with us and show us his garden. Stories of him such as losing his horse and getting caught on film in a bathtub in Europe never failed to amuse us. When we girls started to date, he made sure to check out our boyfriends and inquire as to their intentions.

When he became seriously ill and dependent on a mobile oxygen tank, he never lost hope or his spirits. We all loved him dearly. The void in the family left by death is still keenly felt.

Peter Clemezi (Uncle Peter)
(Married Rose Nardella; Children: Peter James, John, Gary, Robert, Donald)
Uncle Peter was always an exceptionally handsome man. He was a hairdresser with a shop attached to his home. When I was 13 years old, I decided to bleach my hair blonde; it turned bright orange. Uncle Peter came to the house and repaired the damage.

I would frequently baby sit his 5 boys. The experience gave me renewed respect for my Aunt Rose's fortitude and patience. For two weeks every summer, the family vacationed with us in New York. The boys used to try to drag me into the swimming pool or sneak by my bedroom to watch me dress. I had to always have my guard up. They have since grown into remarkable men. Peter James is one of the most good-hearted and generous people I know.

When my Aunt Rose became ill, Uncle Peter devoted himself to her. I have always admired him for that.

Angelo Clemenzi (Uncle Angelo)
(Married Lucia Anselmo, children: John, Mark, Ann, Joan, Elizabeth, Susan)
Like his parents and siblings, Uncle Angelo was devoted to his family. He was a quiet man with many talents. He loved art and music and had a good singing voice. I will always remember him singing "Sunrise, Sunset" with a tear in his voice at my cousin Ann's wedding.

Uncle Angelo had a good knowledge of history and would take every opportunity to acquaint us children with interesting facts. In this way, he was very much like Nonno.

From our grandparents, parents and aunts and uncles, we learned the value of our Italian heritage, the importance of family, tradition, respect, and love. We can never repay them for enrichment they brought to our lives.

313

My Memories

Written by Deanna di Grandi Jones

Memories of Concetta Serra Clemenzi

Nonna:

I have a vague memory; I must have been 5 years old, of Nonna Concetta in the back room at Auntie Sophie's house with a big crane next to the bed. I watched in amazement as they used it to lift Nonna into her wheelchair. I had never seen or imagined anything like it.

I remember her funeral; I was 6 years old. There were so many people there crying, so I cried too. I don't think I realized why I was crying. This is the very first funeral I had ever been to.

Memories Mace di Grandi Jones

Mace:

I have a very vivid memory of when Mace and I were about 8 and 9 years old and we used to climb the walls in the hallway where our bedrooms were in the house our dad built in Staatsburg, NY. We used to put our hands on opposite walls, and then our feet, and then just walk up them. We used to race to see who could touch the ceiling first; he always won.

Mace di Grandi Jones

314

Emma (Clemenzi) Villanti,
A.K.A. The Cake Lady with Beautiful Blue Eyes

Part One
Written by Christopher and Nancy Obert with information supplied by
Sophia and Angela Villanti and Mary Goldrick
Photos supplied by Sophia Villanti, Janice Charowsky and Giovannina Obert

Emma (Clemenzi) Villanti

One day, while we were visiting with Sophie Villanti, she told us a story about her sister, Emma Villanti, and the cakes she used to make. Sophie told us that she would spend hours making these beautiful cakes. They were made only for special occasions and were huge. Sophia then pulled out an old photo album with two photos of the cake Emma made for her parents, Giovanni and MariaConcetta Clemenzi. It was their 50th Anniversary and Emma wanted to make the cake. The cake took about a month to make and contained 80 dozen eggs and an uncounted amount of candy decorations. They said the cake weighed 230 pounds! It had to be transported by truck to the party. Can you believe that? What a cake!

Giovanni and MariaConcetta Clemenzi's 50th Anniversary

315

The Clemenzi cake

We told Sophie that we had another photo of an even larger cake. We showed her the photo of Dominick and Catherine Villanti's 50th Anniversary. She said that Emma made that one too, and it was much larger than the first one. It is hard to imagine all the time, effort and love that must have gone into making those cakes. We wish that we could have seen and tasted them in person.

Dominick and Catherine Villanti's 50th Anniversary

Angela, Sophie's daughter, told me that Emma would make the buildings out of sugar cubes and hold them together with frosting. Angela also said that Emma made cakes for weddings, including her daughter Roberta's, and her niece Christine Di Grandi's. Since Angela is a few years older than us, she did have the chance to taste them, and even acted as her helper at times, as did many other nieces and nephews. Angela said, "She had a wonderful way with children. I remember Auntie Emma always had dishes of candy in her home and she would say, 'take two, one for each hand.'"

316

Part Two
Written by Christine di Grandi Jones
Photo supplied by Sophia Villanti

Aunt Emma vies the greatest artist and bakers! Not sure she was known as the cake lady but Angela (Villanti) and I agree that she was a Master of Creative cake Building! Emma "Marie" also made a remarkable cake for Cardinal Cushing! We all loved watching her make the sugar swans. Some of her nieces and nephews would help out washing the countless cake pans and molds. The large sliding glass doors had to be removed from the house so Emma's masterpiece cake could be transported to the destinations by professional movers in a van. She deputized the young male cousins to guard the cakes... even bought them badges to be deputized! Surely the purpose must have been to keep them from digging in! Many of the nieces were gifted with her famous doll cakes for our birthdays!

Emma and Phil Villanti (son of Dominick Villanti-from Lipari of the Aeolian Islands and Catherine Costa of Leni, Salina) had two children-Roberta October 4, 1941, is the first born of our generation and Philip Alvin June 1947. Phil followed in his father's foot steps and became a self employed roofer. He and his lovely wife Connie live in Danvers.

Roberta is a well traveled and accomplished woman. She has mastered the Italian language (one of many) and teaches English as a second language. She has a love for animals, enjoys photography, gardening, and diverse interests. Her daughters are Danielle January 5, 1971 and Nicole Jaquith March 28, 1975.

Emma was Godmother to 11 children. She loved Children and always made us feel so important. At her untimely death, it was requested that donations be made to the Home for Little Wanderers.

Cardinal Cushing and a very young Angela Villanti

317

Uncle Dominic and Aunt Helen

Written by Christine di Grandi Jones

Helen and Dominic Clemenzi

Thank you Uncle Dominic for the fabulous stone planters that grace my home! You have taken the skill that Nonno taught and have embellished it! Many in our family use and display your hand painted tiles in our kitchens-I think of you each morning as I look around my home.

The joy of my summer visit would not be complete without visiting you and Aunt Helen in Gloucester. I love touring your garden with its most unique scarecrows and artistic sculptures! Your humor is displayed all over your house (even the bathroom) with singing fish, dancing daisies, and the like... Thank you for your generous and warm hospitality covering your table with incredible clam cakes, fresh green beans from your garden, pasta with clam sauce and a bottle of wine! Hearing your tales of teaching my mother to cook brings laughter. Your sense of humor is wonderful!

You have always been so welcoming to family who also come to enjoy the incomparable white sands of Wingaersheek beach. My memory goes back to Dorothy and I as children drawing Mickey Mouse in the sand. Her artistic skills have well surpassed those days. I can visualize her painting of JFK and little John. I also have a painting of Mary Catherine's! Such a talented family!

David, I still have the picture of you and me at age five in our Davy Crocket costumes complete with fur hats! (or was it Daniel Boone?) Thank your for hosting me at your beautiful beach home (if it weren't for my smelly sneakers, I might still be invited!)

Richard, I hope I make it to one of your boating expeditions which I have heard so much about. And thanks to our beloved Bobby, we are still able to tell the stories of our little cousins getting lost on the beach and his not recognizing them-and let us not forget the basket or mushrooms he found in the woods and let his neighbors sample before he did!

Thank you Aunt Helen for caring for Nonna Concetta in her final days.

Battista Clemenzi

Written by Cheryl (Clemenzi) Comstock
Photos supplied by Sophie Villanti and Giovannina Obert

Front row: Amy, Jennifer and James Comstock, John Battista holding Benjamin Clemenzi,
Olga Clemenzi, Carrie Ann and Mark Beane
Back row: Michael and Cheryl Comstock, John T. and Christine Clemenzi, Alex Clemenzi,
Marie and Danny Beane

Battista a passion for gardening he learned from his father John (Giovani) Clemenzi. My father was on oxygen for years which kept him from being able to bend over to garden. He would have rather perished than give up gardening, so he planted his vegetables in several 60 gallon barrels that would enable him to garden at waist level. His green thumb produced a garden that resembled the lush greens of a rainforest. One of my fondest memories as a child, and one that my children also have from their childhood is that of picking and eating fresh vegetables from my father's garden. He always bordered the garden with vines of peas so his children and later his grandchildren (as well as all the children that would visit him over the years) could pick and eat the peas fresh out of the pods.

His garden was located in the backyard but the property was large and it sloped down considerably which meant that to reach the garden he had to walk down a long drive way down hill. Soon his illness would prevent him from being able to get back up that incline to the house. As it became increasingly harder for his lungs to bear the task, we all thought he would have to give up the garden dispute the barrels. His oldest son, my brother John, wasn't about to let that happen. He purchased a used golf cart for him to make the trips to and from and get all around his property in Hamilton. The golf cart soon became another joy for my father and his grandchildren. He would give the kids rides around in it and they too learned to drive it. Even though the cart should have remained on the property only and was illegal to drive on the street, you can bet that 'wasn't going to matter to my father. He would soon begin the practice of using the golf cart to deliver his fresh garden vegetables to various neighbors. He, of course, always planted a surplus so he would be able to share with everyone who came to the house or that he could deliver to.

Another story that speaks volumes about my father's personality is one my mother just shared with me a few weeks ago. After my father died my mother sold the property and house in Hamilton that they had lived in for 50 years. Last month she received a letter from a woman named Laura that had been a neighbor of theirs for many of those years. Laura still lives in the neighborhood in Hamilton. She wrote to my mother saying that she had been out walking her new granddaughter. As she pushed the stroller past my parents old home she had a flood of memories of a time 30 years earlier when she had just moved to that neighborhood. She remembered my father coming out of his house and rushing right over to meet this new neighbor. He reached down and snatched up her baby from the stroller saying "come, come into the house and have something to eat", a practice he would repeat over and over again through the years.

Many neighbors and friends lives were touched by John Battista Clemenzi's and I'm sure they could write their own book just about him and his generous ways and love of people. There are so many wonderful memories of my dad that I couldn't possibly relate them all. What comes to mind most of all is his incredible love of children and people and his desire to constantly surround himself with family.

John Battista Clemenzi, Maria Concetta (Serra) Clemenzi, Olga (Vandi) Clemenzi, Cheryl (Clemenzi), Michael Comstock, Maria Concetta (Costa) Serra and Domenico Serra

I am sending you two essays that my daughters (Jennifer and Amy) wrote at separate times while in high school. The first was written by my oldest, Jennifer shortly before my father died in 1995. She wrote it in a sophomore English class essay but we used it as a Eulogy. The next essay is called "Red and White Stucco" and it was written shortly after his death by my second born, Amy. Both are tributes to how much they loved their grandfather.

John Battista Clemenzi

Interview with Olga Clemenzi by Christine di Grandi Jones

Battista, Cheryl, John, Alex, Marie and Olga Clemenzi

"Where do I begin? The most important thing I can say about my husband, John Battista, is that he was the most like Uncle Dominick Serra. He was close to everyone: Nieces, nephews, children, grand children. He was crazy about every one of them. John Battista Clemenzi was the 5th child born to Concetta and John Clemenzi on October 15, 1922. Aunt Olga said she won't say anything about his escapades, that wouldn't be nice and there were many! When she was 21, she met her future husband at her brother's house while he and the others were doing renovations on Aunt Lena's house. Olga's parents (Maria Morri of San Moreno and Attilio Vandi of Rimini, Italy) made her go to dinner there. "It was not love at first sight!" Her father told her to help out in the kitchen while Enrico and Theresa decided that they should get together and go out that evening. John took them all to a night club. Until that night, Olga never knew there was such a thing as transvestites! She said that Theresa DeAngelis Miranda was even more sheltered than she. (Olga's brother Mario was married to Lena's daughter Rose.) John and Olga dated for one week-then, she did not hear from him for a month! This was around Thanksgiving time. She giggled telling this story because if you dated at that time, it was expected that you would get married. Well, she did not see John until Christmas Eve at Zia Lena's two family house on Rantoul Street in Beverly.

Zia "Azalena" lived downstairs with daughter Rose, her brother Mario Vandi, and their daughter and Theresa and her husband Enrico lived upstairs. He did not like it when he learned that Olga had a date for New Year's Eve. He told her to break it and go out with him instead. John Battista proposed by asking: "Are you going to marry me-Yes or No?" She did not answer. Then, he posed this question: "Do you like children?" To this she replied: "yes." John said "Good! We'll have a dozen!" They went shopping for a ring and became officially engaged. They both worked in Boston - John as an independent plasterer. Each night, John would take her back to Boston for a date to places like the Continental and The Old Howard. They always had pizza! She had one slice and John would eat one or two whole pies! One night John had not shown for their date so she called him on the phone to see if there was a problem. Now, bare in mind that Olga had an engagement ring on her finger. John said to her "Nice girls do not call men on the phone"! And he hung up on her! This resulted in their not speaking for a month! John was 27 years old and his mother was afraid he might marry someone of whom she would not approve! Everyday, his mother Concetta would ask if he was going to get married. He would say "OK, mamma, soon."

Olga and John were married on April 23, 1950. When asked what it was that finally attracted him to her, Olga said because he was exciting and worldly. After all, he had worked in places like Florida and Ohio! If he had

321

not gotten food poisoning while he was away, he might not have come home for this encounter. Olga says He works harder than any man she ever knew and played harder than any man she ever knew! John, his father, and older brother Dominic created a partnership "Clemenzi and Sons." Dominick attended Wentworth College and was instrumental in organizing the business. When John went off on his own to specialize in plastering, he gave his share of the business to his youngest brother Angelo. "He was the Pied Piper of Hamilton" befriending everyone he met and making room at his table in his heart. He built his home on 86 Meyer Road in 1953. It was strong! Olga said it was a bomb shelter! John took great pride in his home and spent endless hours keeping it nice. The neighborhood kids would come over and he'd give them all jobs working outside. Since they couldn't pronounce his last name, they would call him 'Mr. McKenzie'. There were dozens of kids! He'd take them all in his truck and buy them ice-cream. He truly loved children. Olga and John have 17 Godchildren.

Their first child, Marie, was born On April 3, 1951, just one year after they were married. Olga tells how upset John was that she was not pregnant the first month of marriage. The second month when she still was not pregnant, he insisted she see a Doctor to find out what the problem was. The doctor prescribed patience for John. Marie moved to Maine with her husband, Daniel Beane, who was originally from there. They have just celebrated their 31st weeding anniversary. Marie became Post Mistress of Carantun, ME. Danny ran the general store which carried a little of everything including fishing equipment. Their store was on the Appalachian Trail and hikers would stop to shower or stay in the loft set up for travelers. Marie brought fresh baked goods to the store to sell. Carrie Anne was born to Marie and Danny on January 17, 1975. Carrie loves movies and knows all the actors! She is good-natured and will talk your ear off! She is crazy about her brother and his wife and helped with much of their wedding plans. Their second child, Mark Charles, was born March 28, 1978. He is a real' Maine-ite'! Mark attended the University of Maine at Orono with studies in computer science. On January 29, 2001, he married Amanda Wolfe. They live in Essex, MA.

John Thomas was born on May 13, 1953. He is a "good son." John always declared that he would never be a plasterer! John has been successfully employed as a plasterer for years! John's dry sense of humor is loved by his cousins. He stands over 6' tall and his friendship and loyalty to his family is even taller! John married Christine Hoops from Groton, CT on July 27, 1991. What a gorgeous Oceanside ceremony and reception that was! Christine is a teacher in Hamilton. Olga says: "John made a good choice!" She so appreciates their coming to dinner each Monday night. They are proud adoptive parents of Benjamin born July 28, 1993. Their home is in Rowley, MA.

Cheryl Ann was born on August 14, 1955. "She was "The apple of her father's eye." One of Cheryl's most treasured qualities is her love from children. As a teen, she did a lot of baby-sitting. She continues caring for children after having her own children. James Michael Comstock won her heart and they were married on August 18, 1979. Cheryl is creative and has an artistic view. Olga says: "She was the best baby-she never cried! But now, she cries when she is happy or upset" Just goes to show that artistic temperament! Cheryl was eager to start her own family. Jennifer Lynn was born on .November 22, 1980. She graduated in 2003 Magna Cum Laude from Keene State College. Amy Comstock was born on June 8, 1982-another beautiful young woman! She is shares her mother's love for children and her sensitivity. Amy is attending college. James Michael, November 4, 1985 is a "good kid" He is currently in High School and is on the golfing team. He loves sports and is about 6' tall. James is easy going, sweet and quiet. All three of Cheryl and Michael's children are very close.

Alex Joseph was born on August 20, 1959. Alex has always been a true independent person. At age 16, he planned his entire trip to Hawaii with his two friends. His resourcefulness kicked in when the travel company went bankrupt on his last day there. Alex was not quite 20 when he really asserted his independence and moved to San Francisco. He worked for Ghirardelli Chocolate Manufacturer for 21 years. (Cousins loved visiting him there and receiving the chocolate treats when he came back East to visit!) Alex presently works for the Four Seasons Hotels and enjoys the many benefits! The thousands of miles do not keep Alex from being with family. Olga just celebrated her 75th birthday. She is now lives in a lovely condo in Middleton and continues to be very active. Traveling, reading, and being an integral part of family life, keeps her very busy. We can always count on Olga to be at a family function or respond to someone's needs.

John Battista Clemenzi - Eulogy

Written by: Jennifer Comstock
Introduction and ending by Chris Clemenzi

Son, brother, husband, father, uncle, John Clemenzi was all of these, but the role that was by for the closest to his heart and soul was that of Nono. He dearly loved his six grandchildren, Carrie, Mark, Jennifer, Amy, James and Benjamin and he was enormously proud of each one. They were his golden treasure, the most precious thing on earth to him. They all loved him dearly and were very proud of the courage he displayed in dealing with his illness. His granddaughter, Jennifer put her thoughts and feelings into words when she wrote this essay several weeks ago.

When facing an illness, courage can be very hard to find. Sometime during all our lives we will know someone who is ill or even dying. I was only a baby when mg grandfather was diagnosed with asbestos poisoning in his lungs. I only remember hearing the stories about how he had worked with the poisonous dust for so many years. It was fifteen years ago that his doctors told him he had six months to live. Many of his friends and family wondered how and why he is still alive. I know that it is because he has the courage to never give up and the power and will to live.

My grandfather, John Bettista Clemenzi, is truly an extraordinary man. He has gone through many different stages of his illness, and presently, he cannot breathe without an oxygen Mask. A lot of people in his situation would just give up hope and waste away. But, my Nono is not like most people. He is the kind of person who lives life to its fullest and never gives up. He is very active for a man who can only breathe with an oxygen mask. When I go to visit him he is usually out in his garden which is built in barrels so he doesn't have to bend down. He also enjoys walking through his quiet neighborhood, stopping along the way to talk to his friends. Recently, as his illness progressed, it has become more difficult for him to be outdoors. When he can't go outside he enjoys having his grandchildren come and stay with him. One weekend, when we went to visit him and asked him how he was feeling, he replied, "Much better now that you kids are here." My grandfather is a very strong man who has the courage to live.

Two winters ago was the first time my grandfather had been hospitalized for his illness. When the phone rang and I heard my grandmother's voice, "Nono is in the hospital". fear and panic struck over me like a bolt of lightning. When I saw him lying in his hospital bed giving his every strength to sit up and talk to us, I wanted to cry. He was in the hospital for a couple of weeks and then he was sent to a rehabilitation center. We visited as often as we could and every time he looked better and better. His doctors were amazed at his progress and at his strength to live. He was sent home with oxygen tanks and told that he had to use them all the time.

He has been on oxygen for two years now and we have all adjusted to it. At first, he was afraid to go into public places and be seen wearing an oxygen mask. We all assured him that It would he fine and eventually he did it. Now, he is use to wearing the mask, and we're all very grateful that he is lucky enough to have it.

My siblings and I love to spend a weekend at my grandparent's house. My grandmother says that Nono gets excited just knowing that we're coming over. One day while I was sitting in the closed in porch of my Nono's house he asked me if I would remember him after he died. As the tears stung my eyes I immediately replied, "Nono, how could I ever forget you?" He looked pleased with my answer, but I could still see a shadow of doubt in his soft, brown eyes. I didn't know how I could convince him that I could not and would not ever forget him. I hope that he knows how much I care about him and how much I respect him. My grandfather is one of the most courageous people I knout and I love him very much.

Carrie, Mark, Jennifer, Amy, James and Benjamin, I believe that today's snowflakes are Nono's love showering down on you all.

November 29, 1995

323

Red and White Stucco

Written by Amy Comstock

When I think about my Nono, there are many memories that come to mind. Nono always enjoyed spending time with his six grandchildren. Even as his illness progressed he enjoyed being with his family. I spent a lot of my life at the red and white house on Meyer Road in Hamilton. My Nono had died almost four years ago. At that time everything changed. Although everything has gotten back to "normal," I still feel as though I've lost an important person in my life.

One year ago, my family was invited to a birthday party for my Noni. The party was held at Noni and Nono's old house, which I had not been to since Noni moved. The new owners were not related, but they were kind enough to have our relatives over for this occasion. As my family turned down the very familiar road, I started anticipating what it would be like to go back there. I told myself that it was just a house, and now that he was gone, the changes wouldn't matter. We turned into the driveway, and I was shocked to see that the red and white stucco house was now green and white. I started to question whether I really wanted to be there.

As I walked into the house, I was greeted by my extended family. This was very comfortable as it seemed like one of the hundred other parties that had been thrown there. From where I stood, nothing in the kitchen had changed. Jackie, the new owner, handed me a bag and asked me to put it in her son's bedroom, the last room on the right. I started to feel angry as I walked down the hall. We called that the "waterbed room." I knocked on the door, and a 10 year old boy opened it. A large golden retriever stepped out from behind the door. Looking in, I saw that the waterbed had been replaced with bunk beds, and the fuzzy, red carpet had been removed to reveal a wooden floor. I didn't stay there long. I turned and went to put my coat in Nono and Noni's old room. When I walked in, I was bombarded by the changes that were there. Everything was different; even the familiar grey rug was gone. Standing beside the bed, I remembered the day we had come home from Nono's funeral. I had walked into their bedroom that day too. Next to the bed in the rug were the tracks that the stretcher had left when the ambulance attendants were taking Nono to the hospital. Tears came to my eyes as I thought of him. I thought of when he was in the hospital, the last time that I had seen him. I had held his hand at his bedside, while my Mom talked to him. He could not speak, nor could he pick up his head to nod or shake it. My Mom told him to blink his eyes twice if he understood her. He did understand, and he squeezed his eyes shut two times to let us know this. Suddenly, the door opened behind me, and there were people coming in to put their coats down. I was brought back to the reality that I had escaped momentarily.

I recovered from my tears, only to walk down to the kitchen and see my Mom crying as she stood with her cousins. I turned and walked outside, as I began to cry again. I didn't want anyone to know that I was upset, as I was supposed to be the strong one, or that's the position I had unknowingly assigned myself. Three or four minutes passed, but it seemed like hours until my cousin came looking for me. I went back to the house where another cousin had just arrived with a baby. I played with the baby for a couple of hours which was a much-needed distraction. By the end of the night it was starting to be more comfortable to be there.

As we were pulling back down the driveway in the dark, I thought about how I had felt going back to the house. That red and white stucco house held many priceless memories. Part of me was glad that the house looked different, as it was no longer Noni and Nono's house. However, the other part of me wished that everything could have remained untouched, as Nono had left it. I now know that I could handle visiting there again, although I am not anxious to go back anytime soon.

3/30/99

My Godfather

Written by Christine di Grandi Jones

My Godfather, Uncle Johnny, often referred to as "Battista" by his siblings, was the center of many family gatherings. We nieces and nephews loved to visit him and our warm and hospitable aunt Olga. She made us feel grown up by talking to us as if we were important. Uncle John was a BIG man in every way! He was generous, fun, remarkable, hardworking,

Uncle John built his white masonry home on 86 Meyer Road, Hamilton, MA. He kept his grounds well manicured. We enjoyed Easter egg hunts, Eggs tosses and races on his lawns. He built an "Italian room for a big round table for meals and gatherings. Aunt Olga always had an endless stream of food filling their table. Breakfast was always a treat there with fresh sliced melon bacon, sausage, and blueberry muffins-. What a way to start the day!

One event, which stands out quite clearly in my memory, was when I was about age 8. On one of my many overnight visits, my cousins Marie & Johnny and I made a raft and put it to sail on the forbidden pond. Since our navigating skills were limited, we capsized and thought we would drown! We were quite shaken by this 'near death experience' and walked with great trepidation up to the house. Uncle Johnny was raking the stones in his driveway when he saw us sopping wet trying to slip back to the house. Once he knew we were ok, he started swinging the rake handle at his children's bottoms! I was most upset since I never had an uncle mad at me before.

I remember the horse and the barn with an apartment and the big garage where we saw family movies. His pool table was the first and the biggest one I ever saw. We kids retreated to his huge basement to play.

Aunt Olga was particularly famous for her chocolate roll that she would bring to family gatherings. Aunt Olga was tall and trim and wore her long black hair in a French Twist. The only time her hair was down was on Halloween as she prepared herself as the annual scary witch!

Wherever Battista traveled, he looked in phone book to see if he could find any Clemenzi's who might be related. (Recently, I followed his example by using the Internet to find family members in Italy). When my family moved to Dutchess County, in New York, Uncle Johnny struggled to pronounce Poughkeepsie. With a quasi-Italian accent and mispronunciation for which he was famous and cause for much laughter, would say; Po-skip-see. My little children giggled as they tried to teach him how to pronounce it. Whenever Uncle John would visit, he would bring a cornucopia of vegetable from his gardens. He supplies us for the season. Gardening was his great joy. After his taking ill with Asbestosis and needing Oxygen, he would strap on the bottle of oxygen in a basket his daughter made for him and ride his golf cart that his son John gave him and ride down to his lush garden that was now built-up on barrels so he would not have to bend down to garden. There was an article about that in the local newspaper this improvising!
Aunt Olga continues to bring grated cheese to us all!

Many or the extended family members have swirled plastered ceilings in their homes which was John Battista's insignia. His hard working son has carried on his trade, generosity, and sincere concern for others. I will never forget how my cousin John made sure my car was in good shape for my trip back to NY.

Whenever I would come back and visit the Beverly area, Uncle John was one of the very first people I would call and make plans to see. We all love reminiscing about the good times that centered on uncle Johnny!
Our family is richer and closer because of the unifying nature of Uncle Johnny!

Clemenzi Family History

Written by Donald Clemenzi
Photos supplied by Sophie Villanti, Christine DiGrandi Jones, Donald and Gayle Clemenzi

Foreground: Gayle and Donald Clemenzi
Middle row: Brendan, Kiera, Kathy, Margaret, Rose, Peter, Joyce Clemenzi
Back row: John D, John A, Gary, Peter James, Robert and Candace Clemenzi

My parents, Peter Clemenzi (son of Concetta Serra (Clemenzi)) and Rose Nardella created somewhat of a legacy and have given us endless roots. They were married after my father returned from the war in Germany on July 6, 1952 at St. Mary's in Beverly. My mother is said to have worn a satin dress of multi-layers that she thought she'd be wearing in the winter; my father's discharge from the army was delayed and she wore that dress on an extremely hot July day - 100 degrees! My mother's brother, Uncle Mike worked with my father at the A&P and introduced my parents. That started the ball rolling; Auntie Emma, my father's sister) was instrumental in helping my parents get together, as Emma babysat for Rose's younger sister, and knew the Nardellas very well. While my father was away in Germany, my mother wrote to him every single day until he came home. My parents were married for almost 44 years when my mother sadly passed away in 1996. Although she is gone, she lives on in all of us. She loved family, meeting and entertaining in our home. Some of my favorite memories are simply of us sitting in the dining room, listening to my aunts and uncles telling stories – for hours. Having lived these antics only prepared my parents for five boys!

One story they told that vividly stands out in my mind is when my mother and her cousin, Josephine Carnevale, took my grandfather's new car for an unexpected dip in the creek. They were about 8 or 9 years old

326

and they were playing house. My mom pretended to be "the driver" of her dad's new car. She took the car out of gear and it rolled into the water! Neighbors saw Josephine jump out immediately before it went in the water, but no one saw my mother get out into the tall weeds. Our long time friends and neighbors, the Biondinis, thought my mom hadn't gotten out. While my grandmother and great-grandmother were crying in the kitchen, they heard something in my mother's room – it was she, hiding under her bed.

Another story we loved to hear over and over again at the Sunday gatherings was the story of my grandparent Clemenzi's new living room furniture with big square, wooden legs. For some reason, my father, a young boy at the time, didn't like the look and he took a saw to the legs to round them off. Come to think of it, my parents never did buy furniture with square legs… so I assume the story is true.

My family was brought up in Beverly, except for one year when the three oldest boys were little and they lived in Florida for a year. My father still lives in the house where we grew up. His successful business, which he ran and operated, a beauty shop, is now being run by my cousin's wife, Pam Nardella. Although my father and mother worked extremely hard to raise five boys, we have wonderful memories of family. Our family extended to whomever we shared our time, including the station full of fire-fighters next door. Some of them became long-time companions and friends. My mother used to cook for them and we played all the time in the fire house, unless the chief was there! Then, we would hide!

Five boys can create high energy – and we did. We have vivid memories of getting caught digging holes in the foundation of our house, putting holes in doors and breaking the glass on the front door after slamming it; in fact, the local hardware store kept one ready for my dad since he had to replace it so often. My mom was a wonderful cook. I used to love her spinach patties, her homemade pasta and her pies! I remember making gnocchi with her; we'd make pounds of it and it would disappear in a meal or two. Mom always said she'd wanted a daughter, too, but I think we kept her busy enough!

We'd have our more subdued, but no less fun moments with weekly family gatherings. On Sunday's we'd visit Nana and Nonno Nardella or Nana and Nonno Clemenzi. Our cousins have always played together as kids and still get together with our families. The 4th of July parties were an annual event with lobster, swimming and fun. Christmas Eve in Nana Nardella's basement was a traditional celebration of the seven fishes. We now host this with my brothers and their families and Gayle's family here at our house, and the girls put out reindeer food and cookies in hopes that Saint Nicholas soon will be there...

My parents made sure that we were surrounded by family and good times. Nothing was ever more important than family. They took us on annual trips to NY to visit with Auntie Mary's family, my father's sister. We enjoyed seeing our cousins, with whom we've remained close, despite distance and time, taking day trips to the City and touring the mansions of Hyde Park. My parents also traveled with my Uncle Battista and Auntie Olga. I'm sure they had no idea the parties that went on while they were off in Spain or Italy! My parents loved to go to new places, see new things and were looking forward to traveling a lot in retirement. My mother's health failed and my father was by her side taking care of her until her passing. They were, however, still able to spend time at their house in Florida despite my mother's health. They had many wonderful years and memories together; they always let us know that we are their legacy. My parents have always been proud of us five boys.

Peter James is my oldest brother, born February 23, 1954. He attended Bentley College and studied business. He is a successful investor and a great brother, as well as uncle to all his nieces and nephews. Peter has also taken on the role of the eldest brother and has been there for our family decisions, crises and support. He has great family events and family gatherings at his house, especially pool parties that he and his long time friend Punkie (Sandra) host. My daughters love visiting him and we know he loves being with his family.

Cathy and John Clemenzi

My second oldest brother is John Anthony born on March 11, 1955. John is now a wonderful and involved father. Despite the long hours he works, he still never misses time when his family needs him, whether it be helping with the HS band or building Brendan's house with him. He is a successful superintendent of a large construction company. He married Kathy Lyman who has stayed home to raise their 4 children. Their children are Brendan, a software development manager who married Karen Ahern in 2002; Margaret, a hair dresser, will marry Wesley Rollings in October, 2003. Kiera Lee is double majoring at Fitchburg State University to become a teacher; John David is a talented drummer and a sophomore in high school. Our annual Christmas Day meal continues at John's house, and no one misses it!

Robert Michael, my third brother was born on July 22, 1956. He married Joyce Osgood, who works at the Polish Club. Rob works as a handyman and is an expert electrician, and is in high demand; it's how he knows just about everyone and everything that's going on locally. Rob and Joyce have one daughter, Candice. Candice is attending Lesley University in Boston and is studying to become an early childhood teacher. Candice has become very close to us since our girls were born. She faithfully spends time with the girls and they adore her. And when Uncle Rob visits, the girls have a blast, bend a few rules and giggle a lot.

Barbara and Gary Clemenzi

My brother Gary Steven and I are closest in age. He was born October 28, 1959. Three years ago he married a wonderful Brazilian woman, Barbara. They met at work and continue to work together. They have one adorable, very busy little son, Cristofer, who is now two years old and very attached to his "moo" toy. Nicolas, another baby, is coming in October 2003. Gary is the function manager of Creative Catering in Beverly. Easter is now becoming a new tradition at Gary and Barbara's house. Food and family…

And I am the fifth boy. I was born April 10, 1963 and married Gayle Johnson in 1990. We honeymooned in Germany and helped chip away at the Berlin Wall. I am the customer support manager for an international software company and a full time father. Gayle was working as a teacher of the Deaf until the birth of our beautiful triplet daughters who were welcomed to the world on our 8th anniversary. Marissa Rose, Kendra Lynn and Jenna Marie are now five years old and off to kindergarten in the fall. Bringing up three babies at the same time has been fun, exhausting and has given us some of the most wonderful moments as parents and partners.

Donald and Gayle Clemenzi
Kendra, Marissa and Jenna

Our daughters are the light of our lives. Jenna is a very bright, cheerful, outgoing little girl who brings us laughter and happiness; she soaks up the world around her. Kendra brings out the child in all of us; she is skillfully artistic in many ways, fantastically creative and imaginative. Marissa has an unending passion and enthusiasm for life; she takes on the world with the energy and beauty she brings to our home. Our family has been with us since before their birth. Besides everyone listed here, Gayle's parents and her side of the family, we've had visits and help from just about everyone. Auntie Olga, a.k.a. Auntie O especially, has found a very special place in our home and our hearts.

My home is busy, but filled with a deep sense of family and love. We grew up knowing that family is always here and always the root of our life. Family is our priority, our purpose and our foundation. I know that my father is proud of me, my brothers and of our families. My mom loved being with each of her grandchildren and she doted on all of them from the moment they were born. Since she has been gone, she has had four (almost five) more grandchildren born into the family. I know that if she was still with us, she would love to meet and spoil Gary's son(s) and my girls (and all the pink that comes with them!) She is gone, but always with us for each family gathering, in our hearts. Our parents showed us a love that transcends all -- family.

Peter Clemenzi Memories

Written by Peter Clemenzi

As a boy growing up in Beverly, I remember making slingshots with my friends. We used the inner tubes from tires cut into strips and fastened them onto sticks in Y shapes.

Another memory I have is saving up my money to buy a brand new bicycle. It was bright red and I was so proud of myself that I couldn't wait to show it off to my big sister Sophie. I rode it from my house on Elliott Street to the home where Sophie was doing private duty nursing near the Beverly Library on Essex Street.

When I was about 14 years old, my friend Philip had an exciting idea to build our own boat. I asked him, "Where will we get the wood?" and he answered that his father could get it from his job at The United Shoe where he packed the machinery to be sent out. So we got some wood and made our boat with tongue in groove joints. Then we put heavy boulders in it to sink it in the Bass River so that the wood could swell and make the joints tight. Of course this was a secret but somebody told Papa. Being an overprotective father, he went to the river, found the boat and destroyed it right away !

I remember

Written by Peter James Clemenzi

Starting with Nonno, then my parents, aunts and uncles, have been great role models who have instilled the highest of family values in me. I have experienced family gatherings since I was a child. I can remember seven of us cramming ourselves into our car and setting out to visit Aunt Mary. If I saw us coming down the road, I might have wanted to run but instead, while she was working to support her family, she opened her doors and made us feel like we were special, loved, and important. They gave what they had-food, a place to stay, a hug and a smile what ever was needed to make life better –I saw this all the time!

This is what makes me who I am. All of them were a blessing to me and there beautiful examples continue with all of us We are keeping it going… That is what our family was all about and I couldn't be more grateful-seeing it from childhood. I witnessed it even when my parents were on a tight budget, if someone needed a bag of groceries, help with their rent, a place to stay, they made sure they got it! Whenever someone came to our home they were treated as the most important person on earth!! They were and still are a great example of unselfish giving, generosity, and hospitality. This is the true meaning of life, unconditional love………

Memories:

Concetta:
"I fondly remember spending time at Nonna's-cleaning and spending the night listening to her countless family stories.

Uncle Angelo:
Uncle Angelo was my mentor in areas of self improvement-teaching me not to put limitations on self and to dream and visualize and to achieve whatever you want as long as you do not hurt anyone.

Auntie Mary:
Thank you for opening your home to my family. Your home and generosity provided me and my family with a couple of weeks vacation each summer. It was an important time in which a bond was created with my cousins which has developed over the years.
They are my brothers and sisters. I feel that way with most of my cousins. Look how we enjoy each other and our special bond! I get blessings each day with the phone calls that come in to touch base and show their caring.

Uncle Dominic and Auntie Helen:
Gave us a vacation spot and continue to be there. I have recently gotten closer to Uncle Dom and appreciate that relationship. Thank you to Aunt Helen for being so supportive to my mother, calls, notes, and always being up beat! This was precious love.

Auntie Emma:
Her generosity was tremendous. She just about dressed us. She shared her creativity with us.-The time and energy she invested to celebrate her parents. Great tribute and great example!

Auntie Olga and Uncle John:
They opened their home to us as teenagers. It was great to have a safe place to continue to celebrate after a Homecoming or prom

Aunt Sophie:
Oh, what can I say, she is an incredible inspiration on how to live your life to the fullest. She gives herself to family, friends, and strangers. Aunt Sophie continues the tradition of preparing a special birthday dinner of gnocchi for me. This tradition was started by my mother when I was a child and continued until her passing.

Thank you family and especially the "A team" for all your unconditional love!

332

Giovanni and Maria Concetta (Serra) Clemenzi Wedding Day

Giovanni Clemenzi
Sophia, Marietta, Emma, Dominick and Concetta Clemenzi

Marietta and Sophia Clemenzi

Peter, Battista and Giovanni Clemenzi

335

Peter, Dominick, Angelo, Battista and Giovanni Clemenzi

Back row: Peter, John Battista, and Dominick Clemenzi, Dominick Villanti (holding Maria), George Di Grandi (holding Christine), Phil Villanti, Angelo Clemenzi

Seated: Rose Clemenzi, Olga Clemenzi (holding Marie), Helen Clemenzi, Sophie Villanti, Concetta Clemenzi, John Clemenzi Sr. (holding David Clemenzi), Mary DiGrandi, Emma Villanti, Lucia Clemenzi

On floor: Dorothy, Richard and Robert Clemenzi, Catherine Villanti, Philip A. Villanti, Ronald Di Grandi, Diana Di Grandi, Roberta Villanti

Dominick and Sophie (Clemenzi) Villanti (standing)
Maria Concetta (Serra) and Giovanni Clemenzi (seated)
Catherine, Angela and Maria Villanti

337

Giovanni and Maria Concetta (Serra) Clemenzi

1st row left to right: Concetta (Serra) Clemenzi, Mary DiGrandi, Sophie Villanti and Peter Clemenzi
2nd row left to right: Emma Villanti, Dominick Clemenzi, John Battista Clemenzi and Angelo

Sophia and Dominick Villanti

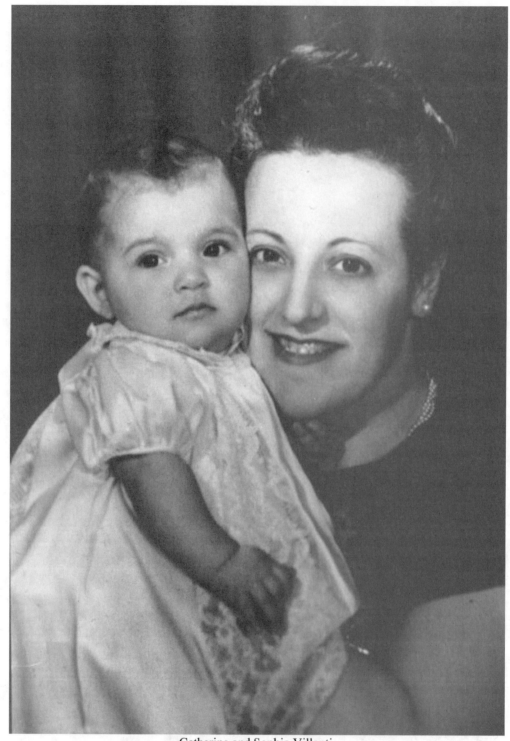

Catherine and Sophia Villanti

Alana Constantelo, George and Catherine Constantelo, Dominick and Sophie Villanti,
Maria and Dennis Parent, Angela Villanti, Kristen Constantelo

Catherine Constantelo, Maria Parent, Sophie and Angela Villanti

Angela, Sophie, George, Catherine, Alana, Kristen, Dennis, Maria

Anthony, Kaitlyn, Jason, Kristen

George & Marietta (Clemenzi) DiGrandi Wedding Day

Deanna Jones, Christine di Grandi Jones (holding) Bettina Jones, Patricia Hohmann
Front: Francine di Grandi and Diana di Grandi

Trisha, Christine and Deanna Jones

Trisha, Deanna and Mace Jones

John, Stefanie, Patricia, Sarah and Robert Hohmann

Ronald, Francine, Patricia, Diana and Christine

John Clemenzi, Philip & Emma Villanti, Mary Carnivale, Dominick Clemenzi

David in arms of Dominick, Helen, Dorothy,
Richard, and Robert Clemenzi

Helen and Dominick Clemenzi celebrated their
50th wedding anniversary on May 6, 1993

Charlene, David, Tina and Eric Clemenzi

Khalil family - Omar, Mostafa, Aisha, Mary and baby Sarah

Aisha, Omar and Sarah Khalil

349

Aaron, Lara, Gail and John Clemenzi

Donald and Gayle Clemenzi
Kendra, Jenna and Marissa

Lucia and her Grandchildren:
Front row: Aaron, Jared, Farren, Ben, Jesse, Joseph
Back row: Asa, Tasia, Lucia, Ariel, Lara, Catrina and Alyssa Clemenzi

Christine, Peter, Peter, Rose, Gail, Donny
Paul, Lucia, John

Patricia Hohmann, Francine di Grandi, Danielle Jaquith, Alana Constantello, Roberta Jaquith,
Peter James Clemenzi, Sandra Thompson, Catherine Constantelo
Gina di Grandi, Mary di Grandi, Stefanie Hohmann, Sophia Villanti, Kristen Constantelo
Sara Hohmann (in car), Robert Hohmann, Anthony Constantelo (blue shirt)

Standing in: back John A, Gary, Peter, Robby, Donald, John T, and Richard Clemenzi
Next row: Diana Di Grandi, Ann Clemenzi, Maria Parent, Elizabeth Clemenzi, Patty Hohmann, Mark
Clemenzi
On couch: Susan Clemenzi, Roberta Jaquith, Mary Kahlil
on floor: Joan Clemenzi, Christine Di Grandi Jones, Angela Villanti

Marie, John and Cheryl Clemenzi

Cheryl, Maria, Alexender and John Clemenzi

John, Gary, Robert and Peter James Clemenzi

MariaConcetta (Serra) Clemenzi Family Notes:

In youth we learn;
in age we understand.

--Marie Von Ebner-Eschenbach (1830-1916)

Caterina Serra and Giovanni Costa Family

Happy Memories

Written by Donia Blanton

Catherine (Serra) and John Costa

Catherine Serra and John Costa were both born and raised in Salina, Sicily but didn't know each other until they came to the United States. They met in Boston. After they married, they lived out their lives in a tiny house in Beverly, Mass. Mom (Maria Concetta) says that even thought the house was small, there was always room for company. Their God parents (Santa & Joe Scimone, from Revere, and their children) loved to come over and would all spend the night... people would sleep anywhere they could find a spot. They kept single mattresses in a storage room for just such occasions and they played the player piano and sang and just had a grand time.

Mom says her dad (John) would come home every Thursday night with boxes stacked high of pastries for the family and for each of their birthdays they would always get a box of Hershey chocolate candy bars. She said it might not sound like much, but her friends were always envious of the treats they got. Her mom and dad would go out on a date every weekend, and attended the Opera whenever it came to town. Mom's sister, Nancy, was the one in charge when her parents were out.

Her dad would have mom sit and pick slivers of steel from his hands when he came home from working as a machinist for United Shoe Machine Corp. in Beverly, Mass. Mom, her sister Nancy and brothers Orazio and John Battista all worked in the leather factory. Her sister Santa worked for GE - in the early days it was the Hy Grade light bulb plant.

Santa's boyfriend introduced mom to my dad through correspondence during the war. Dad came to visit on furloughs and he eventually left the service to marry her. After they were married he brought her to Virginia (the only one to move away from Mass.)

I can remember as children, every three years or so we would go to Mass. to visit mom's family for a week in the summer... Happy memories.

Stories I Remember and Stories I've Been Told

Written by: Nancy Costa Desmond

My Father, Orazio Costa and my Mother, Rose (Femino) Costa grew up on the same street, Williams Street in Beverly. My Mom lived up the street from my Father. Both families were large. My Dad's family had eight children and my Mom's had ten. Speaking with my Aunt Josie (Costa) Scagliarini she told me how the Costa's and the Femino's spent a lot of time together. Apparently they use to play baseball in front of My Mother's house on Williams Street. Every Saturday night my father's parents would go out and the Femino's would go to the Costa's house and sit around the player piano and sing. They would also play cards. My Aunt Sanna (Costa) Augustus and my Aunt Nancy (Femino) Cyr were in the same graduating class from Beverly High School. They continued to stay close for all these years. Aunt Sanna passed away this past February but their little group of friends still get together weekly at Rose Vandi's house to play cards.

Back row: Battista Costa, Orazio Costa, Nancy Costa, Josephine Costa and ?
Front row: ?, Sanna Costa, Rose Femino, Nancy Femino, Mary Costa and ?

Car Memories

My Dad, Orazio Costa was the first cousin to own a car. He had a large Packard. Per "Uncle" Dominick Clemenzi all the cousins would climb in and go for rides. They would go a number of places, for ice cream or wherever. I do not know who was with my Dad at the Sate Fair when he won a car? I am not sure of the year, but he won a brand new Chevy. Does anyone remember that? "Uncle" Dominick also told me how the cousins would all follow each other to New Jersey to visit their cousins. They would tell each other things like "Hurry -up! But go slow."

I love spending time with "Aunt" Sophie (Clemenzi) Villanti. At this time she is our oldest relative. She is someone to really admire. She definitely has some of the best family stories. Right up there with Uncle Dominick and Aunt Helen Clemenzi. Aunt Sophie told me a story of when she had asked her Father if she could take the car and go to New Hampshire. He immediately said, "Yes", but she wanted to take her cousin, my Aunt Nancy Costa with her. Nancy told Sophie her Dad would never let her go. Sophie took it upon herself to go to the United Shoe where my Grandfather, John Costa worked. She went to his boss and had him called to the office. My Grandfather must have wondered what was wrong. Sophie asked him in front of his boss if Nancy could go with her to New Hampshire. Of course he did not dare to say, "No" in front of his boss so they were able to go. Obviously, Aunt Sophie knew the best way to deal with people even as a young girl.

359

Rose (Femino) and Orazio Costa's Wedding Day
December 1, 1945

My Father went into the army and when he was discharged at Thanksgiving in 1945 my parent's decided to get married. They planned their wedding in one week. They were married December 1, 1945. The day of their wedding there was a huge snow storm. They were married at St. Mary's Church and they had their reception at United Shoe Club House today it is called the Beverly Golf & Tennis Club. They had a large wedding party that included family and friends. Unfortunately, my Aunt Josie had just gotten married a week before and she was on her honeymoon so she was unable to attend.

Nancy (Costa) and Keith Desmond's Wedding Day
December 1, 1984

My husband Keith and I were married on what would have been my parent's 39ᵗʰ anniversary, December 1, 1984 and I wore my Mother's wedding gown. The weather was beautiful, not a typical December 1ˢᵗ, it was very warm. The interesting thing was the day I had planned to go shopping for my wedding gown I woke up remembering my Mother had once said to me she would like me to wear her wedding gown. I never went gown shopping. I pulled my Mother's gown out of the pillow case she had put it away in, inside of her hope chest. The gown fit me perfectly. I am so happy I was able to wear my Mother's gown and we were able to share their anniversary date with them.

Fond Memories

Before Keith and I were married, on Fridays he would walk to National Bank to cash his check from Coleman's Sporting Goods, on his way he would always stop and see "Uncle" Dominick Villanti as he was tending his garden in his yard. "Aunt" Sophie would always come out and speak to Keith and say to him, "Are you going to the bank again?" Aunt Sophie would always be quick to invite Keith in for refreshments.

Last year when we went to the family reunion there was an auction. I was standing a ways back from the person holding up the items to be auctioned, but when I heard they had an afghan made by Aunt Sophie I bid on it and I was lucky enough to get it. It turned out to be a baby's afghan which was fine with me. I put it away for my first grandchild. I was just thrilled to have it. Aunt Sophie called me this past winter and asked me to stop over. She had made me a beautiful afghan which I keep on our bed. I love it and will treasure it forever. Thanks Aunt Sophie!

My Mother, Rose Costa also liked to make afghans and give them away. Luckily she gave me a beautiful baby afghan which I kept in my hope chest, because by the time my 1st baby Rose was born she had passed away. My parent's Orazio and Rose Costa were the best. Of course we all think our parents are the best. My Dad worked hard and would do anything for his family. He was very talented and could fix anything. He was also quite the inventor. I remember he made me a machine to help me trace maps to do school work. I can picture it. It was quite inventive. I was only 7 or 9 and at that time there was nothing like it on the market.

Holidays were always lots of fun with a lot of good food. My Mother was an excellent cook. She was also a great story teller and family historian. I learned a lot from her. She was truly my best friend and when she died I lost a part of myself. She knew both sides of the family so well. I try to be like her and tell my children family stories and explain relationships. I always love to hear stories about my Mom. It helps to bring her memory back to life. Uncle Dominick just recently told me how when they were younger probably before they were all married a group of them would get together and it would often take awhile for people to start talking. He said my Mother was often the ice breaker. She had a way of getting the group going. My Mother loved company. She loved it when our house was full of people. All my friends loved my Mother's cooking.

Growing up most of our Sundays were spent at my Grandmother Costa's house. We would all sit around and play cards. My Grandmother's house was very small, but there always seemed to be plenty of room. I can picture her back yard with the big cement bench out side her back door. She had grape vines and huge garden and apple and peach trees. When I was real small she had chickens running around the yard.

The group sitting on the cement bench in Catherine Costa's back yard

The Wednesday before Thanksgiving was always so exciting. We always had a half of day at school and when I got home Uncle Silvio, Aunt Josie and Theresa would always be there. Aunt Josie was always such a good cook and baker. She made the best Polish bow ties. They came every Thanksgiving up until Gram died in 1984.

I have great memories of going to visit Aunt Josie's in Springfield. She always made fresh blueberry muffins and blueberry pancakes. Aunt Josie like my Dad was very talented she could do anything and fix anything. My sister Marieann use to love going to Springfield in the summer and spend time with Theresa. We would go to Forest River Park. They had animals there. One year they had two donkeys there, a friendly one and a not so friendly one, the not so friendly one bit me. Not too many people can say they were bitten by a donkey.

As kids the Costa Family would have family get-togethers at Stage Fort Park - in Gloucester. It was always fun to get together with our family.

362

Orazio Oscar Costa

Written by Danielle Desmond

Orazio Costa with Rose and Danielle Desmond

Orazio O Costa was my grandfather. I had lived with him ever since I was born. We lived on 16 Northridge Rd. I lived there up until I was three. In 1991 my grandfather was diagnosed with cancer. In 1992 we moved to 38 Nelson Ave. I was three and my sister Rose was six. My grandfather struggled to fight cancer for 2 years. I hate the fact that my Grampy died when I was only four and I don't have many memories of him as other people do, but I do have memories of him. I remember everyday after pre-school I would curl up next to Bumpy (the name we would call our grandfather) and watch old cartoons, sleep, or he would teach me something new. I also used to go to all of his doctor appointments. I remember when it was my moms 35th birthday and she took the day off and we had been running around to all of Bumpy's appointments and we decided to go out to lunch after. We went to Friendly's and right when Bumpy got out of the car he tripped on a crack on the ground and fell on his wrist. He insisted that he was fine but we knew he wasn't so we brought him to the hospital and it turned out he broke his wrist. They gave him a removable cast. When we got home my Grampy took off his cast and insisted his arm wasn't broken. We had to take him back to have it recast. Although I only knew him for four years he made a true impact on my life. I know I will grow closer with my grandfather in the years to come with all of the great, heart warming memories and stories that he brought to my family and they will pass them on.

I Love You Bumpy!

Caterina (Serra) Costa Family Photos

Caterina (Serra) and Giovanni Costa
Children: Orazio and Nancy

Catherine (Serra) Costa and Frank Costa

Giovanni Costa

John Battista Costa, Orizio Costa (in uniform) and Maria Costa

Orazio, Frank, Mary, Santa, Josephine, Bob

Orazio, John Battista, Josephine and Mary Costa

Mary, Nancy, Santa and Josephine Costa

Catherine, Orazio Costa and Rose Femino

Rose Femino, Orazio and Sanna Costa

368

Orazio and John Costa

Marieann, Concetto, Rose, John, Nancy and Orazio Costa

Concetto, John, Marieann and Nancy

Orazio Costa, Marieann (Costa) Calder, Nancy & Keith Desmond, Concetto Costa and John Costa

Nancy (Costa) Desmond and her Dad Orazio Costa

Judy (Weislik) Day with her cousin Larry Costa

Keith Desmond, Josephine (Costa) and Silvio Scaglairini

Sanna (Costa) Augustus, Keith and Nancy Desmond, and Larry Augustus

Keith, Nancy, Rose and Danielle Desmond (1997)
With Goofy, Minnie, Mickey and Donald

Back row: David Calder, CJ Costa, Sharon Calder, Johnny Costa
Front row: Marc Calder, Linda Costa, Mathew Costa and Anita Costa

Tyler Costa, Anthony Nolasco, Kiarra Beltre, Jacob Nolasco, Mariah Nolasco, Tori Costa
and Santa Clause

374

Ed and Maria Copeland

Susan and Ray Brown

Thomas, Maria, Donia and Ray

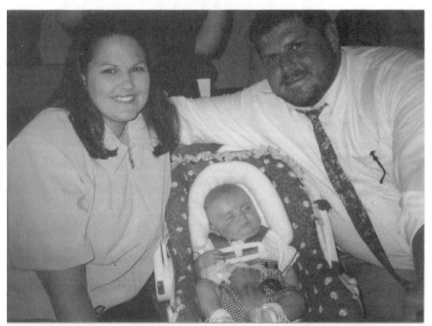

Adrienne, Donald and Dylan Blanton

Maria (Costa) and Ray Brown
Donia, Ray and Eddie

Maria Brown, Henry and Santa Weislik and ?
Ed Brown, Santa Weislik and Dennis Weislik
Ray Brown, Donia Brown and Judy Weislik

Caterina (Serra) Costa Family Notes:

We do not remember days,
we remember moments.

--Cesare Pavese (1908-1950)

Salvatore Serra and Maria Lazzaro Family

Memories of Santa (Serra) Galletta

Written by Mary (Serra) Goldrick
Photo supplied by Janice Charowsky

Santa and Mary
Graduation Day – June 1942

My cousin Santa and I grew up on York Street and went to grammar school together. After school we'd go outdoors to play. We loved to jump rope, play hopscotch and play ball. Santa was very good at volley ball. I always wanted to be on her side in school because her team usually won the game. She was very strong and could serve the volley ball over the net and make a lot of points.

In June 1942 we graduated from Public School #1. Santa was working a short time before I got my job in W. E. Co. After work we'd go shopping or to a movie (to get our dishes!) and on the weekends we go to Coney Island with our sisters and friends or parents. Several times we'd go out on dates with the boys from work. Once when she was asked to go out, she asked me to go with his friend, so she wouldn't have to go alone. This was called double-dating. These were just casual dates until sometime later when Santa met Dominick Galletta. He lived in the Bronx next door to my Aunt Catherine Villanti. They soon fell in love and were married in 1948. Their wedding reception was in a huge ballroom in the Pennsylvania Hotel in New York City. All our relatives from Massachusetts attended their wedding. Santa's wedding gown was just beautiful! It had the longest train I had ever seen. Her sister Bea was her Maid of Honor, Lena and I were the bridesmaids. After their honeymoon, Santa and Dom went to live in the Bronx with his Mom and Dad on Laconia Ave. Two years later Santa gave birth to a lovely baby girl and named her Josephine after her mother-in-law. All went well, until Santa became ill and then died two days before her 49th birthday. She was born August 1, 1927 and died August 11, 1976. We were all very saddened and still think of her and miss her.

A Day at Hampton Beach, NH

July 15, 1944

Written by Christopher Obert and Giovannina Obert
Photos supplied by Janice Charowsky and Giovannina (Serra) Obert

The daughters of Salvatore, Giuseppe and Domenico, rented the upstairs apartment at "The Crawford". It was the first and only time they all got together and rented a place. This was the first vacation for many of the girls. They would go to the beach, visit the shops or go out to eat. My mother told me she remembers that the Beverly Serras planned the trip and did a great job! This was one summer the Serra Girls would never forget. That was especially true for my mom, Giovannina; because on one of their day adventures, the group went on a bus ride to Salisbury Beach. It was on that bus that Giovannina met Norman Obert, her future husband and my father.

Back: Caroline Serra, Bartolomea Serra, Bartolomea Serra, Rose Serra
Front: Giovannina Serra, Santa Serra, Bartolomea Serra and Santa Serra

Santa, Bartolomea and Giovannina

Santa, Caroline, Bartolomea and Giovannina

383

Salvatore Serra Family Photos

Salvatore Serra

Maria (Lazzaro) and Salvatore Serra

Santa, Lena and Bea Serra

Sal & Maria

Christopher Lazzaro & his grandchildren, Bea Serra & John Serra

John and Jean Serra

John, Marie and Jenna Hyla

Salvatore Serra and Maria (Lazzaro)

John Battista Christopher Serra, Dominick Galletta, Santa (Serra) Galletta, Joseph Scibetta, Angelina (Serra) Scibetta, Mary (Lazzaro) Serra, Salvatore Serra, Bartolomea (Serra) Fanto and Thomas Fanto

Mary, Lena and Sal

Angelina (Serra) and Joseph Scibetta Wedding

Joe and Lena, Barbara and Emil, Sal Serra, Betty Ann, Joey

Lynette, Emil and Michael D'Elia

Joe Scibetta, Lynette D'Elia and Lena Scibetta

Lena Scibetta and Michael D'Elia

Mary Serra, Betty Ann Scibetta and Sal Serra

Mike and Betty Ann
Joe and Lena
Barbara Jo, Lynette, Emil, Joe Gerry

Michael and Betty Ann Tagliarine

Lena, Betty and Joe Scibetta

Emil & Barbara, Joe & Lena, Gerrie and Joe Scibetta and Betty Ann & Mike

Gerrie Scibetta and Michael D'Elia

Dominick & Santa (Serra) Galletta Wedding Day May 1948

?, Mary Serra, ?, Bea Serra, Santa (Serra) & Dominick Galletta, Angelina Serra and Joseph Scibetta

Lena and Joe Scibbetta

Lena and Joe Scibetta and their children
Barbara Jo, Joseph, and Betty Ann

Lena and Joe Scibbetta and their grandchildren
Angela Tagliarine, Lena, Brittany Scibetta, Michael D'Elia, Lynette D'Elia, Joe, Amanda Scibetta

Barbara and Emil D'Elia
with Lynette

Brittany and Gerrie Scibetta, John Hyla and John Serra Jr.
Betty Ann and Angela Tagliarine

397

Salvatore Serra Family Notes:

Words form the thread on which
we string our experiences.

--Aldous Huxley (1894-1963)

Maria Carolina Serra and Gaetano DeLorenzo Family

Maria Carolina (Serra) DeLorenzo

Written by Rosa (Rose) M. Czarnecki

Maria Carolina (Serra) DeLorenzo, the youngest child of John Battista Serra and Bartolamea (Lazzaro) Serra came to America last, because her father John Battista Serra got very sick and burial was in Salina, Italy. In America, as a young girl, Maria Carolina worked at Carbone's Grocery Store on Rantoul St. Beverly, Massachusetts.

Gaetano DeLorenzo who lived on another island near Sicily, knew of the Serra family before coming to America. He began a trucking business delivering vegetables to Boston, Massachusetts. Going through Beverly, he stopped for cigarettes at Carbone's Grocery Store and saw a familiar face from Italy. He dated Maria Carolina Serra for 2 months and at 18 years old Maria Carolina Serra and Gaetano DeLorenzo married April 23, 1916 in Salem Massachusetts over a fish market on Front Street. Later, the Italian Church was built.

Maria Carolina, 18 years old and Gaetano DeLorenzo, 22 years old eventually raised seven children: Catherine Jenni, Maria Concetta, Antonio, John Battista, Bea, Joseph and Rosa Marie.

A-Nona (as we called her) Bartolamea always lived with daughter Maria Carolina and Gaetano DeLorenzo and their seven children. A-Nona taught me all the Italian love songs, including Per Um Bacio da More, Oh Marie, Santa Lucia and many more. A-Nona sang beautifully.

While in Italy, A-Nona worked for her uncle, a doctor, and kept a book of remedies for herself. One that stays in my mind was to heal a cut or bruise. She washed it well, trimmed the hair around the cut, and put red wine on the cut and then sugar. After healing, you would never know where the cut had been. My brother Joseph is proof of this.

A-Nona repaired our socks and taught me to make a hem around linen material to make handkerchiefs.

A-Nona always with prayer beads in her hands prayed often. A very lovely, sweet lady, with dark brown hair passed away in April, 1948 at the age of 96-plus. I never saw her dye her hair.

My parents and A-Nona taught me how to live a happy life.

During World War II, my mother worked in a factory on Rantoul Street in Beverly, Massachusetts making airplane parts. A very hard working woman always sweet.

My father, Gaetano Delorenzo, always a hard working man, loved music. He played the guitar and mandolin. Many a Sunday, we gathered around the kitchen table with brother Joseph playing clarinet, and we all sang.

Many pleasant memories are in store with my lovely parents, who I will always adore.

Maria Carolina (Serra) De Lorenzo Family Photos

Caroline (Serra) & Gaetano De Lorenzo 50th Anniversary

Left to Right: Joseph, John, Tony, Gaetano and Maria Carolina,
Catherine Stone, Connie Camarda, Bea Chenery and Rose Czarnecki

Anthony (Chick), Catherine (Kay), Connie
and baby John Battista De Lorenzo

Catherine and Connie DeLorenzo

404

Frank Costa, Gaetano De Lorenzo, **Kenneth & Katie Stone**, Mary DiGrandi,
John Battista De Lorenzo, Sam Madugno
Seated: Theresa (Morretti) Bosco and Bea (De Lorenzo) Chenery

Katie Stone

Beatrice (DeLorenzo) and Joanne Chenery

Chenery Children

Maria Concetta (DeLorenzo) and Anthony Carmada

Anthony, Maria Concetta Carmada with Anthony's Mom

Connie (De Lorenzo) and Anthony Carmada

Joanne (Carmada) and Ray Whiteman

Joe (far left) Michael, Priscilla, Kathi and Alyssa

Rose and Alyssa Czarnecki

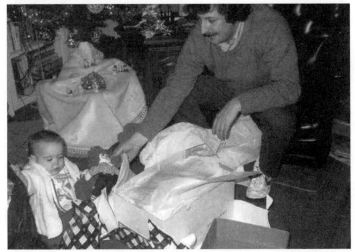

Alyssa and Ron Czarnecki

Maria Carolina (Serra) De Lorenzo Family Notes:

Part Three

A picture shows me at a glance
what it takes dozens of pages of a book to expound.

--Ivan Sergeyevich Turgenev, *Fathers and Sons*

Leaves off the Tree

Serra Family Photos

Miscellaneous Serra Family Photos

Photos supplied by many people listed in the "Acknowledgements" section

L to R: John & Concetta (Serra) Clemenzi, Dominick & Catherine (Costa) Villanti,
Marie (Costa) & Domenico Serra,
Angelina (Serra) DeAngelis, Grace (Lazzaro) & Giuseppe Serra

Lena, Dominick, Philip and Jennie, seated: Catherine (Costa) & Dominick Villanti

Front: Sophie Villanti, John Serra, Mary Serra, Giovannina Obert,
Rose Di Lorenzo and Frank Goldrick
Back: Olga Clemenzi, Peter Clemenzi and Mary Goldrick

Standing: Bartolomea Serra, Santa Serra and Rose Serra
Seated: Santina Serra, Bettina Serra, Giovannina Serra and Caroline Serra

Standing: John Serra, Marie (Serra) Goldrick, Frank Goldrick and
Rose (DeAngelos) Vandi
Seated: Mary (Smythe) Serra, Sophie (Clemenzi) Villanti, Dominick Villanti,
Olga (Vandi) Clemenzi and John Clemenzi,

Jenny (Villanti) Napolitano, Sophie (Clemenzi) Villanti, Olga (Vandi) Clemenzi

Mary Serra, Lena DeAngelis, Catherine Villanti, Caroline DeLorenzo
and Bartolomea Serra

Santa Jones, Jennie Napolitano, Mary Serra, Bartolomea Sienkiewicz,
Sophie Villanti and Lena Congley

Back Row: Giuseppe Serra, Domenico Serra, Salvatore Serra, Gaetano De Lorenzo
Second Row: Marietta Clemenzi, Angelina (Villanti) Congley, Giovanni Clemenzi, Grazia Serra, Maria
Concetta (Serra) Clemenzi, Angelina (Serra) DeAngelis, Colombo DeAngelis
Two children: Margherita Serra and John P. Serra (with dog)

Back Row: Santa (Serra) Jones, Frank Costa (in background), John Clemenzi, Bea (Serra) Sienkiewicz,
Bea (Serra) Fanto, Concettina (Serra) Clemenzi, Bea (Serra) Charowsky and Mary (Clemenzi) Di Grandi
Kneeling: Giovannina (Serra) Obert and Josephine Chifferlli (friend)

420

Jenny Villanti, Bea Serra, Bea Serra, Lena Villanti and Giovannina Serra

Santa Serra, Bartolomea Serra, Santa Serra, Giovannina Serra and Bartolomea Serra

Giuseppe Serra, Santa Serra, Salvatore Serra and Bea Serra

Salvatore, Bartolomea, Dominico
Maria and Maria Concetta

Battista Clemenzi, Mary (Serra) Goldrick, Frank Goldrick, and Rose (DeAngelis) Vandi

John and Mary (Smythe) Serra, Sophie (Clemenzi) Villanti and Giovannina (Serra) Obert

Seated: Joseph "Peppy" and Barbara De Lorenzo, Giovannina Obert
Back row: Rose Czarnecki, Peter Clemenzi, Angela Villanti, BettyAnn Bonaiuto and Sophie Villanti

Enrico and Theresa Miranda, John Battista Clemenzi

424

L to R: Olga Clemenzi, Peter Clemenzi, Sophie Villanti, Mary DiGrandi, Dominick Clemenzi and Helen Clemenzi, Celebrating Sophie's 85th birthday on August 14, 1999

Back two: John and
Middle: Caroline, Bea, Bea, Bartolomea (Lazzaro) Serra and Giovannina
Kneeling: Santa and Rose

Guy DeLorenzo, Joseph "Pep" DeLorenzo, John C. Serra and John Clemenzi

Bea (Serra) Charowsky and Bea (Serra) Fanto

Rose (Serra) Bonaiuto, Santa (Serra) Galletta and Caroline Serra

Catherine "Katie" (DeLorenzo) Stone and Mary (Clemenzi) DiGrandi

Mary (Lazzaro) Serra, Angelina Serra, Maria Concetta (Costa) Serra

Maria Concetta Clemenzi and Mary Serra

John Serra, Bartolomea (Lazzaro) Serra and Angelo Clemenzi

Back: Bea Serra, Bea Serra
Middle: Domenico Serra, Bartolomea (Lazzaro) Serra and Giovannina Serra
Front: John Serra and Santa Serra

Rose DeAngelis and Frank Costa

John Clemenzi, John P. Serra, Jennie Serra, Santa Serra and (kneeling) Gaetano DeLorenzo

Bea Serra, Betty Serra, Bea Serra, Santa Serra, Mary Serra and Lena Serra

Margherita Eggleston and Joe Scibetta Jr.

Olga Clemenzi, Sophhie Villanti, Giovannina Obert and Lucia Clemenzi

Standing: Rose Bonaiuto, Mary Goldrick and Giovannina Obert
Sophhie Villanti, Lucia Clemenzi, Olga Clemenzi, Mary Serra and John Serra

Back: Geremy, Eileen Charowsky, Lorraine Charowsky
Jason Obert, Shari Obert, Amy Ayers, Marissa (friend), Heather Charowsky,
Robert Charowsky & Michelle Obert
Front: Zack, Grace Wilson, Julia Wilson and Laura holding Emma Obert

Giovannina (Serra) and Norman Obert

433

Fun Photos and Art

This section contains collages that Christopher Obert made for a college Photoshop course.
Photos supplied by many people listed in the "Acknowledgements" section

Photos of different families foreground,

with a 1911 painting of lower Manhattan by Richard Rummell in the background.

Photos of the descendents of Dominico Serra foreground,

436

with a railroad poster of 1909 in the background.

437

Collage of photos and other items.

Collage of photos and other items.

Dominico and Maria Concetta Serra and wedding photos of their children

History is in all of Us

Written by Christopher Obert
Art collages created by Christopher Obert

During the time I was compiling this book I was also a full time college student. I took many computer software and programming courses. In one of the courses I created the flyer that was mailed out for the 2002 Serra Family reunion. Here are two more images; I created in Photoshop that I thought you may like…

History is what this book is all about!

To all those that have served their country, God Bless You!

Serra Family Photos Notes:

*The purpose of all war
is ultimately peace.*

--Saint Augustine

World War II and Other Stories

The Serra Family Goes to War

Giovaninna's World War II Postcards and V-MAIL

Written by Christopher Obert

Post Card from neighbor John R. Zulinski Jr.

During World War II, my mother (Giovannina Serra) collected and saved postcards. She kept them in a large scrapbook. When I was young I loved to look through the old cards. There were dozens and dozens of them. I thought that they were so cool. Over time some of the cards fell out and I kept some of them. Ok, I took a few that I liked best, such as the one shown above for War Bonds. Ten of the cards I have were blank, but five had messages on them. Three were from friends and two from family. I have included the two cards and one V-Mail from family members. I wish that I had more to include, but my mom's scrapbook was lost years ago during a move. Thank God that those few cards fell out.

Michael Charowsky World War II Correspondences

Michael Charowsky

V-Mail sent by Michael

Note: V-Mail was a type of mail that was designed to save space during the war.

Marie (Costa) Serra, Michael Charowsky & Bartolomea (Serra) Charowsky

Front of Post Card – Officers Quarters, Fort Hancock, N.J.

Message on the back of Michael's post card…

To: Miss Mary D. Serra, 267 York St., Jersey City, N.J.

Hello Mary,

Well I finally got the cards so I sent them to you. How are you these days? Thanks for your letter. It's pretty nice out here, plenty of everything. Give my regards to everybody. How are you getting along in school, still getting those high marks? I hope so. Keep up the good work. I feeling fine and everything is Ok. Well so long and be a good girl.

Michael

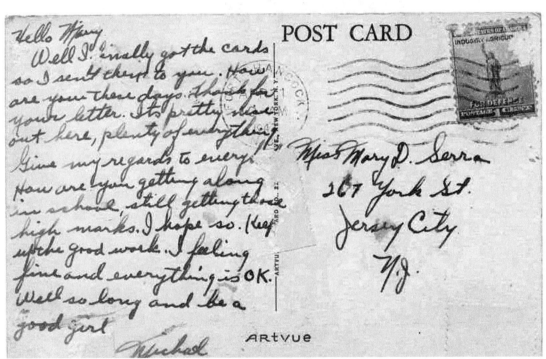

Back of Post Card

449

John B. Costa WW II Post Card

John B. Costa

Front of Post Card – Tank Driver!

Message on the back of John's post card…

To: Mr. & Mrs. S. Serra, 267 York Street, Jersey City, New Jersey

From: Pvt. John B. Costa, Co. D12th 2nd Ing. Regt., Camp Lee VA, USA
(difficult to read)

Hello Uncle & Aunt. How are you and the family? I am fine and hope you all the same. I ment (sic) to write you sooner but I didn't have time to write to you. How's is everything in Jersey City? I hope everything is Ok there.

John B. Costa

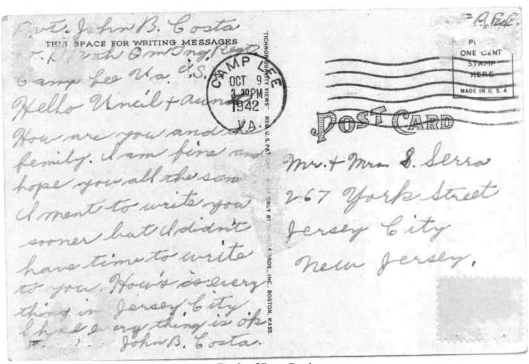

Back of Post Card

More of Giovannina's Postcards

As you can see, the topics on the front of these cards varied widely. Some of the most popular were humorous cartoons, but others offered a religious or military look at what was happening around the world. One thing that you may have noticed on the back of John B. Costa's Post Card is that it was delivered without a stamp! I have noticed that if the Post Card was from a service person the cards did not need postage. I hope you don't mind me adding these post cards to the family book, maybe they will being back a memory!

Postcard to Miss Marie Serra from "Lorette"

Blank Postcard

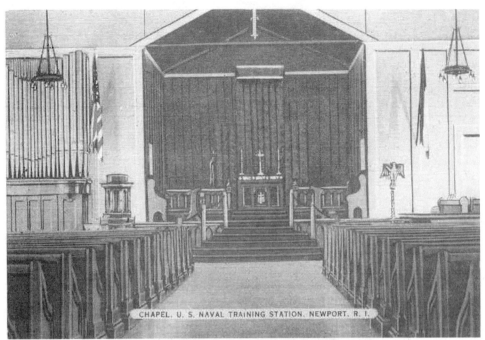

Postcard to Dominic Serra from Fredrick DeSanti

Blank Postcard

Domenico "Dominick" Serra Air Raid Warden

Written by Christopher Obert

Domenico Serra

       As I was doing research for this book, I found out that Domenico Serra was an active patriot. During the Great War (World War I) he worked at the Hyatt Ball Bearing Company. Dominick Charowsky told me that when he went into the Air Force, he had a conversation with Domenico and he told him that his job was considered to be war essential and that he was given a deferment. I do have a copy of Dominico's "Registration Certificate" card, but that only proves that he registered. It does not say whether he was deferred or not. I do not believe that Domenico needed a deferment, since he was 26 years old in 1914 when the war broke out, and 29 years old in 1917 when the United States entered the war but I am not sure of the rules at that time.

Dominico's "Registration Certificate" card

Hyatt Ball Bearing Company 1916 - Domenico Serra (marked at left)

454

When World War II started, Domenico was living in Jersey City. President Franklin D. Roosevelt declared that America was in "a state of unlimited emergency". The United States was aware of possible attacks along the east coast and New Jersey was in direct danger. Each city was responsible for organizing and recruiting its own Civil Defense organization. It was this organization's duty to supply the towns with the means to handle any emergency which could arise. Dominick Charowsky told me that during his previous conversation, Domenico told him that during WWII he was doing something with the downtown waterfront civil defense. I found out that at this time, the local Civil Defense organizations created the role of the "Air Raid Warden". I found out through Mary Goldrick, Domenico's daughter, that Domenico Serra was one of these Wardens for Jersey City.

Air Raid Warden for Jersey City Certificate

When I was writing this story, I asked Mary Goldrick for some input, and here is what she told me:

"Chris, all I remember was my father putting on his helmet, gas mask and arm band, which signified he was an official Air Raid Warden. He patrolled the streets in our immediate neighborhood during blackouts. Cities near the Atlantic and Pacific coasts practiced these blackouts because the threat of bombing and the glare from the city lights made ships anchored near shore easy targets for submarines. When the siren sounded he made sure people stayed in their homes and no lights from their houses were visible from the street. If so he blew his whistle and told them to put all lights out till the siren sounded again and the air raid was over. They were all practice drills only as I recall, as we never saw or heard planes in the sky in Jersey City."

I found some more information on the role of the Air Raid Wardens on The Rutgers University Library Special Collections web page. Here is a little of that information:

Civilian Defense Director, State of New Jersey, Rules and Regulations No. 8

The Air Raid Warden shall function under the direction of the Chief Air Raid Warden, who shall be named by the Local Defense Council. The Air Raid Wardens shall be responsible for calling to the attention of the proper law enforcement representative of any evidenced failure to comply with blackout rules and regulations – warning the occupants of buildings of danger – report over designated telephones to Control Center any vital information such as fires or fallen bombs – assist in fighting incendiary bomb fires – detect and report the presence of gas – advise the civilian population by clackers or other short-range warning devices (i.e. tin pans) of the presence of gas – direct persons in the streets to shelters during an air raid of explosives, incendiary bombs or gas attack – administer elementary first aid – assist victims in damaged buildings.

The Air Raid Warden shall not have police power, but shall report all infractions. He shall not act as a police officer and resort to force to secure compliance….

The insigne of the Air Raid Warden: Seven diagonal stripes, alternate red and white.

The minimum hours of training required are as follows:

First Aid	10
Fire Defense	3
Gas Defense	5
General	5

What are the Chances!

Written by Giovanni (John) Battista Serra
Photos supplied by Giovannina (Serra) Obert and Tony Serra

Giovanni "Johnny" Serra

In May of 1945 I got on a naval transport called the S.S. Sea Devil; we sailed for fifty one days with a convoy made up of one hundred and twenty cruisers and destroyers that were loaded with ammunition and supplies. Our transport arrived at the Island of Okinawa on July 3rd and, we disembarked on the 4th, I was there for thirteen months, I was with the 147th Naval Construction Battalion. While there, they were building what we called tank farms, a few of the bases that were built were called Acorn 44, Kedina and Yana Baru. I believe Kedina is still in operation. I was a Naval Guard. One night I was on guard duty when a sailor came up to me and asked me if I knew where the barber shop was, I told him it's at the top of the hill up by headquarters, he than replied, "You don't recognize me do ya?" and I said "No, do I know you?" He said, "You should, I'm your cousin Anthony De Lorenzo from Beverly Massachusetts." I was stunned at first and I didn't know what to say! What are the chances of two cousins meeting over seas!! He told me that he wasn't actually looking for the barber shop but, that he was looking for me, and that he got my name from headquarters. My Father and his Mother are brother and sister. He told me that if I wanted to visit with him to come up to were he was staying on the island because he was going to be leaving very soon. I did visit with him and, during our time together I asked him if he would contact my mother and father when he got back to the states and let them know that I was alright, he said he would and we parted ways, I will never forget meeting my cousin on the Island of Okinawa. I also remember the first typhoon that hit the island and, it was a bad one! The winds were one hundred and fifty miles an hour and there was a lot of rain, I had a buddy named Irving Zywotow, Irving and myself decided that we had better find safe cover and soon! He said "lets go into the caves on the island" I didn't feel right about that so I suggested that our best bet would be to go up to the chapel that was built into a cove. We did just that and when we got into the chapel we slept by the altar. I never prayed so hard in my life!

The next morning when we woke up the typhoon had passed and there was some light rain but, the worst was over, no more winds. No one was killed by that typhoon, some men got injured but, over all no deaths. It took me thirteen days to get home on the S.S Sea Bass and, I was sea sick most of the time. We reached San Francisco and we got liberty for five days, then they put us on a train headed for N.Y., Ledo Beach, Long Island. We took another train to Courtland St. but the trains from Courtland St. to N.J. were on strike! So I took a taxi cab home. The first person I saw was my mother, she was waiting on a customer in the grocery store that we owned at the time "Serra's Grocery Store". She took one look at me and brought me upstairs to where we lived 267 York St. Jersey City N. J. I took off my uniform and soon after got a job! My papers said Honorable Discharge and my medals were Asiatic Pacific Medal, American Theatre Medal, Letter of Commendation Occupation- Sub Auth Bu Pers Victory Medal. My title while serving was Machinist's Mate Third Class (CB) V-6

Giovanni "Johnny" Serra

John Serra (marked at left) Sea Bees Guard Troop

S.S. Sea Devil

459

Joseph "Norman" Obert U.S. Navy WWII Stories

Written by Chris Obert from the stories told to him by his father Norman

Joseph "Norman" Obert

Norman served on three ships during the war, The USS West Point started out as the SS America, the nation's newest and largest luxury liner. It was converted into a troop transport in 1944.

The USS Humphreys was a converted WWI destroyer. One of its missions was to go into the Admiralty Islands and act as a diversion. At the same time, on the other side of the island, the main group would be landing. While their troops were loading onto the small rubber boats, a Browning Automatic Weapon accidentally went off. A soldier had filed off the safety! The Japanese were now aware of their presence. The Japanese waited until the men were close to shore to attack. The Captain of the ship ordered flank speed into the harbor, firing both 4-inch guns at the same time (something they never did). They saved as many men as possible, then backed out as quickly as possible. Although the mission did not go as planned, it was successful. The diversion that was needed was realized as the USS Humphreys stormed to the rescue.

One of the main functions of the Humphreys was to deliver troops and supplies to the beaches. They would use wooden transports called "Higgins Boats" to accomplish this. The transports would be filled with men, then go onto the beach, unload, and return for another load. On one mission Norman was coxswain (pilot) of a Higgins boat delivering U.S. Cavalry troops. Upon reaching shore and as the front hatch was lowered for unloading, the Japanese fired a weapon into the barge. The shell exploded, killing all on board except Norman and the two gunners, who were protected by metal shielding. They had to abandon the barge and go ashore. They had to engage the Imperial Japanese Marines who were holding the island. During hand to hand combat, Norman was wounded in the hand. A Japanese soldier, with his bayonet attached to his rifle, lunged at him. Norman's hand was cut, but the Japanese soldier was not so lucky. After the battle, the U.S. controlled the island and Norman was returned to the Humphreys.

This is a photo of a "Higgins" boat used by the USS Humphreys.
(It is possible that this photo shows Norman at the wheel)

The third ship Norman served on was the USS Telfair. The Telfair was a Haskell Class Attack Troop Transport ship. One undertaking my father told me about was their mission into Okinawa. There were 40 ships traveling in formation. There were 10 ships in a row, followed by a second row of 10, then a third, then a fourth. The Telfair was near the middle of the third row, following the command ship in the second row. One minute the other ship was there, the next it had exploded. The ship was hit by a Kamikaze. Norman was a Gunners Mate and had just finished cleaning his twin 20's. He was about to cover one of the guns when the ship blew up. Normally it takes 2 or 3 men to cock the 20's, but Norman did it himself and began firing at the incoming Japanese planes. He told me "when you are frightened, you gain strength". One plane, which he was shooting at, passed so close overhead that if he stood on the gun he could have reached up and touched it. He told me "you could see my shells going right into it". Another plane got caught in the crossfire between Norman and his 20's and a US Navy plane. My father told me "my shells were buzzing by the Navy plane and his were buzzing by me". He said "It was both incredibly exciting and frightening. I will never forget it!"

USS West Point (SS America) AP-23

USS Humphreys APD-12

USS Telfair APA-210 (LPA-210)

Army Memories

Written by Peter Clemenzi

I served in the army in Germany from December 1949 to June 1952 in the armored division on the M 24 tank. I was a sergeant in the constabulary and it was our job to make sure the Germans didn't have any weapons. The uniform was quite impressive looking with a gold colored scarf.

One day on maneuvers we had stopped to set up camp when all of a sudden we heard a shot being fired. The bullet ricocheted off a tank and hit me in the spine. I had to be taken to Nuremburg Hospital, the only building left intact in the city after the devastation of the war. I needed surgery to remove the bullet and stayed in the hospital about two weeks.

While stationed in Germany I did some traveling in Europe. That is when I first visited Rome and met my father's cousin Annunziata Tortora and her sons Marcello and Luciano. Luciano was a young man at the time and he took me to see the sights in Rome and also to Turania, my father's hometown where I met my Clemenzi cousins. Turania is a very small town in the mountains with narrow cobblestone streets and I remember the cemetery was on a mountainside because there is so little flat land in the area.

I returned to the United States in June 1952 and married Rose Nardella on July 6 of that year.

SMSgt. Dominick Charowsky

Taken from his U.S. Air Force Retirement Ceremony Report June 18, 1996

Dominick Charowsky

SMSgt. Charowsky was born 1 August 1952 in Jersey City, New Jersey. He entered the Air Force at age 17 following his boyhood dream to work on airplanes. After basic training at Lackland AFB, Texas, he attended technical training school for turbo-prop aircraft at Sheppard AFB, Texas.

His first assignment was at Little Rock AFB, Arkansas in 1970. Crewing C-130Es he traveled extensively throughout Europe while on rotation to Rhein-Main AFB, Germany. In May 1971 he volunteered for an assignment to Vietnam. On July 6, 1971 he was assigned to the 90th Special Operations Squadron at Nha Trang AFB, Republic of Vietnam. During his assignment with Special Ops, he flew on and maintained EC-130E aircraft. These aircraft were fitted with highly sophisticated and classified electronic equipment, he logged many hours over North Vietnam and North Korea as well as penetration evaluation missions to almost every Asian country. The normal combat tour of duty is twelve months. Sergeant Charowsky volunteered to be his own replacement, staying in Vietnam for three consecutive tours.

With the fall of Saigon in 1973, he was officially relocated to Kadena AFB, Okinawa to continue flying Special Ops Black Bird missions. He left the Black Birds for Ching Chung Kang AFB, Taiwan, back to crewing trash hauling C-130Es. With his clearances and background in Special Ops, he was assigned as a flying crew chief on the Grey Ghost Flight aircraft. While there, his aircraft was deployed to support the captured USS Miaguez.

In early 1974, the entire C-130 wing was moved from Taiwan to Clark AFB, Philippines. Having sewn on Staff Sergeant by now, he was asked to transfer over to the slick C-130s to help train their crew chiefs. Between his Vietnam, Taiwan and Philippine assignments, he flew to every airfield in the entire Pacific and Indian Ocean Regions.

Upon returning to the States, after five years of duty in Sea East Asia, he was assigned to the 89th Consolidated Aircraft Maintenance Squadron (CAMS) at Andrews AFB, Maryland. There he performed crew chief duties in the Presidential Support Flight crewing the Vice President's aircraft.

In 1977, SMSgt. Charowsky requested and was selected for another special assignment to the Special Mission Flight at Langley AFB, Virginia, as a flying crew chief on the four Air Force C-130s assigned to the Central Intelligence Agency, CIA. In 1978, the Langley flight moved to Pope AFB, North Carolina to make room for the new F-15 wing being assigned to Langley. He continued as a flying crew chief on the CIA birds until making Technical Sergeant in early 1978. He then moved back to trash hauling C-130Es again.

Dominick Charowsky on location.

While supervising the heavy maintenance section at Pope AFB, he developed a method to shorten the repair time required to fix a truss mount crack that was affecting all Air Force C-130s. The Air Force's repair method called for removing all four engines, which caused the need for a functional check flight (FCF) and altogether took one week to accomplish. Sergeant Charowsky's method took 24 hours without removing the engines, thus eliminating the need for the FCF. After the factory and the depot team's visit to Pope to see his method with their own eyes, the Deputy Commander for Maintenance and Wing Commander personally dispatched Sergeant Charowsky to all other C-130 wings to demonstrate and teach his repair method.

Following Pope AFB, Sergeant Charowsky was assigned to McGuire AFB, New Jersey in late 1979 to try his hand at recruiting. In mid 1980 he was reassigned to the 438th Organizational Maintenance Squadron. While at McGuire, Sergeant Charowsky held many positions in maintenance, including Shift Chief, Flight Chief, Senior Maintenance Controller, Mobility NCOIC and acting Aircraft Maintenance Unit (AMU) NCOIC.

During his tenure at McGuire, he led maintenance teams to deploy for the conflicts in Grenada, Lebanon, Panama, Saudi Arabia, Somalia and Croatia. In addition he led maintenance teams to deploy on countless worldwide relief missions, for operational readiness inspections and exercises. Sergeant Charowsky led the maintenance team representing McGuire AFB in the worldwide aircraft maintenance Rodeo competition. His aircraft brought home the trophy for best engine running offload times. Sergeant Charowsky was request by name from the Headquarters Evaluation Team to be a maintenance judge for two other International Aircraft Rodeo Competitions. Sergeant Charowsky was asked to lead the maintenance team deployed to Pope AFB to supervise the repair and return of three of McGuire's C-141Bs that were damaged while on the ground from wreckage of a mid-air collision of an F-16 and C-130.

His biggest accomplishment at McGuire was discovering the cause of why C-141s from three different bases were experiencing multiple engine flameouts both in-flight and on the ground. His discovery affected 85% of all C-141s and prevented a potential disaster. Sergeant Charowsky is currently Aircraft Maintenance Superintendent in the 621st Air Mobility Maintenance Squadron.

Dominick Charowsky

SMSgt. Charowsky has an Associate's Degree in Aircraft Maintenance Technology and a Bachelor's Degree in Aviation Maintenance Management. His military awards include: Purple Hearts, Meritorious Service Medals, Joint Service Commendation Medal, Air Force Commendation Medals, Air Force Achievement Medals, Air Force Outstanding Unit Award, Air Force Good Conduct Medals, National Defense Service Medal, Vietnam Service Medal, Air Force Overseas-Short Tour, Air Force Overseas-Long Tour, Air Force Longevity, NCO Professional Military Education, Small Arms Expert Rifle, Small Arms Expert Pistol, Air Force Training Ribbon, Republic of Vietnam Gallantry Cross with Palm and the Republic of Vietnam Campaign Medal.

Larry Ayers – U. S. Navy

AQ3 L. Ayers

Larry Ayers

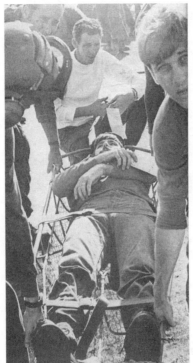

Larry (on cot) taking part in an emergency drill.

USS Saratoga CV - 60

Dominick Villanti

Frank Goldrick

L to R: John Batistia, Orizio and Maria Costa

Dennis Vandi

Santa (Serra) and Harold Jones

John and Tony DeLorenzo

John Serra

Steven Lorusso

Jerry Eggleston

Norman Obert (center) and some of his mates

Harold Jones, Santa (Serra) Jones,
Bea (Serra) Sienkiewicz and John C. Serra

John Serra

Enrico Miranda, in his Italian Army uniform
during World War II

Anthony DeLorenzo

John C. Serra

Ray Brown

Dominick, Mary and Battista Clemenzi

Frank and Mary (Serra) Goldrick

Serra Family War Notes:

474

Death is Nature's expert advice
to get plenty of Life.

--Goethe (1749-1832)

A Family's Journey

Serra Family Reunions & Get-Togethers

Serra Get Together
Beverly Sept. 6, 1936

Back Row: John Battista Clemenzi, John B. DiLorenzo, Theresa Miranda, Marietta Clemenzi, Nancy Costa, Katie DiLorenzo, Emma Clemenzi, Connie DiLorenzo, Sophie Villanti, Rose (Vandi) DeAngelis

Middle Row: Peter Clemenzi, Rose ?, Rose DiLorenzo, Bea DiLorenzo, Bea (Nonna) Serra, Bea Serra, Carrie Serra, Santa Costa

Front Row: Angelo Clemenzi, Bobby Costa, Margie Serra, John Serra

Serra Family Get Together - Sept. 6, 1936

Notes:

Santa (Costa) Krauskas and Norman Obert have been concerned that with the passing of years the cousins belonging to the Serra Clan have become very numerous and have grown far apart so that many no longer know or recognize each other and their children. Santa and Norman have talked this over on several occasions and finally had a meeting with Beatrice (Serra) Sienkiewica and Rose (Serra) Bonaiuto at the home of Angelo and Lucia Clemenzi. It was decided before much more time passes that something should be done to reacquaint the many new and old members of the Serra Clan.

Everyone agreed the thing to do was to have an old fashioned type family picnic like we used to have when we were kids. Everyone bring their own provisions and refreshments. There is plenty of room to cook-out so if you want, bring your own habachi.

The picnic will be held at the home of
        Angelo and Lucia Clemenzi
              11 Hart Street
          Beverly Farms, Mass.
on the Labor Day Weekend. It was decided we would use Saturday, September 2, 1972, as the date, so that if it should rain that day the picnic can be held Sunday, September 3, 1972, and there would still be the following day, September 4 for travel time for anyone coming from a distance.

Now remember the picnic is for the entire Serra Clan which also includes husbands, wives, children and grandchildren. In other words anybody related to or married into the Serra Clan or any offspring of a Serra.

There is a pool so bring swimsuits and towels. We hope to have rock music for the young people. There is room for dancing. There are swings for the little kids. There is plenty of woods for hiking, you can play basketball, badminton or a game of cards, you can bird-watch or just sit around and enjoy each others company.

There is also plenty of room at the Clemenzis for anyone needing a place to sleep. Come early. We hope to start by 11 A.M. and continue as long as you want through the evening. Come and stay all day or part of the day. We are hoping all the families will find it possible to come. A map to the Clemenzis is provided Should you run into trouble finding us call 922-1296 or 922-3143.

                    See you on the 2nd of September.

                        Santa (Costa) Krauskas

                        Norman Obert

                        Rose (Serra) Bonaiuto

                        Beatrice (Serra) Sienkiewica

                        Rose (DeAngelis) Vandi

                        John Battista Clemenzi

Many of the cousins can provide sleeping quarters if needed just call.

Invitation letter from 1972 reunion

Serra Family Reunion - September 3, 1972

Notes:

LOOK WHAT'S COMING!

" A REMINDER "

11 HART STREET, BEVERLY FARMS, MASS.   01915

S· ATURDAY AT 12:00 P.M. TILL WHENEVER

E   VERYONE IS WELCOME

R   EMEMBER THE DATE AUGUST 2 nd, 1986

R   EMINDER TO COME, FOR A FULL DAY OF FUN

A   MAGIC SHOW YOU WON'T WANT TO MISS, MUSIC,
    DANCING AND VOLLEY BALL, OR IF YOU PREFER,
              T H E   P O O L

R   EMEMBER TO BRING YOUR BOOZE, CHAIRS & TOWELS

E   XPENSES WILL BE SHARED BY ALL

U   NLESS RAIN COMES, THEN IT'LL BE AUG. 3 rd, 1986

N   UMEROUS HOURS OF FUN AND SOCIALIZING

I   CE CREAM AND BALLOONS FOR THE KIDDIES

O   N THE GROUNDS OF 11 HART STREET, BEVERLY FARMS, MASS.

N   O ONE SHOULD MISS THE FUN

              C O L D   B U F F E T

    APPROXIMATE PRICE:

        $7.00 AGES 14 YEARS TO ADULT

        CHILDREN UNDER 14 YEARS FREE

Invitation letter from 1986 reunion.

Serra Family Reunion – August 2, 1986

Nearly 300 Serras gather for reunion in Farms

By CORIA HOLLAND
Times staff

BEVERLY — What takes $487 worth of cold cuts, 375 ears of corn, an ice cream truck and a magician?

The Serra family reunion.

Last Saturday, nearly 300 Serras from as far as Rome, Italy and as close to home as Beverly showed up at the day-long event held at the home of the late Angelo Clemenzi on Hart Street.

John Clemenzi Jr., a retired businessman, organized the reunion which attracted relatives from New Hampshire, Texas, New York and Massachusetts. The last family gathering took place in 1972 in Beverly Farms, when 425 relatives celebrated until 2 a.m., Clemenzi said.

This reunion was cut short by rain, but that did not take away from the celebration, Clemenzi said with a smile.

"The party couldn't have been better. The weather was with us for a little while. I enjoyed watching the kids the most. We had a magician and to just see the expressions on the kids' faces was wonderful," he said.

Olga Clemenzi, John's wife, said she enjoyed getting reacquainted with relatives she had not seen in years.

"Everyone was so happy. There was no malcon-

Domenico Serra, center, and family clockwise from tent. No one said this is wrong or that is wrong. The family even brought picture albums. We looked at the pictues and thought, 'God, those pictures had been taken 100 years ago," she said.

A husband-wife magician team from Maryland and an ice cream truck hired especially for the children were featured at the reunion. The bushels of corn were donated by Lucy Angelini of Wenham.

right: Anthony, Concetta, Catherine and Joseph.

The Serras are descendants of Domenico Serra, an Italian immigrant who traveled to America at 15 in 1903. He found work in construction and helped build the United Shoe Machinery building at 85 cents a week.

Serra saved his money and returned to Italy three times — each time bringing back a family member: his mother and one of his eight sisters and brothers.

The Beverly Times Newspaper clipping

483

Serra Family Reunion – August 2, 1986

Photos by Chris & Nancy Obert

Robert "Bobby" Charowsky, Dominick Villanti, Janice Charowsky

Liz Clemenzi and Anthony Garreffi

Serra Family Reunion – August 2, 1986

Heather Ayers and Michelle Obert

Maria (Charowsky) Dombrowski and Christina Dombrowski

485

Serra Family Reunion – August 2, 1986

Carol Ann (Serra) Downing and Daniel "Dan" Downing

Charlotte (Simms) Serra and Mary Lynn (Serra) Gonzalez

Serra Family Reunion – August 2, 1986

Photos supplied by the Keenan Family

Sarah, Josie and Patrick Keenan

Lucia Clemenzi, Patrick, Josie, Sarah, and Gavin Keenan

Serra Family Reunion – August 2, 1986 Notes:

Serra Family Reunion - June 29, 2002
Press Release

Written by Christopher Obert

On June 29th there will be a party 101 years in the making. It is on this date that the Serra Family Reunion will take place. Domenico Serra immigrated to the United States, as a boy of 12, in 1901. He came to the United States from the island of Salina (a small island north of Sicily). He traveled from the port of Naples, Italy on the ship "Liguria". He made the trip with several friends from his village. It was a long hard crossing in steerage, but they were determined to get to America. America offered many opportunities, so Dominic saved his money so he could bring the rest of his family to America. In 1907 he went back to Italy to get his brothers and sisters. He brought Joseph, Angelina, Anthony and Maria Concetta first. The second trip he intended to get his parents and the rest of the family. Unfortunately his father, John Battista, got sick and died in 1910 or 1911 before he returned to Italy. So he went back to get his mother Bartolomea, his brother Salvatore and sisters Catherine and Caroline. In 1912, Dominico made his third and last trip back to Italy. While there, he married Maria Concetta Costa. After the wedding the two of them returned to America to start a new life and begin a family. Each of the other Serra brothers and sisters did the same, start a family and teach it the old style belief of God, Country and Family. Today, 101 years later, the Serra family is gathering to remember and honor those that gave so much. It is because of their courage and sacrifice that all of these families are here, living in freedom and prospering in the greatest country on Earth.

Serra Reunion 2002 Facts:

Who: The Extended Serra Families
What: Family Reunion, Celebrating 101 years in the USA
Where: Pingree School, Hamilton, MA
When: June 29, 2002
How Many: almost 300 people
Families From Where: New Hampshire, Maine, Virginia, New Jersey, California, Arizona, New York, Texas, Pennsylvania, North Carolina, Connecticut and the following towns in Massachusetts: Amesbury, Beverly, Chester, Springfield, Northampton, Haverhill, Topsfield, Methuen, Danvers, Boxford, Bradford, Salem, Jamaica Plain, Byfield, Rowley, Middleton, West Newbury, Wenham, Gloucester, Peabody, Westborough, Billerica, Lynn, Westford, Lowell, Athol, Quincy, Ipswich, Longmeadow, Georgetown, and Manchester by the Sea.
Food: Hot and Cold Buffet
Events: Sing-a-longs, raffles, family tree display, Salina display, games and lots of smiles

Reunion Committee: Jerry & Margherita Eggleston, Angela Villanti, Bill Eggleston, Betty Bonaiuto, Sharon Turcotte, Frank Bonaiuto, Joe Bonaiuto and Chris & Nancy Obert

Sharon (Eggleston) Turcotte gives the family directions

2002 Serra Family Reunion Newspaper Story

Reunion 101 years in the making

By MIKE LaBELLA
Staff Writer

More than 250 guests from as far away as the West Coast came to a special Obert family dinner.

They gathered at the Pingree School in Hamilton two weeks ago for a family reunion planned in part by Christopher P. Obert of Haverhill.

Since retiring from Lucent Technology last summer Obert, 40, has been turning over leaves on the family tree of his mother, Giovannina (Serra) Obert.

"I'm doing this partly for our children so they'll know there's more to our lives than just the here and now," Obert said.

Conducting the research has meant countless hours of work. Obert gathered volumes of information about the family including names, dates, and places, then entered all of it into a computer. A genealogy software program did the rest and the final result was 44 pages of family history which Obert

Relaxing after their family reunion, Christopher and Nancy Obert and children Shari and Jason.

wants to convert into a book for family members to enjoy.

"You fill in the information and the genealogy program creates a tree for you," Obert said.

Obert says the story really begins in 1901, when at age 12 his late grandfather Domenico Serra immigrated to the United States from the island of Salina (a small island north of Sicily).

Immigrants like Serra came

by the thousands to Ellis Island seeking a new life.

Young Serra had traveled from the port of Naples on the ship "Liguria" along with several friends from his village.

"It was a long hard crossing in steerage, but they were determined to get to America," said Obert. "Dominic saved his money and in 1907 went back to Italy to get his brothers and sis-

ters. The rest is history."

Obert mailed invitations to 150 Serra family members. In return they mailed him stories and photographs he used to chart his family's history.

Photographs and memorabilia from the Serra family will be on display in an emigration museum being created on the island of Salina according to Obert's cousin, Christine Di Grandi Jones of Hyde Park, NY. The museum will honor Italian families that left Salina for America and Australia during the early 1900s.

"Salina is a volcanic island and during that time a disease had destroyed olive crops which many residents relied upon for their income," she said. "So many of them left to find work elsewhere."

Christopher and his wife have two children, Jason, a senior in the carpentry shop at Whittier Tech, and Shari, a junior at Boston College majoring in English and History.

Newspaper clipping from the Haverhill (MA) Gazette July 18 – July 24, 2002
Used with permission.

2002 Serra Family Reunion Letter from Salina

COMUNE DI MALFA

(Provincia di MESSINA)
BIBLIOTECA COMUNALE "Cav. Giovanni CAFARELLA"
Via Fontana , 2   98050 MALFA –ISOLA DI SALINA- EOLIE
E mail : bibliomalfa@virgilio.it / Tel. 090.9844372

TO MRS.
CHRISTINE DI GRANDI JONES
AND SERRA FAMILY
NEW YORK (U.S.A.)

Oggetto: visita nelle Isole Eolie alla ricerca delle proprie radici.

Sono stato lieto di avere conosciuto la signora Christine e suo marito in occasione della recente visita nelle Isole Eolie e, in modo particolare, a Malfa , nell'isola di Salina, alla ricerca delle proprie radici.

Ho visto il lavoro approfondito e dettagliato svolto dalla signora Christine per ricostruire l' albero genealogico della propria famiglia le cui origini derivano proprio da Malfa, dove è stato istituito il Museo dell'Emigrazione Eoliana ,nel quale sono raccolte le memorie storiche degli eoliani nel mondo.

A tal proposito si stanno raccogliendo i fondi per acquistare un nuovo immobile per conservare e custodire altro materiale che è stato raccolto e che si continuerà a raccogliere.

E' stata gradita , anche, la vostra visita nella Biblioteca Comunale di Malfa dove, oltre ai libri ed ai documentari, avete potuto ammirare foto e quadri sulle Isole Eolie.

Mi auguro che altri componenti della numerosa famiglia Serra possano visitare le Isole Eolie e conoscere i luoghi dove sono nati i loro nonni.

Ho appreso che giorno 29 giugno avverrà a New York una riunione dove vi incontrerete tutti. Sono delle iniziative interessanti ed apprezzabili che suscitano anche commozione e dimostrano il legame che esiste nel vostro ambito familiare e grazie alla vostra unione avete avuto una forza maggiore per inserirvi con successo nella società americana.

Nel porgervi i miei auguri e congratulazioni vi invio cordiali saluti

Antonio Brundu

Bibliotecario e addetto culturale del
Comune di Malfa

MALFA, 28 giugno 2002

Letter sent to the Serra Family from Antonio Brundu, Cultural attaché of Malfa

Serra Family Reunion - June 29, 2002
Photos by Eggleston Family, Chris Obert & Tony Serra

Some of the almost 300 people attending the 2002 Serra Reunion

The Extended Serra Families at the Pingree School, Hamilton, MA 2002

Serra Family Reunion - June 29, 2002

Front to Back: Nancy Clemenzi, John Clemenzi, Laura Clemenzi, Gail Clemenzi,
Kristen Constantello, Stefanie Hohmann, Patricia Hohmann, Gina Di Grandi
Mark Clemenzi, Elizabeth Clemenzi (standing),
Wayne Wendell (behind Elizabeth), Danielle Jaquith

Back Row: Tom Richard, Beth Richard, John Costa, Concetto Costa, Angela Costa,
Richard Costa, Frank Costa Jr. and Frank Costa Sr.
Front Row: Taylor Richard, Seated: Wives of John and Richard and Norma Costa

Serra Family Reunion - June 29, 2002

Angela Villanti and Janice Charowsky

Background: Billy Dombrowski and Bobby Charowsky
Giovanina (Serra) Obert, Mary (Serra) Goldrick, Sophie (Clemenzi) Villanti
Grace Wilson and Kimberly Dombrowski

Serra Family Reunion - June 29, 2002

L to R: Janice Charowsky, Patricia (Di Grandi) Hohmann,
Christine (Di Grandi) Jones and Catherine (Villanti) Constantello

Dennis Vandi, Sophia Villanti, Anthony Garreffi,
Christine Di Grandi Jones, John Menichello, Dan DeLorenzo

Serra Family Reunion - June 29, 2002

Back: Dennis Vandi, Katie Kuntupis, Marilyn Kuntupis, Mary Vandi
Front: John & Charlotte Serra and Rose Vandi

Lorraine Charowsky and Larry Ayers

Serra Family Reunion - June 29, 2002

Shauna Buckley, Gabriella Smith and others create some spin art

Marilyn Kuntupis, Dominic Miranda, Faye Sienkiewicz, Paul Sienkiewicz,
Marjoriel Panorelli

Serra Family Reunion - June 29, 2002

L to R: Joe Bonaiuto (sr.), Maria Rose Bonaiuto, Bea Fanto, Mercy Constantelo,
Helen Clemenzi and Dominic Clemenzi

Joe Scibbetta, Lena Scibbetta, Bea Fanto, Emil D'Elia and Barbara Joe D'Elia

Serra Family Reunion - June 29, 2002 Notes:

Everything you see I owe to spaghetti.

--Sophia Loren (1934 -   )

Mangia

Nothing says Serra more than Good Food

Malvasia delle Lipari®

Information supplied by Christine DiGrandi Jones

The Island of Salina produces a fine wine. It is called Malvasia delle Lipari®. The grapes are grown and processed on the island. The vineyards are located next door to the Serra homestead. This wine has the flavor and spirit of the island and would be a fine addition to a great Italian meal. I do not believe it is easy to get bottles of this small company's wine but I wanted to supply you with what information I have on the wine. I hope that if you get a chance to try this wine you enjoy "A Taste of the Island!"

Malvasia delle Lipari®
Denominazione di origine controllata
D.O.C.
Imbottigliato all' origine da
Pino Carrà – Via Umberto, 7- Tel. 090/9844051
MALFA - ITALIA

Italian Anise Cookies

Information supplied by Mary Goldrick

If you need a nice dessert to go with the Malvasia delle Lipari® wine.
Here is a nice recipe for some good old Italian Anise cookies.

Ingredients:

1 ½ Sticks Butter (softened)
½ Cup granulated sugar
3 eggs
3 tsp. Anise Extract (Pure)
3 tsp. Baking Powder
3 Cups Flour
Pinch of Salt

Preparation:

Preheat oven 350°
Cream butter and sugar together until fluffy
Beat in eggs one at a time
Add anise extract
Mix in baking powder, salt and flour until dough forms to a ball and all traces of flour are gone
If dough is a little sticky add more flour 1 tsp. at a time, so dough is easy to handle
Roll into balls, size of walnuts or smaller and place on an un-greased cookie sheet.
Yield: approx 3 dozen
Cook for 15 minutes until slightly brown and cool on cake rack.
Frost when completely cooled.

Frosting for cookies

1 Cup Confection Sugar
Add 1 or 2 Tbs. milk or cream a little at a time and 1/8 tsp. Lemon Extract (Pure) flavoring
Add more milk if thinner icing is desired.
Add more powdered sugar if icing is too thin.
Dip cooled cookies in frosting and set aside to harden.
One or two drops of food coloring may be added if colored icing is desired.
Dip into colored sprinkles before icing hardens if desired.

Bartolomea Serra Recipes

Submitted by Marge Eggleston

Here is a recipe that my grandmother, (your great-grandmother) BARTOLOMEA SERRA taught many of her grandchildren when she lived in Beverly.

"S"erra Cookies

Ingredients:

two pounds of confectionary sugar
two pounds of flour
six eggs
one tablespoon of baking powder
one teaspoon of salt
two Italian cinnamon sticks

On a table or board, mix the sugar and flour together by hand. Add the baking powder and salt and mix again. Now mix in eggs, one at a time also by hand. Add cinnamon sticks which have been hand grated. Again, hand mix entire ingredients. Take approximately two tablespoon full of the mixture and hand form until about one-half inch thick and one-half inch wide. Place on a greased cookie sheet and form dough into an "S" shape. Of course, the "S" signifies "SERRA". Place sheet in oven at 350 degrees F until the bottom of the cookie are lightly brown......about 20 minutes.

Bartolomea made her own cookie sheets by cutting the top and bottom from a gallon olive oil container and flattening out the sheet.

Another famous recipe my mother, Gracie serra, used and taught her children is for ravioli. I mean true ravioli; the kind one would die for; she may have learned it from her mother-in-law, Bartolomea Serra.

Ravioli

Ingredients:

6 cups of flour
3 large eggs
one-half to one cup of warm water with one tablespoon of salt added

Sift flour on a board and make a mound about 8 inches in diameter. Form a hole in the center of the mound. Crack eggs into center of mound one at a time adding some amount of the warm water with each egg and gradually mixing the eggs with the flour using fingers. Once the ingredients are semi-mixed, knead thoroughly, adding small amounts of water until mixture is soft and smooth, this takes a bit of work. You have now finished the pasta part of the raviolis. Wrap the dough into a small ball, wrap with a damp cloth and set aside.

Filling
1 pound container of ricotta cheese
1 half pound of Romano cheese
1-half teaspoon black pepper
4 eggs

Mix all ingredients together in mixing bowl using wooden spoon. Add additional seasoning such as parsley and oregano to taste. Roll out small portions of the pasta dough as thin as possible but still thick enough to be able to handle. Spoon out portions of the filling onto the rolled out dough. Cover filling with a section of the rolled out dough and seal edges around filling using a standard eating fork, to pinch both sheets of dough together. Place in kettle of boiling water to which some olive oil and one tablespoon of salt has been added. Cook for fifteen to twenty minutes. Serve with tomato sauce, meat balls and sausage. (boy am I hungry!!!)

Rose Clemenzi's Easter Bread

Submitted by Donald and Gayle Clemenzi

This Easter Bread recipe is Rose Clemenzi's. Everyone always looked forward to eating it. Today Margaret, Rose's granddaughter, takes over the tradition and makes it every year.

Ingredients:

2 cups warm milk
7 cups flour
2 yeast cakes
5 eggs (four yolks and 1 whole)
1 lemon rind
1 cup sugar
1 stick of butter
1 Tbsp vanilla
1 Tbsp anisette
1/2 tsp salt

Preparation:

Mix milk & yeast thoroughly.
Add 2 cups of flour. Work out all the lumps.
Let it set 1 hour.

Add 1 rind of lemon, 4 yellow of eggs and one whole egg, 1 cup sugar (to taste), one stick of melted butter, 5 cups of flour, 1 Tbsp vanilla, 1 Tbsp anisette, 1/2 tsp. salt.

Mix the dry ingredients together. Beat the eggs and flavoring together well.
Add melted butter to the egg mixture.
Add this mix to the flour; it will be crumbly.

Add yeast mixture and mix well. Knead on board until it is of fine texture. (less is better)
Put in large, greased bowl or pan; turn over so it will be greased & coated. Let it rise until it doubles in size.
Break it down and make into loaves, twists or breads.
Put on greased cookie sheets and let them rise again.
Bake at 325 or 350 until done - about 30-40 minutes. The bread will be golden brown.
When they are still warm from the oven, brush them with a beaten egg to give a golden sheen.

Baked Whitefish

Submitted by Nancy and Christopher Obert

Here is our favorite fish recipe. It reminds me of all of the old fish dinners I used to have with my family.

Ingredients:

2 lbs. whitefish fillets, skinless
2 small onions, sliced
1 Tbsp. butter or margarine
3 Tbsp. white wine
Dash salt
Dash black pepper
1 clove garlic, minced or pressed
1/3 cup dry white wine or 1½ Tbsp. lemon juice
3/4 cup whipping cream
1/2 tsp. dried oregano leaves or 1-2 tsp. fresh oregano chopped
1/3 cup grated Cheddar cheese
1/3 cup grated Parmesan cheese
2 Tbsp. white bread crumbs
1/2 lb. cooked shrimp

Preparation:

1. Sauté onion in butter in heavy pan over medium heat. Do not brown. Spread onion over bottom of a shallow backing dish.

2. Arrange fish fillets over onion in pan, overlapping thin edges. Sprinkle with salt and pepper. Add garlic.

3. Pour wine or lemon juice over fish.

4. Add whipping cream and oregano. Cover with foil.

5. Bake at 425°F for about 10 minutes. Uncover.

6. Add Cheddar cheese, Parmesan cheese and bread crumbs. Distribute shrimp evenly over top.

7. Bake, uncovered, for another 10 minutes or until top is golden, cheese is melted and the fish flakes easily.

Recipe for "Gi Gi" (Deep Fried Round Balls)

Submitted by Mary Goldrick

My mother made these every Christmas Eve when we were growing up. Everyone loved them. I helped roll them out and fry them. It sounds complicated, but easy, once you get the knack. Make them often to learn as I did, you will enjoy the taste as we did and still do.

Ingredients:

6 cups flour
3 tsps. baking powder
1 cup sugar
3 heaping Tbs. Crisco
3 Tbs. olive oil
6 eggs if small, 5 if large
Approx 1/3 cup of sweet wine "Marsala"

Form a well of flour and mix sugar and baking powder into it
Add Crisco, olive oil and wine and mix together with fingers
Add eggs one at a time and mix with rolling motions until dough is slightly sticky, but not too soft or hard
Form a loaf and cut off a chunk and roll out on slightly oiled surface in a long rope about as thick as your finger
Keep loaf covered in cloth napkin so as not to get hard crust
Cut into ½ inch pieces and fry in hot oil- Mazzola or a good vegetable oil at about 400 degrees using a basket
Stir gently so as not to burn, the oil will foam so lift basket up occasionally
When slightly brown, remove and place in deep bowl lined with paper towels to absorb extra oil
When cooked, dust with powdered sugar or coat with maple syrup or honey
They should be flakey and tender
Store in covered tin so as not to harden

Pasta with Ricotta Cheese (NO Grated Cheese)

Supplied by Mary Goldrick

Ingredients:

1 can Ricotta – small 2lb size
4 cups flour
1 egg
¼ cup milk
pinch of salt

Make a well with flour, add egg, milk, salt and ricotta cheese, mix with fingers
Knead lightly to keep together
Roll out, cut into pieces-long strips- and boil in water
Top with tomato sauce
Delicious!

Pecan Balls

Submitted by Mary Goldrick

Ingredients:

2 cups sifted all purpose flour
½ lb. (1 cup) soft butter
2 cups finely chopped pecans
½ cup granulated sugar
¼ tsp. salt
2 tsp. Vanilla extract
Confectioner's (powdered) sugar

1. In a large bowl, combine all ingredients (EXCEPT Confectioner's sugar), with hands
2. Mix until thoroughly blended – Refrigerate 30 minutes
             Preheat oven to 350 degrees
3. Using hands, roll dough into balls 1¼ inches in diameter (about the size of a walnut)
4. Place one inch apart on un-greased cookie sheet
5. Bake 15-20 minutes or until cookies are set, but not brown (I like a little brown)
6. Let stand 1 minute before removing from cookie sheet, then remove to wire rack to cool
7. Roll in confectioner's sugar while slightly warm
8. Cool *completely* before putting into tin container or they will sweat and get very soft
9. One recipe makes about 40 cookies

*Double this recipe to yield approximately 100 balls (Make one batch at a time)

Enjoy your baking!

Marietta's Meatballs:

Submitted by Mary Clemenzi di Grandi

Ingredients:

1/2 pound ground pork
1/2 pound lean ground beef.
1/2 cup of Italian Pecorino cheese. (A necessary ingredient)
1/2 cup of Italian bread crumbs.
2 celery stalks chopped very finely (use a chopper).
1/2 teaspoon Fennel seed to taste.
A few finely chopped sprigs of parsley.
2 small eggs or 1 jumbo egg.
Add water if needed to moisten the mixture.

Be sure your hands are cleaned and mix it all up.
Kneading it and squeezing the mixture through your fingers.
Roll between your palms to the size of golf balls.
(If you are making it for soup, make them tiny and do not brown just drop in hot soup)
Cover bottom of heated frying pan with olive oil.
When oil is hot, place meatballs in pan leaving enough space for turning.
Turn them over as soon as they are golden brown.
Brown on all sides.
You have to stand there and watch them so they do not burn.
Remove from pan and drain on paper towel or drop in sauce if there are any left after the kids eat them!

Enjoy!

PS I do not measure anything!

Tomato Sauce with meat

Submitted by Christine di Grandi Jones

Ingredients:

1 pound of lean ground beef
1 large sweet onion
4 One pound cans of crushed tomatoes
1 pound of fresh mushroom
3 tablespoons of olive oil
1-tablespoon oregano
1 tablespoon dried parsley
4 bay leafs
1 tablespoon of minced garlic
½ cup Sliced black olives?

Cove bottom of a large pot with olive oil.
When the oil is heated, lightly sauté one large chopped sweet onion and 1 pound ground beef.
Add 2 teaspoons of minced garlic while lightly brown ground beef
Gently stir in half pound sliced mushrooms
Add 4 large cans of diced tomatoes…(Forgive me, ancestors, for not growing my own fresh tomatoes!)
Add about a cup of red wine if desired.
If you keep sipping the wine while preparing the sauce, it will taste better!
Sprinkle a few tablespoons of oregano and finely chopped Uncle John's parsley
(or resort to two tablespoons of dried parsley)
Add bay leafs.

Do you wanna try putting in the black olives?

Let sauce simmer low for about a good hour.
Ready to pour over your favorite pasta!
Don't forget to add lots of Parmesan cheese!

When cooled, I fill zip lock bags in perfect serving sizes and freeze for quick use later.
(Do not heat in the plastic)!

*(You can adjust the amount of meat & diced tomatoes according to the desired thickness and quantity you wish to make. Small can of tomato puree may be added for a thicker sauce).

I use this same meat base for chili and sloppy Joe's! Just add red beans and lots of chili powder!

Sophia's Cheese Cake

Submitted by Christine di Grandi Jones

Grease 10 inch spring form pan

Prepare the crust:

Grind graham crackers crumbs to about one cup.
Mix in 1 tablespoons sugar and half teaspoon cinnamon, and 1 stick of melted butter (or margarine).
Mix it up and pat it against the bottom and half way up the sides of the pan.
Line the outside bottom and sides of the pan with aluminum foil and put in oven for 15 min. at preheated oven at 350 degrees.
Take out of oven and set aside while preparing the filling

Prepare filling:
Separate 5 large eggs.
In large bowl place three 8 oz packages of Philadelphia cream cheese at room temperature and the five egg yokes.
Beat egg whites until stiff gradually adding ¼ cup of sugar. Put it to the side.
With the same beaters (without washing them) start beating the cream cheese and the five egg yokes **slowly.**
While beating, cream cheese/egg yoke mixture add pure juice of one lemon, one teaspoon of vanilla extract, ¾ cup of sugar, one teaspoon of ground lemon rind (Zest), 3 tablespoons of all purpose white flour, and ¾ cups of sour cream.
When it is all blended, fold in the beaten egg whites, into the cream cheese mixture.
Pour mixture in the baked shell and bake at 325 degrees for 60-65 minutes.

Once it is baked. Turn off the heat and leave in closed oven for one hour.

Top with anything you like.
I prefer Comstock pineapple pie filling for my topping, you can even use powdered sugar.
Put topping on after the pie is chilled or when ready to serve.

Must keep refrigerated.

Serves as many people as can fight for it!

Irish Soda Bread

Submitted by Mary Goldrick

Ingredients:

3 cups flour
½ cup sugar
1 Tbs. baking powder
½ tsp. baking soda
pinch of salt
1 cup golden raisins (Soften first in a little water)
½ cup caraway seeds (optional)
1 egg
1½ cups buttermilk
A little butter for brushing on top of loaf

Mix all ingredients in order as listed
Form into a ball, brush top with butter and make cross on top with a knife
Bake at 375 degrees for 35 minutes or so, test with toothpick
Makes 1 small loaf
Cook completely, slice and eat with butter
Tasty with coffee or tea. Enjoy it!

Scotch Bread

Submitted by Mary Goldrick

This recipe was given to me by my husband Frank's Scottish grandmother, Elizabeth (Young) McElroy. Frank's maternal grandmother was born in Salt-to-Sea, Scotland. She gave me this recipe when we were first married. In 1962 when we lived in Newark there was a bread strike, you couldn't buy a loaf in any store in Newark or Jersey City. Frank's grandmother made us Scotch Bread in place of bread. It was the first time I ever ate it. It's more a cake than a "bread". What a treat, I thought. I've made it every St. Patrick's Day and most holidays since. It's a favorite of Kathleen's especially and all the Goldrick family.

Ingredients:

2 ½ cups flour
½ lb. butter softened (2 sticks)
½ cup sugar

Using a metal spoon (not wooden), cream the butter
Add sugar, then cream together until fluffy
Add flour and mix with the side of spoon until mixture is mealy, crumbly
Pour mixture into 8x8 inch pan, non-stick
DO NOT grease pan
Pack down *tightly* with back of spoon
Bake in preheated oven 350 degrees for 30-35 minutes
Edges should be slightly browned
Remove from oven – while still hot sprinkle top with granulated sugar
When completely cooled, cut into squares

*Double recipe to make 2 pans – easier to mix one at a time

Chicken and Onions

Submitted by Sophie and Angela Villanti

Ingredients:

One fowl cut in pieces or chicken breasts and/or thighs
Vegetable oil
Lots of onions, quartered
Salt and pepper
Rosemary (optional)
1/2 cup white wine
Grated Romano or Parmesan

Sear the chicken pieces in the oil in a soup pot for about 10 minutes. Add remaining ingredients, cover pot, turn heat down to low and simmer several hours. The onions will caramelize and form a delicious sauce.

Boil the rigatoni in another pot, drain and cover with the onion sauce. Serve chicken along with the pasta, top with grated cheese.

This is a recipe my mother learned from her mother in law, Catherine Costa Villanti. It has been a family favorite in the Villanti clan for many years and I've served it to many friends who all love it. This is great on a cold fall or winter day.

Anisette with Almonds Biscotte Cookies

Submitted by Bea Fanto and Lena Scibetta

2 ½ cups flour mix in 1 ½ teaspoon baking powder. In another bowl cream together ½ cup salted butter, 1 cup sugar, mix together until light and fluffy. Add ½ tablespoon Anise seed or 1 teaspoon Anise flavor. Add 3 eggs, two tablespoons of water, 1 teaspoon orange extract, 1 teaspoon vanilla extract. Beat thoroughly, blend in flour mixture and add one cup chopped toasted almonds if desired. Chill dough until firm about 2 ½ hours. Divide dough, shape in flat loaf 2 inches wide, ½ inch thick. Place loaves 6 inches apart on greased baking pan. Cook 375° for 20 minutes, remove slice ¾ inch return to oven, brown on all sides.

Additional Serra Family Recipes:

Love is a symbol of eternity.
It wipes out all sense of time, destroying all memory
of a beginning and all fear of an end.

--Madame De Staël, *Corinne*

As Time Goes By

Messages to the Past, Present & Future

"Nancy, Shari and Jason, I love you more than anything!" - Chris Obert

"Mom and Dad, thank you for all the gifts you have given me!" - Chris Obert

"To Aunt Bea & Uncle Mike, Aunt Charlotte & Uncle Johnny, and Aunt Mary & Uncle Frank; thank you for all the good food and good times we had every time we visited New Jersey" - The Obert Family

"To America and Ellis Island, thank you for opening your doors to our grandparents, Domenico & Maria Serra, it will not be forgotten!" - The Obert Family

"Chris, thank you for writing the family tree!" – Mom, Giovannina (Serra) Obert

"I would like to thank God that both my parents were at my wedding" – Mary (Obert) Fortin

"To my grandchildren, if you walk on the moon someday, think of me while you're there…" - Chris Obert

"Mom, If I could take a way all your pain and sadness I would without hesitation, please take care of yourself, I Love You Mom" - Tony Serra

"I want to thank you Christopher, your wife Nancy, your daughter Shari and son Jason, for all your tedious work on the Serra Family Tree project. You are leaving a wonderful legacy for all of us and all those Serras yet to come" – Mary (Serra) Goldrick

"To my daughter Michelle, I am so proud of you. You are a wonderful mom" – Mom, Mary (Obert) Fortin

"To my granddaughter Emma, You are the light of my life. Nonna loves you very much" – Nonna, Mary (Obert) Fortin

"To Eric, watching you love my granddaughter Laura and her mom makes my heart very happy" – Mary (Obert) Fortin

"To Lori and Gary, You make me proud to be your step-mother" – Mary (Obert) Fortin

"To Roger, my world is nothing without you babe. I love you with all my heart. I know we'll have many more happy years to come" – Mary (Obert) Fortin

"Chris, I am so proud of you for taking on this massive project! You have done a wonderful job! Thank you also for being the best husband and father to our two children. I love you so much!" – Nancy (Blanchette) Obert

"Shari and Jason, You two make me so proud to be your mom. I don't think you realize how much my life revolves around each one of you. I love you both and hope your lives turn out to be everything you hope and dream about!" – Mom, Nancy (Blanchette) Obert

"Kudos to Christopher, Nancy, Shari and Jason Obert! Your diligence and constant endeavor has made it possible for us to own, read and enjoy the "Serra Story". Congratulations on a job well done!" – Aunt Mary (Serra) Goldrick

"To my wonderful husband Frank, for your caring and sharing a lifetime of love and happiness. I could not have managed without you. All my love and devotion always!" – Mary (Serra) Goldrick

"Our heartfelt thanks to our daughter Kathleen and husband, Robert (Wilson) for making us the proud grandparents of two beautiful girls, Grace and Julia. They have given us untold happiness and joy." – Mom & Dad, Mary and Frank Goldrick

"To our dearest son Mike and his lovely wife Pam, we give you all of our love and devotion. May God bless and watch over you always." - Mom & Dad, Mary and Frank Goldrick

"To my sister, Jennie (Obert) for the many years of encouragement and guidance while I was growing up. You truly helped to shape my future. May God Bless You always. With gratitude and love!" – Mary (Serra) Goldrick

"To my family, love each other and be good to each other." – Mom, Giovannina (Serra) Obert

"I never forgot and I always used what I learned from my mother and father, and I was always very happy that I did!" – Giovannina (Serra) Obert

"Always put God, Jesus and the Blessed Mother first." – Giovannina (Serra) Obert

"To Ryan and Angela, I love you" – Mom, Patricia (Obert) Ponticelli

"We love you Emma" – Mom and Dad, Michelle Obert and Stephen LaFrance

"Bye" – Emma Obert

"To my family, I love you" – Geremy Ayers

"To my Grandparents, thank you for all you have done for us" – Geremy Ayers

"God Bless the Entire Serra Family" - Norma (Obert) Ayers

"Thanks to Mom and Dad for all their love and support, and making me the person I am today. Love You" – Norma (Obert) Ayers

"To my husband Larry and all of our children, thanks for all the smiles, I can't smile without you." – Norma (Obert) Ayers

"Special thanks to our brother Chris. His hard work and dedication made this book possible. We love you" – Mary, Norma, Ed and Pat

"To everyone in New Jersey, especially Aunt Mary and Uncle Frank, I'm so glad we've been able to be so close to you, never letting the miles between us get in the way of that loving relationship. It feels as though you live right nearby. Thank you for always opening your homes and your hearts to us. I love you all. God bless you. Love" – Shari Obert

"Mom & Dad, I love you both so much. Thank you for all you have done for me and for always believing in me and supporting me. You mean so much to me and always will. Love, xxoo" - Shari Obert

"Dad, I am so proud of you. You've spent so much time and energy on this book, doing so much more than most people will ever realize. Your dedication definitely shows; this book has turned out to be amazing. I love you Daddy. Love" - Shari Obert

"To Ed Obert, thanks for being the best big brother!" – Chris Obert

"To all of my cousins in Massachusetts who showed me such good times at the beaches, at their homes everywhere, Thanks to you all I had a great childhood!" – Lena (Serra) Scibetta

"Most of all to my Uncle Dominick who took us to Coney Island when we were young and made sure we did not get lost, by whistling for all of us to gather around him before getting on the train." – Lena (Serra) Scibetta

"To God, Thank You so much for everything" – The Entire Extended Serra Family

*Writing is pretty crummy
on the nerves.*

--Paul Theroux (1941-   )

Family Autographs
and Notes

Family Autographs and Notes:

Family Autographs and Notes:

Family Autographs and Notes: